The Christian Enigma

The Christian Enigma:
Back to the Message

Rev. Dr. Thomas D. Lynch
Rev. Dr. Cynthia E. Lynch

Interfaith Academy Press
San Miguel de Allende, Guanajuato, Mexico
Honolulu, Hawaii, U.S.A.

About the Cover

Casillas Rodríguez, General Luis Rey. Photograph taken as a colonel in Kashmir, India. Winter 1949. From a personal interview by Thomas D. Lynch with Casillas's son, Dr. Luis Rey Casillas Celis. 26 Apr. 2013.

Cover and interior design by Jon Sievert

Copyright 2014 by Thomas D. Lynch and Cynthia E. Lynch. All rights reserved. No part of this publication may be reproduced, stored in an information storage and retrieval system, or transmitted in any form by electronic or mechanical means without the prior written permission of the copyright holders. Reviewers may quote brief passages in a review. Every reasonable effort has been made to obtain permission for copyrighted material included in this work, and to ensure accuracy at the time of publication, but prices, locations, and other pertinent publication elements can change. Any errors that may have occurred are inadvertent and will be corrected in subsequent editions, provided notification is sent to the publisher. The authors and publisher do not accept and hereby disclaim any liability to any party for any loss or damage caused by errors, omissions, or any potential disruption or problem due to application of information contained in this book, whether such incidences result from misuse, negligence, accident, or any other cause.

ISBN 978-0-9856475-1-3

Interfaith Academy Press
San Miguel de Allende, Guanajuato, Mexico
Honolulu, Hawaii, U.S.A.

International Academy for Interfaith Studies
www.interfaithacademy.org

Printed and bound in the United States of America

Contents

Preface vi
Acknowledgements viii

Part 1. Rediscovering the Message

1. Introduction 13
2. Religion in Crisis 22
3. Genes, Social Evolution, and God 41
4. The Omega Interpretation 66
5. Jesus and Process Theology 93
6. The First Interfaith Theologian 111
7. The Gospel of Mary 127
8. The Issue of a Personal God 152
9. The Essential Message 173
10. The Message Through Parables 195
11. Getting Off Message 220

Part 2. The Enigma of Spirituality

12. Introduction to Spirituality 241
13. Practical Spiritual Knowledge 249
14. Discerning Between Good and Evil 277
15. Spiritual Love 302
16. Conclusions about Spirituality 321

Appendices

A. References and Suggested Readings 328
B. Spiritual Coordinate System 355
C. Versions of the Golden Rule 360

About the Authors 362

Preface

Some usage and terms in the book need preliminary explanation. We capitalize critical words for emphasis. For example, Son of Man and Kingdom of Man are capitalized because they are critical concepts. We prefer the phrase *Kin*dom of Heaven rather than Kingdom of Heaven in order to avoid the sexist language in contemporary translations. We feel the need, though, not to change the term Kingdom of Heaven when it reflects the words used in the time of Jesus. We capitalize pronouns when they refer to Jesus and Sophia. And we try not to use pronouns when the subject is God because we see God as beyond gender.

We often boldface direct quotes to set them apart from the text and emphasize their importance. In Part 2 of the book, we italicize key questions in order to highlight them.

In the first appendix we include a set of references and suggested readings. This bibliography (Appendix A) should facilitate readers pursuing their own research on the topics explored in this book. Within the text of the chapters we provide sources in parentheses, and these sources are tied to the references in Appendix A. But in writing this book we tried to minimize the citing of sources in order to make the text more easily readable.

The two other appendices contain supplementary information related to spirituality. Appendix B is a brief explanation of how empirical research could be conducted on the topic of spirituality. Appendix C presents versions of the Golden Rule found in various world religions.

In this book, we cite and refer to the Holy Bible, but, although we recognize there are many versions of the Bible, we use the King James Version published by the World Publishing Company of Cleveland and New York (year not provided). The Bible we selected was in English, but we realize that the text was first published in Greek and later in Latin. Another problem beyond the many versions of the Bible is the fact that language changes over time, and thus it becomes difficult for modern English speakers to understand earlier versions of English, such as that spoken in 1611. So we often quote the 1611 version, but sometimes we modify that language to use contemporary words such as "you" instead of "thou." We apologize to the purist, but we think our efforts make it easier for the contemporary reader to understand the quotations. We also apologize to those who prefer other versions of the Bible, but we believe our choice of this version is reasonable and our modifications enable better communication to our readers.

From a standard religious point of view, the story of Jesus and His message is fact that should not be contested. From an objective point of view, the story of Jesus and His message should be considered speculation because the four evangelists who wrote what we call the New Testament gospels were clearly biased in their opinions, not present at the events they describe, and wrote decades after those events took place. The interpretation of their accounts by later church leaders, which we label the Alpha interpretation, has made a remarkable impact on the world. However, this book offers an alternative speculation that we think is more feasible. In our interpretation, Jesus was a man, not God, but a man who deserves the utmost respect and admiration for the thoughts He brought to the world.

We do not view our book as an academic effort but rather our presentation to a general educated public of what we argue is an alternative interpretation of the message Jesus brought to us. We hope we accomplish our purpose in a manner that is readable yet informative.

Acknowledgements

Writing and eventually publishing a book is not the work of one or more authors; it is a group activity. Thus, we wish to recognize those people who were part of this group activity, while we stress that any faults in *The Christian Enigma: Getting Back to the Message* should be addressed solely to us the authors.

Early proofreaders and commentators were Michael Keasts and Robert deGast. They caught mistakes large and small. Their work was vital as it helped us produce a much better book. In addition, we prepared 16 hour-long power point presentations based on the book's contents that we showed to an English-speaking discussion group at the Empowerment Center in San Miguel de Allende, Mexico, over a period of several months. One might think this audience of mixed nationalities could not add anything to the book, but that would be a mistake. The participants in these discussions were remarkably useful in their active and probing questions. They helped us gain even greater insight into the proper content, including wording, for this book.

Several people played a significant part in producing the book at its later stages. Sharon Steeber was the copy editor and proofreader of the book's pages. She was awesome in making suggestions on how to improve the readability of the material and making sure the references were correct. She was outstanding, and we offer her our heart-felt gratitude. Jon Sievert converted the copy-edited pages into the final version you read in this book. He should be called Saint Jon for his remarkable patience and certainly his professionalism as we went through many detailed corrections.

Dr. Luis Rey Casillas Celis, a retired economist from the World Bank who now lives near San Miguel de Allende, contributed the picture of the young Jesus in India. The father of Dr. Casillas took the picture as a colonel in the Mexican army shortly after World War II while attached to the United Nations. Colonel Casillas (who later became a four-star general) photographed the painting of a young Jesus he saw in a monastery in the Kashmir area of northern India. The director of the monastery told him the painting of Jesus was made when Jesus visited the monastery. The picture is not ideal in that you can also see a reflection in the photo, but it nevertheless may be the only authentic image of Jesus in existence.

Part 1

The Spirituality Enigma

Chapter 1

Introduction

Our purpose in writing *The Christian Enigma: Back To The Message* is to argue that Christianity, almost from its beginnings, took a very wrong turn. We need to return to the original message Jesus tried to bring to us but that, through the centuries, we have misunderstood and thus ignored. We believe Jesus' message was intensely spiritual and most Christians have seriously missed it from the beginning. This book explains why that message was misunderstood and restates the message of Jesus as we interpret it. We refer to the misunderstood message as the Alpha Interpretation and to our restatement as the Omega Interpretation.

He Speaks, Not Spoke

In 1838, Ralph Waldo Emerson presented a lecture at his *alma mater* Harvard Divinity School. As a result, he was banned from Harvard for nearly thirty years because his lecture questioned the divinity of Jesus. In *Democracy Matters*, the American philosopher Cornel West argues that Emerson was the most famous intellectual of his day, and he quotes Emerson's words that day in 1838. Those words serve as a guiding motif for this book:

> *The stationariness of religion: the assumption that the age of inspiration is past, that the Bible is closed; the fear of degrading the character of Jesus by representing him as a man; indicate with sufficient clear-*

ness the falsehood of our theology. It is the office of a true teacher to show us that God is, not was; that He speaketh, not spake. The true Christianity – a faith like Christ's in the infinitude of man,—is lost . . . .

Let me admonish you, first of all, to go alone; to refuse the good models, even those most sacred in the imagination of men, and dare to love God without mediator or veil . . . .

Yourself a newborn bard of the Holy Ghost,—cast behind you all conformity, and acquaint men at first hand with Deity . . . . Look to it first and only . . . that fashion, custom, authority, pleasure, and money are nothing to you,—are not bandages over your eyes, that you cannot see,—but live with the privilege of the immeasurable mind. (quoted in West, 74 – 75)

Our book is based on the assumption that the Bible is not closed. We do argue that Jesus was just a man, but we also argue that He was the most remarkable individual who has ever existed. In a larger respect, what He accomplished is even more remarkable because He did so as a mere mortal. We do believe that we present Jesus in this book not as He spoke, but rather as He speaks to us in our present time. Jesus believed in humanity's infinite potential, and we think that belief is lost in the current understanding, the Alpha Interpretation that is called Christianity. His goal was to show a path so that infinite human potential could, and will be, realized.

This book argues that you, the reader, should refuse the current interpretation of Christianity, the Alpha Interpretation, even though it is most sacred to so many. This book dares you to instead love life (God) using the spiritual wisdom of Jesus and to do so by going deep within yourself. Do not let conformity rule you. Jesus told us to transcend fashion, custom, authority, pleasure, and money because they are nothing. Jesus taught us to open our eyes to see and our ears to hear. With your God-given mind, guided by your loving heart, reach into yourself, continually transcend to your ultimate truth, and let that truth guide your actions in life.

Confronting the Unfathomable

The father of Thomas D. Lynch, one of the authors of this book, was God; at least many people in New Guinea worship him as God to this day. That makes one of the authors the "Son of God," or more accurately, the adopted "Son of God." (Please excuse our humor.) Yes, this sounds absolutely crazy, but it is true. During the mid-1940s, people in isolated regions of New Guinea saw planes in the sky and often the planes would drop cargo in large crates to various remote places (Glines).

Thinking God, or the gods, sent them wonderful gifts, the people in this isolated region started worshipping the person who sent them, and that was then U.S. Army Air Corps Colonel Thomas R. Lynch, father of Thomas D. Lynch. (Only a few years earlier than his wartime experiences in the Pacific, Thomas R. Lynch had adopted his son.) As part of General Douglas MacArthur's military force, Lynch was assigned to air logistics, meaning he was responsible for much of the allied air traffic in the South Pacific during the latter half of World War II.

The religion that worshiped Lynch, as God, was known in the Pacific as the Cargo Cult or Cargoism. It was, and still is, a religious movement among some of the natives of the islands of Melanesia in the South Pacific (Glines).

In the early decades of the twentieth century, Europeans arrived on the islands and also brought cargo, that is, material goods for their exploration of the islands. When the ships left, the strange people left behind equipment and unused supplies in wooden boxes (Glines). From this abandoned cargo, Cargoism started. Then, during World War II, the arrival of massive numbers of soldiers and airmen, also with huge cargoes, proved the validity of Cargoism theology to the people. They were rewarded for their faith and their predictions were confirmed. A time of plenty had arrived, and there was no longer a need to work because everything would be provided from above.

Members of the Cargo Cult believed a new age of blessing was here and the God-sent special cargo heralded its arrival. The cultists believed that their deities (Col. Lynch apparently was among them) would continue to send them goods just like those used by the military forces. They believed the goods came from heaven, which for them is located in the sky immediately above Australia. They believed that this cargo came to them packed in crates addressed to specific individuals.

Members of the Cargo Cult in the 1940s prayed much in the way many mainstream Christians today pray as a result of their Alpha Interpretation of God. Christians commonly pray for salvation, meaning for an after-death passage to heaven and for material blessings and well-being in their lifetime. To the native people of New Guinea, God was like a modern-day automated teller machine (ATM) in which you present your password (prayers) and out come material blessings.

When the cargo did not arrive as expected, the cultists did not lose faith. When it stopped coming in the postwar period, they simply kept praying, and they continued to expect that their "mana" would drop from heaven. The followers of Cargoism in time assumed the lack of material wealth from the sky was because they had not performed the correct ritual or had neglected the gods.

Not surprising, in the twenty-first century, the worship of cargo is waning, but occasionally a persuasive leader manages to spark renewed interested in the religion. Typically, this renewal occurs when a leader claims that, in a dream or vision, some supernatural power told him or her a messiah will soon return bringing huge supplies of manufactured goods. This return will usher in a new era when believers will have their identity, dignity, and honor restored. Inequality, suffering, and even death, will cease. The riches of the wealthy and anyone who defrauded the believers will then belong to the cultists.

The believers think that religious ritual stimulates the arrival of cargo and that the gods respond only to correctly performed ceremonies. Cult leaders and sometimes whole communities demonstrate that they have received news about the coming of cargo by falling into ecstatic states. Correct ceremonies by the believers have included marching with wooden rifles, flag-raising ceremonies, and imitations of the American military dress and behavior under the command of Col. Lynch.

In the heyday of the Cargo Cult after World War II, proper ceremonies included the building of airfields, radio masts, and lookout towers. Cult leaders contacted the gods using what appeared to be wireless telephones often carved out of wooden posts. They carved headphones out of wood and wore them while sitting in fabricated control towers. They waved landing signals while standing on their runways. They lit signal fires and torches to light up runways and lighthouses. They even built life-sized mockups of airplanes from straw and created military-style landing strips. They expected cargo to appear on altars or other holy places where they believed their deity would appear (Glines).

This story illustrates that there is a natural tendency for any people, when the remarkable confronts them, to make up explanations to deal with a seemingly impossible set of phenomena. What makes thunder and lightning? What happens to us when we die? Why do we sometimes win or lose battles? Why am I sick? Why did my mother die? Why are there very strange big things moving across the heavens? Why did this cargo come to me, and how do I make it come again?

What is more challenging for us to understand than the concept of God? Human minds create answers where explanations are lacking. We are curious and creative as a species.

If there are questions about the unknowable, then the human mind naturally fills the gap as best it can with explanations our minds can grasp. We are very slow to give up on our invented theology, and sometimes we do not, even when confronted with new knowledge and discoveries that provide better explanations.

The most obvious way to look for answers about God is to see and understand God as some sort of super-human, super-animal, or feature of nature, such as the sun, mountain, sky, and so on. In time, these explanations may seem inadequate, but those who criticize such explanations must realize that the problem is not God. Rather, it is the impossible challenge of trying to articulate the vast subject of God with our limited minds, experiences, and language.

Speaking in accordance with our values as authors, college professors, and Interfaith Ministers, we think it wrong to demean or even argue that one way or another of worship is foolish. Instead, we believe we should honor each particular understanding of God and let each set of people evolve their understanding as they process more information through living.

As long as a particular religion is tolerant of other religions and does not force its viewpoint upon others or somehow hurt people or creatures, then we need to respect those belief systems, even if we think they are mistaken. Unfortunately, many Christians have not agreed with that position, and often they still do not agree with it today. Repeatedly, conflict and harm have ensued.

Like some of the indigenous tribes of New Guinea, many Christians also worship an ATM version of God. They adhere to the Alpha Interpretation of Christian theology, wherein they need only believe that Jesus is the Son of God and their personal savior. Somehow that means they will be forgiven for all their wrong doings and, when they die, will go to a place called heaven, and thus acquire eternal happiness.

This belief is a remarkable misunderstanding of the message that Jesus taught. It's a situation much like that of the New Guineans who misunderstood what Col. Lynch was doing in World War II.

An Insightful Understanding

As academics, we find that when we confront students with a difficult question and they have no clue as to what the correct understanding is, some students react by making up an answer with their imagination. We argue that the Alpha Interpretation is such a made-up answer, but it was made-up by intelligent people trying to understand the conflicting stories about Jesus, just as the New Guineans tried to understand the reality of cargo planes.

Rather than use our imaginations to make up a Christian version of a Cargo theology, we argue that students of the teacher Jesus should just read His message as He left it to us, and interpret it within the context of His times. His teachings are the Omega Interpretation, which we explain in Chapters 4, 7, 9, 10, and 12 through 16.

Jesus spent a great deal of time explaining how each person should approach life. For Jesus, God was largely a mystery, as many other aspects of our lives are a mystery. Being a mystery does not mean the mystery is unimportant or non-existent. It just means we do not know, or we have an incomplete answer.

Nevertheless, Jesus did have an insightful understanding of God and heaven, and we believe that understanding is important to us in our time. Although we believe that Jesus was just a man, He was a man who deserves the utmost respect and admiration for the philosophy He brought to the world. Because of our admiration of Jesus, we capitalized pronouns referring to Him in spite of the fact that we do not consider Him to be God.

Organization of this Book

In this two-part book, we explain that the Christian religion is in serious crisis largely because Christians insist upon using the Alpha Interpretation of the gospels rather than the Omega Interpretation based on Jesus' actual teachings. Jesus had a goal (*telos*) in His ministry, which was to bring to humankind what He considered "food" for the human soul, not an "easy pass" to a place called Heaven. With that spiritual sustenance we can transcend beyond our normal materialistic and ego-centered human existence into a spiritual life.

In Part One, we answer the following questions:
- Where did Jesus get His ideas?
- In what way is Christianity in crisis today?
- How did the current dominant interpretation of what is called Christianity come into existence?
- What was the purpose of the ministry of Jesus?
- What was His real message, which we argue is a very practical explanation of how to live a spiritual life?

In Part Two, we detail His spiritual teachings by addressing the following questions:
- What is spirituality?
- How is it practical?
- How should one discern between good and evil?
- What does it mean to live a spiritual life?
- What is spiritual love, and in what way is it critical to spirituality?

Many religious people consider the story of Jesus and His message as fact that should not be contested. However, as long-time students of religion, we believe the usual story of Jesus and His message should be considered speculation. People clearly biased in their opinions and probably not present at the events when they occurred wrote what is called the New Testament gospels. The interpretation of their accounts by later church leaders has made a remarkable impact on the world. But we believe our alternative interpretation, the Omega Interpretation, is more feasible.

Chapter 2

Religion in Crisis

Religion, especially the Christian religion, is in crisis because increasingly it is difficult for a knowledgeable and thoughtful person of reason also to be a person of faith. For example, there are many inconsistencies in the New Testament, and the existence of inconsistencies can present a problem for readers, especially those schooled in critical thinking.

When it comes to emotional subjects, such as religion and politics, most of us look for evidence that affirms our values and opinions. Those facts that do not fit our preconceived point of view we ignore. As a result, a logical inconsistency, over time, can become a problem, then a crisis, as we realize we are no longer able to maintain our previously held belief. In such a crisis, we might even reach a more radical conclusion, such as abandoning religion, in spite of the fact that more satisfying alternatives are possible.

Let us emphasize that we approach this subject as persons of faith and reason. We do believe atheists have strong arguments, as do church reformers, such as retired Episcopal Bishop John Shelby Spong. He also argues that the Christian religion is in crisis. Bishop Spong focuses his critical observations on the Christian religion only, but many of his views apply to religion in general. If the atheists' and reformers' arguments are correct in even some respects, thoughtful people of faith need to reassess their approach to religion.

Evolution of Religion

For a more comprehensive discussion of the evolution of religion, we suggest you read *A History of God* by theologian and former nun Karen Armstrong and *The Evolution of God* by journalist Robert Wright. Many facts and observations here come from their works.

For thousands of years in what scholars call prehistory, hunter-gatherer groups lived and worked together in family and tribal units that mutually supported and defended each other. Commonly, one or more in the group became the religious leaders. They specialized in caring for the sick and often praying to what the group felt were superior forces or beings to help members of their tribe with the challenges of their lives. Those leaders also prepared and led the group or an individual in key social ceremonies, such as births, coming of age, weddings, and deaths. Today, among indigenous peoples, these religious leaders have various names, but scholars call them shamans.

Around 7,000 years ago, some of the hunter-gatherers settled near rivers and lakes where, in time, they domesticated animals and developed agriculture. These developments anchored the hunter-gatherers to one place, and their population grew because their innovations were successful. Eventually, the first small cities came into being, as we explain in Chapter 3.

Typically, the political leader of these small cities would be closely allied with the religious leader. The political leader would require everyone to worship as the religious leader directed. In return, the religious leader politically supported the secular leader. In some cases, the secular leader or a close family member was also the supreme religious leader.

Thus religion continued to perform all the functions it had with hunter-gatherers, but a new function was added, that of helping the group to work as a cohesive people, and eventually as a nation, and then, in some cases, as an empire. Religion became the glue, or at least a significant part of the glue, that held the now larger group together under the leadership of the political leader. Sometimes in such groups, the political leader was considered a god or a direct descendant of the gods.

The added title of "god" bestowed upon the political leader even more credible authority and placed him above any laws or rules the group might have. Not surprising, many, if not most, political leaders of various peoples around the world used the concept of god to their political advantage. Clearly, this arrangement worked sufficiently well in many places and can still be seen in the world today.

Because of the intellectual curiosity of human beings and the need to have concrete answers to difficult questions, each religion developed its own mythologies. These mythologies addressed the basic questions of humankind, such as where we came from as a species and how we should behave within our group, including what roles and behaviors are appropriate and inappropriate. Before science came into existence, religion served not only as the glue for society but also as the context where most of the important and often unanswerable questions were addressed.

In summary, religion from its beginning served several functions. It provided a social means to celebrate and observe major events in our lives, offered medical assistance to the people, and was the binding force that helped political leaders maintain power and authority over a large group of people. It also set the cultural traits that helped the tribe consider itself unique. Moreover, religion answered the larger questions that seemed beyond human understanding. Of course, the rise of science and philosophy greatly mitigated some of those roles. For example, modern medicine has largely preempted the healing function of religion. But even that role continues to some extent in those cultures that rely more on religion for healing than on mainstream medicine.

First Religious Awakening

At some point during prehistory, humans started believing there was a god or a group of gods. This point marked what Karen Armstrong terms the First Religious Awakening, and we believe it was vital to human evolution. With religion humankind found it easier to evolve from the hunter-gatherer stage of social evolution to our complex modern civilization.

At this moment in the chapter, many atheists might be saying our analysis of the early development of religion may be correct, but it does not prove God exists. Our purpose in this book is not to prove that God exists. Instead, we stress that religion in the past aided human social evolution and that there are still social roles for religions in the present and future. That said, some of those roles urgently need updating, given the realities of globalization and recent scientific discoveries. Later in this chapter, we address this topic more fully.

Typically, an important role for the gods after the First Awakening was as a higher power that could help people with their daily challenges. Such challenges might include, for instance, making the hunters' spears fly straight so that their game was killed and the family could eat that night.

As the period of the First Awakening continued over thousands of years, humans evolved from disparate nomadic groups into what anthropologists call civilizations. Often, the priest class in those emerging civilizations created a narrative that imbued the political leader with legitimacy and provided a set of rules with which society could better function as a political and social unit.

Second Religious Awakening

As populations and densities of peoples increased over time, from about 800 to 300 BCE, a Second Religious Awakening (referred to as the Axial Period by authors such as Armstrong) occurred throughout the world. However, it did not in all circumstances replace, or even modify, the First Awakening. Nevertheless, it was a significant change for almost all religions of that time. As more cities, nation states, and empires appeared, brutal wars and conflicts among peoples grew more common, especially as humans discovered how to make better tools of war, such as using metals for their weapons.

To address this brutal aspect of humankind, which often resulted from the ego's desire to dominate others, key religious leaders, especially in the Middle East and Asia, reformed their religions to stress the value we now commonly call the Golden Rule. That is "Do unto others as you would have them do unto you."

This value, using similar but not the exact wording, spread around the world until today it is found in almost all religions. (See Appendix C for a list of the various versions of the Golden Rule.) Older religions, such as Hinduism and Judaism, adopted this value, and it is easily still seen in their teaching today. In some cases, religious leaders created whole new religions, such as Buddhism and Christianity, that stressed this value as central to their teachings.

Besides teaching the Golden Rule, the Second Religious Awakening also focused on the concept of Oneness. This religious reform changed our understanding of the deity from an entity that lived someplace else, such as in the sky, a mountain, or natural object, to one within us and in all places simultaneously. God was not in any one place, but was everywhere. With the Second Awakening, instead of God being a big capricious man with a beard who lived in the sky and hurled thunderbolts down on people, God became a great mystery or unknowable power that humans could never totally understand because of "His" infinite nature.

Not all the world's religions embraced this Oneness aspect of the Second Awakening to the same extent they did the Golden Rule. Some religions, such as Christianity, had Oneness at its core from the beginning, as can be seen in the New Testament: "But to us there is but one God, the Father, of whom are all things, and we in him; and one Lord Jesus Christ, by whom are all things, and we by him" Corinthians 1, 8: 6. (Chapter 4 addresses Oneness as a vital part of the Omega Interpretation of Christianity.)

However, soon after Jesus passed from the scene, the influence of particularly the Roman theologians and earlier leaders, such as the Apostle Paul, prevailed, and the leaders of Christianity no longer taught the concept of Oneness. With Paul, the new Christian faith started to revert to the First Awakening belief, which said God existed in a place called heaven. Other religions, such as Hinduism, strongly committed themselves to this Oneness belief as they evolved over the centuries. In Hinduism, as this reform came into being, the multiple gods increasingly melted into the Oneness and were redefined as being infinite aspects of the Oneness.

With the Second Awakening and its stress on Oneness, some religions continued to play the same major roles as before, but yet another role developed. For example, in Buddhism the primary stress lay on spirituality, often using meditation as the means to foster that spirituality. These religions helped individuals grow in spiritual wisdom and in their ability to make ethical decisions. In this way, the purview of religion enlarged to include the teaching of spirituality and ethics.

The Second Religious Awakening ultimately influenced the beliefs held within each of the world's major religious traditions. However, not all the groups within each tradition incorporated both aspects, or even either aspect, of the Second Religious Awakening. Still, segments of almost all religions (often called the mystics) have totally adopted the Second Awakening reforms. There are also segments (often called fundamentalists) in almost all religions that have maintained the First Awakening and have not accepted any, or at least not all, of the Second Awakening's reforms.

One side effect of the Golden Rule is that it led some individuals to challenge the very notion of the existence of God.

For example, many who questioned God's existence had initially prayed and asked Him to save the life of an innocent loved one. If their heartfelt prayers were not answered affirmatively, they, having embraced the values of the Golden Rule, believed that a loving caring God could not, or would not, let a person suffer needlessly. They reasoned that an indifferent God could not exist. They asked: How can I worship a non-existent God? To them a belief in God was fruitless and even foolish.

But to those people who embraced both the Golden Rule and the Oneness aspects of the Second Awakening, the logic that led others to atheism was not compelling. Their understanding of God, as being both within and outside a person, led them to understand suffering as primarily a state of mind.

In fact, few from this segment of each religion reached the conclusion that God was non-existent. They considered life to be a long set of experiences, a process, that a wiser person uses to learn from and grow spiritually. Even the so-called worst of experiences, such as a death camp, could be an opportunity for a person to grow. Rabbi Harold Kushner and death-camp survivor Viktor Frankl suggest that the bad things happening to good people are not a reason to declare God non-existent. (See Appendix A for their book titles.) Instead, their books suggest such occurrences offer a time to look deeper within, search for how to grow spiritually and thereby attain a more profound understanding of God, ourselves, and life.

The major religions of our present time reflect a spectrum of beliefs in which some accept all the Second Awakening reforms, some accept one aspect, and some none. The segments of organized religions that adopted all the second reforms are the ones often called mystical or spiritual.

Not all religious people are spiritual, and not all spiritual people are religious. For example, when asked if they are religious, this latter group answer that they are SBNR, meaning "spiritual but not religious," a term used by the U.S. Census

Bureau as a data point for religious identity. When pressed to explain why they consider themselves to be SBNR, they say they dislike, and even distrust, organized religion. Some in this group go so far as to assert that they are spiritual persons but do not believe in God.

Among the mystical or spiritual wings of religions, there exists a remarkable parallel in beliefs and values (Lynch and Lynch). Each has a wisdom literature — for example, Psalms, the Upanishads, and so on—and the stories and teachings in the literature are remarkably similar to each other. Also, although the rituals differ among the various mystical and spiritual wings, all tend to demonstrate joy and awe as they practice their rituals.

To us, each religion is merely an attempt to understand God from a particular set of perspectives that derive from the cultural, political and social realities of various eras and places. Human nature, which cannot be escaped, colors each individual's understanding of God and, in some cases, a person's decision to say God does or does not exist.

However, from looking at many religions and searching for what they have in common rather than their differences, almost anyone can transcend to some extent the varying perspectives and, in particular, grasp the common spiritual message (Lynch and Lynch). We find the spiritual wing of each religion to be valuable because this is primarily where we find affirmation for our beliefs.

For example, our beliefs that God loves all of us and that there is not one religious path but many, correspond to what the mystical wings believe. A corollary to these assertions is that we believe an active effort to proselytize or convert others to a particular religion is misguided. In contrast, we do believe that helping people who want help with their spiritual problems, as well as those who want help to develop spiritually, are proper and necessary roles for religion. By looking at what religions have in common, one can better answer difficult religious questions or at least have a better insight into what the answer might be within one's faith tradition. From our own seeking to understand God and spirituality, we believe a person is wiser to use the wisdom from many religions rather than try to perceive God through the perspective of one religion.

God as a Human Creation

Many very intelligent people argue that God is a human creation. They assert that God is merely a shared social concept and is, therefore, an illusion. To them God does not exist in any real sense. We both agree and disagree with their arguments.

We agree that much of what religious leaders say about God is a human creation, but we disagree that God does not exist. If we have learned nothing else from philosophy and science, we should understand that what we call "knowledge" changes. It is always evolving because of new discoveries and more advanced insights.

As we move through time, knowledge exists as a process in which we humans continually learn more about the universe and ourselves. Why can we not accept that our understanding of God will, and even should, change as we ourselves evolve and acquire more knowledge? Many of us cannot accept that our concepts of God directly flow from our very human experiences, which necessarily limit what we can know.

Atheists point to the many religious traditions and stress how they differ significantly. These differences account for why some atheists conclude that God does not exist and religion is nonsense. But we again point to the mystical and spiritual wing of all the faith traditions and note how remarkably similar they are. We conclude that these similarities affirm, but certainly do not prove, that God exists. Neither atheists nor persons of faith have a definitive argument for or against the existence of God. Such an argument does not exist and, we suspect, never will.

Some atheists argue that humankind should declare God non-existent. We argue that just because one's conception of God is derived from human imagination does not negate the existence of God. Similarly, because scientists use their imaginations to develop scientific theories, we do not say that scientific theories do not exist. Such a statement is as absurd as is saying God does not exist because human imagination developed our past and current understandings of God.

A belief in God brings benefits to society and its individuals. Studies of prehistory tell us that many humans evidently felt a need in their lives for the concept of an external power, a god or multiple gods. Even though some religious beliefs are based on imagination, we maintain that many aspects of religions are still quite useful to society. In particular, we argue in more depth later in this book that the spiritual aspect of religions is not only individually uplifting but also a potentially powerful force to help us all live together in a sense of Oneness.

The Challenge from Globalization

Because of increasing globalization, rapidly advancing scientific discoveries, and the growing emphasis put on critical thinking, some atheists challenge our argument about the positive roles for religion. They argue that, as a result of globalization, the peoples of the world are experiencing a clash of cultures. They note, for example, that the Judeo-Christian Western culture is clashing with the Islamic culture, and the result is war and attacks on innocent civilians.

Some in Islamic cultures believe that the Judeo-Christian culture demands all peoples of the world adopt the values of Western culture. One example is women's rights. The segments of Islam that have not progressed beyond the First Religious Awakening maintain beliefs that often include a strong bias against the civil rights of women. In fact, fundamentalists of all religions, because of how they understand their Holy Scriptures, look at women as inferior to men.

Some fundamentalists of various religions even believe that having women attend school is an act against God. If they were to adopt different beliefs, they argue, they would no longer be good members of their faith tradition. In the Islamic culture, to push back against unwanted effects from the Judeo-Christian culture, certain individuals and sub-groups resort to violence.

Although some believers from both the Islamic and the Judeo-Christian religions view this clash in cultures as a reason for violence, we think the clash is not as serious as they claim. One of the core values of Western culture is freedom of religion, and Western culture shows a large tolerance for the customs and religions of others. In addition, many in the Islamic religion note that Muslim Holy Scripture specifically teaches religious tolerance toward Jews and Christians. Of course, there are limits to each religion's capacity for tolerance, but we have reason to hope for peace and active cooperation among at least the more liberal and moderate segments of these religions.

Nevertheless, these clashes of culture do inspire radical Islam, radical Christianity, radical Judaism, radical Hinduism, and radical religious groups of all types to commit violence against other religious groups. This tendency to resort to violence is particularly likely if there is no established history of tolerance among the groups. The result of such clashes is fear and hatred, with each group easily rationalizing its violent acts, such as the use of bombs against civilian populations.

Those who make a globalization / culture clash argument for the negative influence of religion on society note that religions may have been a uniting force in some circumstances in the past, but today religions are the major motivation for wars and violence. To them, the fact that religions are based on faith becomes particularly important. They charge that "people of faith" follow their religious leaders without critical thought. If those leaders call for violence, then "people of faith" respond with violence against those of "the other religion."

The solution to this globalization / clash of cultures is not, as atheists suggest, to promote "the God illusion," the notion that the existence of God is an illusion. Even if religion is the primary excuse for violence in the world, it is not realistic to think, first, that religious groups would come to believe that God is an illusion and, consequently, give up their religions, and second, even if they did, that peace would then prevail in the world.

Since prehistory, people have taken advantage of others, and some groups will always find reasons to visit violence upon other groups. Religion is only one of the many excuses people use to rationalize violence. If we had no religions, some individuals would simply create other reasons to justify violence. Such is the nature of the human animal. What is promising is that the religions that have embraced the Second Awakening actively attempt to move us beyond being merely human animals to being spiritual beings. Such beings do not seek or rationalize violence against others.

Religions, especially those that adopted the Second Religious Awakening, play a positive role in fostering peace in the world. In fact, as has been pointed out here, their existence has permitted society, with its more complex groupings, to evolve increasingly toward Oneness. Unfortunately, the fundamentalist wings of these same religions do not embrace the Second Awakening reforms, and that remains a problem in need of a solution.

One contemporary example that shows religions serving as an instrument for peace in the world is the Parliament of Religions. This international group meets every four years in various countries for the purpose of encouraging religious tolerance and understanding. One of its efforts is to focus on the problem that there are many versions of ethics in the world today. These differing and conflicting approaches make the resolving of disputes among groups much more difficult. The Parliament's main recent suggestion for reform is that the religions of the world unify behind a single global ethic and use it to resolve conflicts. Swami Vivekananda (1863—1903), who opened the first Parliament of Religions in Chicago in 1899, famously said, "All differences in this world are of degree, and not of kind, because Oneness is the secret of everything."

The Challenge from Science

Another source of crisis in religion derives from modern scientific theories and discoveries. Some religious people consider modern scientific discoveries in fields such as paleontology, geology, and physics as direct challenges to the teachings in Scripture. They assert that certain scientific findings imply an attack on their religion. For example, some fundamentalists believe that teaching the scientific theory of evolution in schools is an act against God.

They believe the creation story in the first five books of the Christian Old Testament (what Jews call the Torah) must be accurate because they hold it sacred. For them, teaching other than the Biblical account in public schools is an attack on God's Holy Scriptures. They resent any argument that those scientific discoveries suggest the events narrated in Scripture are metaphor at best and mere fiction at worst. They argue that, at a minimum, creationism should be treated equally with evolution, in spite of the fact that creationism has, to be generous, a weak scientific foundation.

A brief note of irony arises in the inconsistent use of science by many fundamentalists. Science, namely modern technological advances, over time also has created more ways for people to kill each other on an ever-increasing massive scale. Although many fundamentalists fight against certain aspects of science when those aspects challenge the stories in their religion, they quickly embrace the use of the more sophisticated weapon systems that science creates to hurt others. One application of science is incorrect, but another is correct. Their logic of being anti-science because of fundamentalist theology but pro-weapons as products from science is easy for them to understand but difficult for us.

The Challenge from Critical Thinking

Many of these same fundamentalists also argue against teaching critical thinking in schools and universities. They disapprove, for example, of religious studies courses in college where professors critically examine religious texts and point out serious logical inconsistencies within and among the texts.

Those who think Holy Scriptures cannot be in error and should be interpreted literally believe that inconsistency in the scriptures is impossible. Yet it exists. For fundamentalist believers, the answer is to ignore and even attack the scholars who dare point out the inconsistencies. Or they create remarkable and difficult-to-believe rationalizations to explain away the inconsistencies.

Positive Influences

Although globalization, modern scientific discoveries, and critical thinking are contributing to the current crisis in religion, they do not have to undermine religion's relevance. Globalization, if done properly, should increase the standard of living and quality of life for most people in the world. Science, if done properly, should advance what we know, and that should help improve the quality of life for all of us. Critical thinking, if used properly, should help humankind make wise decisions and avoid stupid mistakes. Religion, if done properly, should advance peace within the individual and society. Given their likely positive impacts on society, one can safely assume that globalization, science, and critical thinking will and should continue to exist, as will religion.

In all likelihood, the fundamentalist wing of the various religions will continue to resist globalization, science, and critical thinking. Probably the fundamentalists will be successful in some places in the world. Subsequently, those places will, in all likelihood, fall further and further behind economically and socially. In time, the resistance of the fundamentalists will become increasingly difficult for them to maintain unless they have absolute political control.

The more radical elements of the fundamentalist wings of religion may not survive this crisis in religion if they resort to violent attacks against their larger societies. Those societies will defend themselves from the attacks. The larger societies will isolate and remove the dysfunctional elements of religion; the larger societies have the economic and military advantage, and they really have no choice but to do so. Therefore, globalization, science, and critical thinking will influence which elements of religion change and survive.

A Call for Reform

Some current or former functions of religions will have to change in order to survive. While we do think religious leaders should continue to speak out on political and social issues, we also argue for the American innovation of separating church and state. We suspect the separation of church and state will slowly continue to be adopted as a reform in more nation states. As a result, the existence of established state-financed religion is likely to diminish.

We suspect that increasingly the religions will be disestablished as required state religions and will cease being subsidized by the taxpayers. Why? Because in time religious leaders will grow to appreciate that separation of church and state actually strengthens their religion, as separation means that the church becomes disassociated from the negative and unpopular policies of the state.

We hope and suspect that the Golden Rule element of the Second Religious Awakening will gain momentum and become a standard for human behavior. With increasing globalization of commerce and greater exchange of information, active partners in globalization will help people realize that one group "doing unto another group before anything can be done unto them" ruins trust among peoples and is not economically or socially viable in the long term.

For peoples and nations, to reap the maximum benefits of globalization over long periods of time, fairness to all participants will have to be the common value. The Golden Rule, which is common to almost all religions, is an excellent general value and one that would result in fairer agreements among globalization partners.

We also hope and suspect that the Oneness element of the Second Religious Awakening will gain momentum because of the important value called "doubt." Doubt, or skepticism, exists as the core value in the scientific process of acquiring knowledge. Sustained usage of the scientific method means that doubt, as a value, is stage center in our world.

As we note earlier, the findings of science conflict with many aspects of the First Religious Awakening, such as the myth stories of religion. But, significantly, science is not in conflict with the Oneness aspect of the Second Religious Awakening. The spiritual and mystical wings of the major religions also embrace doubt as their core value. The second lesson in spiritual wisdom (see Chapter 13) is that a person must always be a seeker. That means a person must always be questioning old knowledge and searching for new knowledge, including religious and spiritual knowledge.

As in science, Oneness requires a person to accept that there are always unknowns. For a spiritual person, doubt and inquiry are vital to learning more, challenging what is accepted as known, and pushing back the frontier of ignorance. This necessity for ongoing inquiry is consistent with a world that increasingly values the products and knowledge that science provides.

An Interfaith Approach to Religious Reform

We argue that every religion and every person of faith needs to address the crisis identified here. An interfaith approach is one of many means to address and resolve this crisis induced by globalization, scientific discoveries, and the use of critical thinking. We believe there is not just one acceptable approach to learning about God. Instead, there are many approaches or paths.

We also believe there are false paths even within some of the established religions of the world. One such false path is the Alpha Interpretation within Christianity, the topic we discuss in Chapter 4.

Being the best person one can be and fulfilling that potential is very beneficial for each person and the society of which he or she is part. We believe that being the best includes being a spiritual person, following the Golden Rule, and applying Oneness to one's life. We think these goals can be attained easily in Christianity by using the Omega Interpretation; doing so with the Alpha Interpretation is much more difficult and in some cases may be impossible.

To foster greater spiritual growth, people are wise to employ an interfaith approach, meaning they need to learn more about their own religion as well as other religions. With that knowledge, they are better equipped to ask challenging questions about spirituality and to discern the difference between weak and strong answers.

The past few decades brought a remarkable improvement in the religious studies literature from outstanding scholars. In addition, there has been a great growth in the literature concerning atheism, such as books from scientists Richard Dawkins and Sam Harris. To develop spiritually, people need to read and understand not only the Holy Scriptures of religions other than their own but also the literature of atheism. A useful approach in learning spiritual wisdom is to find what the various religions have in common rather than how are they different.

Summary

The Second Religious Awakening, started by religious leaders from almost every religious tradition, needs to continue to influence modern religions until it successfully changes their theology. We especially feel that change is important for Christianity because we believe Jesus embraced all of the Second Religious Awakening and that it was later leaders of Christianity who digressed from it.

People, especially people of faith, need to accept the Golden Rule and incorporate it into their daily lives, just as Jesus did. In addition, people of faith need to accept the concept of Oneness, including embracing the use of doubt and the understanding that religious knowledge also grows and evolves as does scientific knowledge.

Religions have critical functions to perform in society. They should continue to help people who wish to mark and celebrate major events in their lives. They will also provide physical and mental medical assistance in cooperation with other professionals, such as medical doctors. In addition, they will continue to offer political and social commentary on the issues of the day and help communities address their social concerns, such as with their charities. The most important function for religion, though, is to help individuals grow spiritually, if they wish to do so, by helping them address the challenging questions rather than just accept the religious dogma of the past.

The religions of the world, especially Christianity, are in crisis because many of their more thoughtful followers are increasingly abandoning their religions. This exodus stems from at least three realities. First, globalization and the resulting clash of cultures influence and even foster violent conflicts among the religious peoples of the world. Second, scientific discoveries inadvertently challenge religious myth stories and fundamental beliefs of many religions. Third, critical analysis of texts shows the Holy Scriptures of many religions contain inconsistencies, and the fact of these inconsistencies can call into question religious faith itself.

The identified crisis in religion is serious because it does challenge the existence of religions that nevertheless serve important functions in society. This crisis needs to be addressed rather than ignored. Our intention in this book is to confront the crisis head-on as it applies to Christianity, and we hope concerned individuals will do the same for the other religions of the world.

Chapter 3

Genes, Social Evolution, & God

Saying that God uses evolution as a key biological and social tool seems entirely reasonable to us. Our education, including our graduate and post-graduate study, plus our research, has cultivated in us a cautious acceptance of theories. We have a strong doubt for anything based entirely or almost entirely on "trust me" assertions. But we do accept tentatively what scientific thinkers call knowledge because of the rigor of their tested assertions. Therefore, given the scientific knowledge available to everyone, we find absurd the fundamentalists' argument that the Bible must be interpreted literally.

Metaphors and the Learning Process

To our thinking, the stories in the Bible are metaphors, a means to take a difficult or abstract subject and make it easy to understand. In the time of Jesus, people were more accustomed to stories that taught a point through allegory or symbolism. Our challenge as modern day readers is to understand exactly what the metaphors mean to teach us.

In particular, the story of creation, which Jewish tradition tells us was written down by Moses, makes sense only if it is intended as a metaphor. Even if God had told Moses the creation story in the same way contemporary science explains creation to us today, we cannot imagine Moses had the conceptual background necessary to understand that science-based explanation. God had to simplify it for him—tell it in a figurative way—and, we should add, God must simplify it for us.

Anyone who has taught knows that the act of learning is an evolutionary process for the student. You cannot teach advanced physics before elementary physics nor teach Spanish 4 before Spanish 1 to a child in grade school or high school. We like to think of God as the Supreme Teacher, and therefore, God would have chosen to use a metaphorical explanation for what was really important about creation—not only for Moses in his time but also now for us.

If you believe the Bible is for all people through time but insist on interpreting it literally, then you have to deny or reject remarkable discoveries in the accumulated knowledge we call the, social, and above all, physical, sciences. On the other hand, if you believe the Bible is essentially a metaphorical communication that still teaches significant lessons for each of us in our own eras and circumstances, then the Bible becomes a useful tool.

Although Moses was raised as an Egyptian prince, he would not have been comfortable with the Egyptian version of the creation story (see the author Ions in Appendix A), given his Jewish roots. Nor would he have understood our current scientific explanation. He needed an alternative story. His human characteristic called curiosity would naturally fill in the blanks. He would have used his imagination or previous experiences, or he would have relied upon the Jewish oral stories of his day to explain creation.

Although we suspect Moses would have used the combination of his imagination and older oral Jewish stories, we believe it possible that God "told" the story to him, however that telling was done. We also recognize the claim of scholars in religious studies that the Torah was written and rewritten over the centuries by Jewish priests, often to accommodate political needs of their times (Silberman and Finkelstein).

Devout Jews believe God gave the tablets with the Ten Commandments to Moses on Mount Sinai, and that Moses wrote the Torah. We believe that who wrote it and when it was written is not as important as its usefulness to our lives. This usefulness exists primarily because of the Torah's allegorical content, not its literalism.

The sticking point for many who insist on a literal interpretation of the creation story is the theory of evolution. However, evolutionary theory, including social evolution, can be seen as consistent with a belief in God and His intention. According to that theory, evolution over an extensive time period builds significant physical and social characteristics into our genes, and those genes influence our behavior today. Specifically, humans have what we call an inclination towards Social Oneness and what the noted biologist and theorist E. O. Wilson calls "Group Selection" (French 81).

The genes for Social Oneness have been built naturally into humans through the process of social evolution. Those genes help us to be successful in our social behavior, and that success permits us to live better and longer, just as genes give us the ability to stand upright, have fast reflexes, and eyesight to see distances. Even though the genes for Social Oneness are a natural part of our makeup, throughout our lives we need to cultivate the use of wisdom, especially spiritual wisdom, to determine how best to address our yearning for, and predilection toward, that Oneness.

The Concept of Self

Anyone who has taken a philosophy class probably knows Rene Descartes' famous phrase *Cogito ergo sum*, which commonly translates from the Latin as "I think, therefore I am." We believe that a better translation is "I am cognitively aware, therefore I exist." For each of us, we know we exist because we have the ability to sense, and that is all we can be absolutely sure about. More specifically, again because we can sense, most of us believe there is a "self," or what some call the ego. Consequently, many of us can identify with what we think is our individuality, especially in Western culture. But some groups think such identification is an illusion, as we explain later in this chapter.

Moral Development of the Self

The late Harvard professor Lawrence Kohlberg noted that, as we grow as individuals from childhood to adolescence and eventually to adulthood, we experience several stages of moral development. He formed his theory, Stages of Moral Development, by building on earlier work in child development done by Swiss psychologist Jean Piaget (Satterly).

Kohlberg believed that, just as children try to make sense of their life experiences as they grow, naturally proceeding through stages of moral development, so too adults grow in their moral understanding. The way to understand moral behavior is to understand how individuals make sense of their world (Kohlberg). He proposed that individuals construct their own moral epistemology, in other words, standards and criteria to use for knowing or comprehending what they think about morality.

Kohlberg observed that, as individuals mature, they can move through three levels of moral development. Each level is divided in two, making a six-stage staircase (Simpson 1974). The individual "advances" to a higher stage, "better" than the preceding one, by moving up the staircase (Kohlberg). However, not everyone moves up the staircase, and some do not even go beyond the first step.

To Kohlberg, the central stages, Three and Four, represent what he called Conventional moral thinking because that is where he thought the majority of people stop. Conventional moral thinking refers to a person observing common social norms because civilized life requires some kind of accepted order. Movement from *Conventional* to *Post-Conventional* thinking changes a person's understanding of laws, rules and institutions from simply generating order, to a holistic system based on that person's ideal of cooperation.

Kohlberg's Theory

Level	Stage	Focus
Post-Conventional	6. Follows a self-chosen autonomous path based on articulated principles. 5. Obligated to the rules because of felt social contract and the ideal of the greatest good for the greatest number.	Humanity or God
Conventional	4. Loves the rules because they bring order to life. 3. Acts to be liked and well thought of by family and peers.	Immediate circle of significant others
Pre-Conventional	2. Acts to achieve a reward and honor a deal. 1. Acts to avoid the pain of punishment.	Ego

Source: Kohlberg, 1976.

Kohlberg's Stages of Moral Development, which start at stair step Stage 1 and end at Stage 6, help us understand a person's reasoning when faced with ethical dilemmas. The theory provides a framework for seeing the connection between what adults do and their level of moral development (Trevino 1986). The six stages of moral development start with the ego and move continually upward from the individual ego toward universal ethical principles or laws. In *Pre-Conventional* Stage One, a person's orientation focuses on how to avoid punishment. For example, many drivers obey the speed limit laws because they do not want to be stopped by the police for speeding and do not wish to pay a large fine.

In Stage Two, individuals identify the self with whomever they reach agreement. Individuals accept the fact that they have a meeting of the minds between and among two or more other persons and themselves, and subsequently they act to honor that agreement. Essentially, they ask "What is in it for us based on our agreement?" In Stage Two, people think of the self within the context of those agreements. For example, a person may offer to look after your dog while you travel, in exchange for staying in your beachfront home for two weeks.

In the Conventional Stages, Three and Four, individuals identify the self as an extension of their family and friends; social norms drive their sense of morality. For example, a brother or sister will gladly offer to help a sibling in a time of need. In Stage Four, our self becomes identified with our group, which can be a tribe, a profession or even citizenship. Here we have an orientation that maintains authority and social-order.

In Post-Conventional Stage Five, we see the self as the whole, usually meaning the world population but sometimes only our nation. In this stage, we are concerned with doing the greatest good for the greatest number within that population. We have what Kohlberg calls a social contract orientation. In this stage, a person might join a cause that will help him or her identify with good for the larger society, for instance, protecting the environment or rescuing animals. In Stage Six, our understanding of self embraces an abstract principle such as an ideology or ideal, like justice, unconditional love, or Oneness.

The orientation becomes principled-consciousness (Kohlberg). For example, the principle of justice becomes the motivator for our every action, regardless of the harm it may cause us personally. Thus the Stage 6 thinker identifies self with justice, or compassion.

Kohlberg's model shows the human thinking process as it becomes more complex and sophisticated. In it, humans develop and evolve (Trevino 1986:604). That is to say, the emphasis on moral thinking rests on the reasons individuals use to justify a moral choice or action rather than on what they actually choose to do. Individuals make moral judgments regarding their rights and duties based on a rationale that flows from their understanding as to who they are in the narrow or broad sense of self (Trevino 1986; Colby *et al.* 1980).

For many reasons, some of us do not grow morally through all the stages; we get stuck in one or another of the early stages and remain there for the rest of our lifetimes. (For a more complete and updated explanation of the Stages of Moral Development, we suggest you read James Rest *et al.*, *Postconventional Moral Thinking: A Neo-Kohlbergian Approach.*)

Spiritual Development

Kohlberg's theory also has implications for spiritual development. In His teachings, Jesus spoke a great deal about what He called the Kingdom of Man and the Kingdom of God / Kingdom of Heaven (except when quoting Jesus, we use the term Kindom of God to avoid sexist language). Those two "Kingdoms" represent polar opposites to most people, but we consider them a unified process and use the term "a unity of opposites" (see Chapter 5).

These concepts are parts of a process in which a person can evolve from the mindset or consciousness rooted in what Jesus called the Kingdom of Man and grow into the consciousness called the Kindom of God. Neither is an actual physical place.

The Kingdom of Man corresponds especially to Kohlberg's Stages One and Two. In it, the individual identifies himself or herself as the ego and thus extensively uses the pronouns "I, me, my, and mine" while placing extreme value on having material wealth, power, and satisfaction for the ego. Perceived behavioral needs and desires control such a person. For instance, a person may have many cars, shoes, or hats not because he needs them but because he wants them.

Please do not misunderstand us. We agree with Kohlberg and others who see love of the self, defined as ego, as an important first stage in an individual's moral development. But it is just the beginning in the process of spiritual growth. We must consciously grow into the other stages. Some people, however, do not move past Stage One or Two. If we are to be the best persons we can be, we must continue to grow morally, and that also means spiritually.

When Jesus advocated against our exclusive focus on the Kingdom of Man, He was saying we need to start with Stage One, but, more significantly, we need to go far beyond it. We pass beyond Stages One and Two into Kohlberg's Stages Three and Four by expanding our focus beyond our immediate self and eventually loving our neighbors, communities, and even our enemies. We progress to the higher stages of Five and Six by loving all that is the universe, meaning we move toward what we call in Chapter 2 the Oneness aspect of the Second Religious Awakening.

LEVEL	FOCUS
Post-Conventional	Humanity, the Infinite or God
Conventional	Family, Tribe, Friends and Significant Others
Pre-Conventional	Ego: I, Me, My, and Mine

Source: Based on Kohlberg, 1976.

When Jesus advocated for the Kindom of God, He gave us a goal and an ideal we can approach, both individually and collectively, if we care deeply for others and our environment. Realistically, not many of us will reach Stage Six on the Kohlberg scale, and Jesus understood that fact, as indicated by the stress He placed on saving the special one lost sheep over the ninety-nine (Gospel of Thomas Saying, 107 and Luke 15:4-7). Saying 107 reads:

> "Jesus said, 'The kingdom is like a shepherd who had a hundred sheep. One of them, the largest, went astray. He left the ninety-nine and sought the one until he found it. After he had gone to this trouble, he said to the sheep, "I love you more than the ninety-nine."

Note the special one lost sheep is the one that reached the Kindom of Heaven but also deviated from it after achieving it. To God, such a person is worth a special effort to save and is much more valuable than the other 99 who have never reached the Kindom.

What is important is that each of us advances with awareness through the various stages, to the extent we can. Even a small shift of the global population toward Stage Six thinking, with its emphasis on Oneness, and, more importantly, above Stage One moral thinking, will make a radical and positive difference to our world. That shift is what we believe Jesus meant by creating a Kindom of God on earth.

The Infinite, Within and Without

In His teachings, Jesus says that we, as individuals and as a people, need to expand our love to others while including our love of the ego-self. In the Hindu tradition, the larger loved self is Self with a capitalized "S," and that meaning is similar to Kohlberg's Stages Five and Six. We draw parallels between

Jesus' message and the Hindu tradition: Self, with a capital "S," is our union with the Infinite, or God, and the Self resides both outside and inside the person. In this view, we all have the divine spark within us, and our challenge is to grow that spark into a glowing light. In our quest for greater spiritual wisdom, we would also grow that light through our expanding love.

Buddhists approach the notion of self differently. To them, self/Self is an illusion that retards a person's evolution when the individual identifies with it. Buddhists are pragmatists, but they also see ultimate reality in a manner similar to Heraclitus (see Chapter 5). That is, they conceptualize reality not as things (such as rocks, chairs, and persons) but rather as a continuing flow of events that are always becoming. There is no "thing" such as a self but rather a series of events focusing on an ever-changing object, such as a person. In other words, think of ultimate reality as a motion picture rather than a picture.

The goal of Buddhists is to end or minimize suffering caused by endless desires. They see wanting or desires as directly related to the illusion of self (Cleary). Stop wanting, and you will stop your suffering. The Buddhists teach that we should stop identifying with objects, wealth, and power in order to eliminate desires that lead to suffering. This statement is an oversimplification of Buddhism that we hope does not mislead the reader, but the key point here is that the ego-self is considered to be a problem. (For an in-depth explanation of Buddhist thought on Self, see Mark Epstein, *Psychotherapy Without the Self: A Buddhist Perspective*.)

To summarize, individuals can identify themselves in various ways, from (a) being ego-centered and excluding others, to (b) being focused on abstract principles, or to (c) even denying a self/Self exists. Our great religious traditions tell us that being ego-centered and excluding others are what we must avoid. Instead, we must aspire either to identify with something much larger than our limited ego-self or deny the ego entirely. We argue that such insights have helped humankind to evolve socially as a species. We also argue that this evolution needs to continue because it is thus far only partially successful.

Social Evolution

Scientific knowledge regarding how and when our species evolved is incomplete. What follows is one commonly held understanding of that evolution.

About 15 or 20 million years ago, our ancestors in Africa, before we became *Homo sapiens*, were fruit eaters. Meanwhile, an unrelated group of small forest monkeys, also in Africa, developed the ability to digest unripe fruit. This new digestive ability of our rivals for food put our ancestors at a big disadvantage because their primary food supply was greatly diminished. The small monkeys would eat the unripe fruit while our ancestors were still waiting for the fruit to ripen.

To adapt and find alternative food supplies, the humanoids had to move to the edge of the forest where there was more food. But there was also more danger from carnivorous animals, such as big cats, canines, and other savannah predators. Through evolutionary adaption, our ancestors increased in body size and associated in larger social groups for protection. The evolutionary change from individual hunters to small groups to large groups provided them with not only more eyes to detect enemies but also a better ability to defend themselves through their greater numbers and cooperation within the group.

Basically, we are told that, around six million years ago, the ancestors of *Homo sapiens* split off from the lineage that became chimpanzees. For almost all of our relatively short existence—short given the age of earth—we lived in nomadic groups that found food by hunting and gathering.

The need to be in large working groups created the classic human problem that exists to this day. Members of the group had to be intelligent and flexible enough to balance their individual needs with those of the group. Humans working in groups must cooperate and exercise some individual restraint. They must understand behavior of other group members and manage their place in an ever-shifting array of alliances that members form in order to function in the large groups.

Perhaps the first behavioral modification that helped create this bonding within groups was reciprocal grooming. For example, monkeys and great apes (and some human teenagers) today spend up to a fifth of their time grooming each other. Although this bonding behavior still exists, it long ago proved insufficient. So another evolutionary development was necessary: speech (Krubitzer and Huffman).

The need to understand social dynamics in the acquisition of food and how to navigate terrain in groups spurred and rewarded humanoid evolution. It also resulted in increasingly larger primate brains. There is a correlation between brain size and the size of a species' social groups. The cognitive abilities that permit social group interaction are associated with the outer neocortex of the brain. In most mammals, the neocortex accounts for 30 to 40 percent of brain volume. In higher social primates, it is 50 to 65 percent. In humans, it is 82 percent (Krubitzer and Huffman).

No strong correlation exists between the size of the neocortex and the performance of tasks like hunting, navigating, or creating shelter. However, understanding one another, especially in the context of groups, does require advanced cognitive abilities. The only way humans could manage being in groups beyond about 50 in size was by learning to speak. They had to understand group behavior and develop communication skills.

Evolution to Survive

For humans, group living became essential for survival. Some in the group had to hunt and gather, and others had to literally keep the "home" fires burning as they specialized in domestic duties, such as cooking and child rearing. One of the consequences of such social living was that individual behavior became highly flexible and tailored to changing circumstances. For example, a woman in her short life span might have to bear and rear children, but also forage for food and defend those children from predators.

In human evolution, changing global weather patterns also had a profound impact, leading us to move continually and band together in supportive groups. In addition, caring for our children, who matured much more slowly than other young animals, was a remarkable challenge, also forcing us to coalesce in family and tribal groups.

The harsh realities of nomadic life meant that the numbers of *Homo sapiens* in the world grew very slowly until about 3,000 years ago. Then humans started to plant crops, tend them, and grow enough food to support greater populations. As we point out earlier, those populations created cities, and they evolved into what we now call civilization. The technological innovation of horticulture rooted us to particular places and encouraged us to specialize in tasks and to trade over longer distances.

The Importance of Being Selfless and United

In human history, super-cooperative and selfless humans replaced less united groups that were dominated by selfish individualistic members (Judson 90 – 98). From an evolutionary perspective, this replacement happened over a long period of time when the cooperative group practiced monogamy or allowed a limited numbers of wives for each husband and when the group shared food. Such practices reduced the ability of the selfish members to out-reproduce their more generous members. If one or two males monopolized all the females in the group in polygamous relationships, over thousands of years any genes in the gene pool involved in selflessness would quickly disappear, and over time the social group would be less stable (Callaway). Thus, with time, monogamy enhanced specie selflessness and polygamy enhanced selfishness.

From a social rather than an evolutionary perspective, perfect examples of these sometimes worse and sometimes better cooperative behaviors within the group existed in the ancient Jewish nation. When its members followed God's commandments, designed to foster Oneness, they were able to defeat their enemies; and when they did not follow God's directions, their enemies won. Two dramatic examples of the Jewish people being seriously harmed are the conflicts with the Babylonians and the Romans. Clearly, God's actions, described in the Torah, often made the Jewish people more cooperative and selfless toward each other and even toward other peoples, even though the Jews sometimes broke down into rival warring groups.

The Torah helps us further understand the importance of being united, especially in a more civilized environment, such as a nation, rather than being divided into smaller social units. The Torah points out that God gave the descendants of Abraham a leader in the person of Moses. God instructed Moses to form and unite the 12 Hebrew tribes, who descended from Jacob (Israel), the grandson of Abraham, into a large social group and eventually into a nation. Most Jews and Christians know about the covenant between God and the Jewish people. In short, God made an agreement with descendants of Abraham. It was simple and direct: "Believe in Me and follow My rules. If you do that, I will take care of you. If you do not, I will punish you."

Jews did not always abide by the covenant that established the importance of unity, and they fought among themselves. As we point out earlier, when the Jews failed to follow God's directions, they lost battles and eventually even lost their nation twice. Clearly, the political motivation that underscores the Torah is evident: individuals and groups, such as tribes, must think in terms of the Oneness of Israel.

The Torah recounts other developments that show Jews becoming a definable social group (a nation and a people). God defined for them identifiable group characteristics, such as circumcision and wearing their clothing in a manner different from others. God also provided a set of ethical rules to enable group living, and He set dietary requirements. Above all, He required the Jews to live together in harmony and defined what it meant to be righteous and just within a group setting.

Nevertheless, the Torah chronicles extensive warring and murder. The opening book of the Torah relates that one of the first brothers of our species committed murder. Murder and warfare were common in the six-million-year history of humankind; one estimate cites possibly 15 percent of those born in a given year died because of war or murder (Callaway). The fighting took place both among and within social groups.

The Torah is a story with divine social lessons: Social Oneness is important if you are interested in surviving as a group or even surviving as an individual. In more scientific language, genetic predisposition for selflessness is likely to dominate when there are fewer examples of group disparities and discord. The Torah's story of the Jews confirms the science.

The Torah also cites examples of Jews stoning and killing their own people when members of the community violated the group's norms. In this way, the more selfish or non-conforming Jews were purged from the group. To the modern person, such actions seem remarkably harsh and wrong. However, non-conforming individuals weaken the whole group, especially when a group's survival is at stake. The Torah is a lesson in forming a cohesive group. If the group did not eliminate non-conformers, it would not have won its battles and would not have become a nation able to sustain itself.

People who followed the group's rules, formal and informal, contributed to the group's collective strength. In sum, this adherence constituted an evolutionary social advantage that helped the group survive. Again, the fact that the Jews are still a social group after more than 3,500 years supports this scientific hypothesis.

Evolution and Jesus

As we state in Chapters 1 and 2, we believe the prevailing and dominant Alpha Interpretation of the New Testament is not correct and misleads people as to the mission and message of Jesus. We believe that Jesus instead was trying to teach the Jewish people to understand and apply the concept of Social Oneness, and also advance the evolution of the individual. His ministry was about the Kindom of God, which, as we point out, was not a place but rather a selfless state of mind, meaning a consciousness that developed through an evolutionary process.

Jesus understood the larger message of Oneness in the Torah, a message we describe here, and He realized that contemporary Jewish religious leadership was not adequately bringing that message to His people. He knew that almost every individual has the potential to be ego-centered, selfless, or some combination of both. As we note in Chapter 9, His ministry aimed to move His people away from a dominant ego-centered consciousness and toward a selfless consciousness.

Generally, we humans are more selfless than we give ourselves credit. Two "punishment games," as they are called in teaching psychology, illustrate that point. These two simple games show how people react in what many would consider ideal ego-centered situations. In the first game, we are told to assume one person is a dictator who has $1,000 and the second person has no money at all. On average, over many games with different people playing the two roles, how much money would the dictator share with the second person? Realistically, the "dictator" does not need to give any money to the second person (Fehr).

In the second game, we still have two people playing, but

a rule is added. If the second person does not like the offer made by the first person, he or she can refuse the offer. If the second person refuses, then both persons get nothing. On average, over many games, how much would the dictator give to the poor person? From a pragmatic viewpoint, there is now an incentive to share, but how much is shared?

The science of economics—the "dismal science" as the historian Thomas Carlyle termed it in the nineteenth century—is predicated on the pessimistic thinking of individuals like the philosopher John Hobbes. He argued that the basic nature of humankind was poor, nasty, brutish and short. Most Hobbesian economists would guess that in the first game, the dictator would maximize his potential wealth and keep the $1,000. In the second game, they would probably believe that the poor person would reason "something is better than nothing," but that the average figure settled upon would be much larger for the dictator and smaller for the poor person.

Empirical observation of the game while it's being played reveals that the suppositions of the Hobbesian economists would be wrong. Some people seem to have a selfless gene, a gene that might have developed because of social evolution. In the first game, many people are generous enough to share with someone they don't know. In the second game, many people were willing to forgo getting anything themselves in order to punish someone who made a demeaning or ungenerous offer. Humans seem to have evolved an aptitude for conforming to the prevailing cultural norms and making sure those norms are enforced. Apparently we have genes that foster selfless behavior toward others.

Selfless vs. Selfish

Scientific evidence suggests there is a genetic underpinning to being friendly. An extreme case can be seen in a condition identified as Williams Syndrome. A person with Williams Syndrome tends to have poor cardiovascular functions, a small, pointed "elfin" face, and be incautiously friendly and nice to all other people. Such people can learn the phrase "Don't talk to strangers," but they can't translate it into action. In other words, they cannot choose to be unfriendly, as can people in the general population.

Individuals with this condition are missing a small segment of chromosome 7, and that means they are missing more than 25 genes. Almost all people have 46 chromosomes in 23 pairs, one set from each parent; a person with Williams Syndrome has one normal chromosome 7, but the other chromosome 7 of the pair lacks 25 genes or more (www.williams-syndrome.org). Somehow this insufficiency results in overly "nice" people.

We suggest that what happened over thousands of years is that humans developed both the selfish (ego-centered) and selfless (non-ego-centered) sets of genes. Centuries of social situations taught us that working cooperatively was helpful, but not in all situations. So choice became essential for deciding when to be selfish and ego-centered and when to be selfless and non-ego-centered. Often individuals made those choices not using rational thought and wisdom but instead depending upon their stage of moral development.

Selfish genes dominate some individuals and selfless genes dominate others. Therefore, in any population, some people tend to think only of themselves (ego-centered), while others tend to think of what is better for their group or what is best to advance their cause (non-ego-centered). This observation parallels Kohlberg's theory in the Stages of Moral Development. He asserted that, in any normal population, there will be a mix of people reflecting the various stages of moral development. But, he said, very few will be in the highest stage.

The practical implications of this finding are important. We are born with built-in selfish / selfless tendencies, but we are also born with the mental capacity to turn on or off either set of genes. *Freewill* does exist, but each of us has a default setting. If you are naturally selfish, you can train yourself to become more selfless. Conversely, if you are naturally selfless, you can train yourself to become more selfish. In both cases, changing requires time and concerted effort.

Apparently, we are also born with what we call a Social Oneness Virtue. Like selfless and selfish, we are genetically hardwired with inclinations to be individualistic and social, but some of us are more individualistic and others more social. In other words, at one extreme are people who think greed is good, while at the other extreme are people who consider such a thought demonic. Still others, the majority, have a mix of such thoughts that vary by circumstance.

So, like other virtues, Social Oneness is on a continuum, as the Greek philosopher Aristotle taught us. Absolute Individualism, or what we call "Inadequate Social Oneness," is at one end of the continuum; Absolute Social Collectivism, or what we call "Too Much Social Oneness," is at the other end. The Golden Mean of a virtue is the "right" action that rests some place between the two extremes or vices, but such "right" action depends on the practical circumstance of the moment. An example of Absolute Individualism is found in the people willing to harm anyone who does not allow them to live life as they wish. Living life as they wish, for instance, might be their decision to ignore traffic rules. An example of Social Collectivism is found in the people who live in a nation with extensive rules of behavior that strip individual members of any self-identity.

Social Oneness Virtue

Inadequate	<>	Too Much

In the diagram that illustrates the Social Oneness Virtue, the <> symbol represents the Golden Mean for a particular situation. The proper place for the Golden Mean is decided with the assistance of wisdom. The poles of "Inadequate Social Oneness" and "Too Much Social Oneness" are the extremes of the continuum. Both are considered "sins."

The biologist E. O. Wilson argues that this selfish/selfless continuum, or "unity of opposites," developed in humans over a great deal of time. He theorizes that two rival forces drive human behavior: "group selection" and "individual selection" (French 81). The group selection theory of evolution holds that alleles (parts of genes) can become fixed or spread over time in a population because of the benefits they bestow on the group, even sometimes to the detriment of the individual. In individual selection theory, the individual embodies the selection of thousands of selfish genes, each trying to perpetuate itself (Dawkins).

The Role Of Freewill

People fall naturally somewhere along this continuum as they deal with the type and severity of social situations. They can also override their genetic programming because they have both sets of selfish and selfless genes and because they have a mind with freewill that can reprogram their behavior should they choose.

In other words, Jesus was correct. People as a whole, and certainly some people in particular, can move along this continuum, away from selfishness and Absolute Individualism toward selflessness and greater Social Oneness. With effort, many of us, and maybe most, can move from the Kingdom of Man toward the Kindom of Heaven, but that does not mean we will choose to do so. However, shifting the population even somewhat up-range toward selflessness means greater peace and social harmony is likely to result, as the Bible helps us understand.

America's progress in Civil Rights demonstrates that people as a group are capable of social learning. Certainly racism continues to exist in the twenty-first century among some

Americans, but the U. S. population has shifted significantly toward selflessness, in spite of the fact that some people still define their group as being "better" or "superior" than other racial groups.

For each of us as we exercise freewill, life is a series of situations we approach with our enhanced genetic social programming, but time and place also influence what we choose to do in those life situations. What might be the "correct" decision toward Social Oneness for an individual or group depends on the context of the situation. Often we should be more selfless; but sometimes we need to be more selfish.

We must use wisdom and critical thinking on a case-by-case basis when we make those life decisions. For example, using limited family resources to send children to school is a selfless act on the part of the parents and may seem like a selfish act on the part of the children. The parents lessen their limited resources which they could otherwise use for needed purposes, such as buying a new car, whereas the children get to enjoy the experience of college with people their own age. Nevertheless it might be the wiser long-range decision for all in that the children will be in a better financial and social situation in the future to help their parents because of their education.

From the perspective of public policy, we must narrow the chances of allowing negative situations that bring about selfish behavior because such behavior can hurt the larger good of the community. For example, public policy can establish that a homeowner need not give up his home for the purposes of building a road that will improve commerce. If such a public policy existed, few public roads would be built and commerce in an area would be significantly harmed. We must cultivate the development of wisdom within our society so that individuals and groups are more likely to make effective choices, which normally would mean deciding in favor of greater Social Oneness.

In teaching us to love our neighbor and our enemy, Jesus

was not telling the geneticist to cut out those 25 genes. Jesus recognized that freewill is one of God's important gifts to us, but He also knew that freewill choices are best if they are wise ones within the context of our circumstances. Many of us might think loving behavior is always best, but there are situations where we need to apply more judicious behavior. For example, we are always wiser to select our friends so that they inspire our positive behavior and not our bad behavior.

Jesus was trying to encourage the general public to have much more love – at least tolerance and acceptance – toward others. He saw that lack of such traits is the more serious problem affecting human behavior. If many more people aimed for the Golden Mean on the continuum of Social Oneness, then there would be greater peace in the world. Many of us act in a selfish manner toward others, especially if they fall outside of what we identify as our social group. The existence of racial and ethnic prejudice illustrates this. Almost all of us need to expand our self-identity to include everyone and everything. But we must also not forget that the persons most likely to hurt us are those who are closest to us, sometimes including ourselves. We hurt ourselves, for example, when we fail to meet deadlines or forget to study for an exam.

Writing as educators, we firmly believe people need to develop their intelligence and skills as much as possible. Doing so gives them greater abilities that enhance not only their lives but also the lives of others. But obstacles, such as a lack of money, can preclude that development. For people living in social or economic poverty, this endeavor to develop their knowledge and skills can be very difficult and sometimes impossible.

In some cultures, the desire of its people—especially minorities and women—to develop their intellectual, physical, or spiritual self seems like an extremely selfish undertaking, one done at the expense of the family's welfare. Given that individuals can contribute more to the group's well being when they are better equipped or trained to do so, this perspective is normally shortsighted. Developing the intellectual, physical, or spiritual self for as many people as possible is not only good for the person but also for the whole of society.

Sometimes the selfless gene encourages a young woman at the micro level to sacrifice her education for her immediate family's economic well-being. Social pressure and her own genes tell her she has "no real choice." Clearly, at the macro level, what is wrong is having public policies that force women and men into situations that offer poor choices. Our societies certainly do not flourish when public policies oppose personal development.

The story of Martha and Mary in the Gospel of Luke (10: 40-42) is appropriate when discussing wise choices, especially at the micro level. Jesus was visiting a house where Martha and Mary were part of a gathering. Mary was listening to the words of Jesus while Martha was busy preparing food and serving the group. Eventually, Martha complained to Jesus about Mary not helping. Jesus answered: "Martha, Martha, you are careful and troubled about many things: but one thing is needful: and Mary has chosen the correct path, which shall not be taken away from her."

The social selfless gene is important; serving others is indeed important. However, learning, especially from the Master, is radically more important. From a spiritual perspective, there is nothing more important for any person—Mary, Martha, or anyone—than learning from the Master who can teach us spiritual wisdom. Martha was making the free choice not to learn but suggesting that Mary should also make the same mistake.

So where do we find such wisdom? It takes effort to find, but it is found in the spiritual literature of every faith tradition. Wisdom is also found in the halls of the academy, our libraries, our bookstores, and on the Internet. In all cases, when you look for wisdom, you must seek and you will find, because it is always there. Jesus taught us that the challenge is to recognize it, separate it from the material that is not wise, cherish it, and apply it to our everyday lives.

Another Call for a Social Oneness Virtue

In sum, the concept of evolution, and especially social evolution, is consistent with the teachings of the Torah and Jesus. The Torah helps us understand how humankind moved along its social evolutionary path. In addition, the New Testament teaches us that the ministry of Jesus was built on the Torah's message, and that message fostered the social evolution of humankind. Looking at history discussed in the Torah, we can see how the Social Oneness Virtue helped the Jewish people when they applied it and hurt them when they ignored it.

The concept of self is central to religious and moral thought. The scope of its meaning varies among religions but the various meanings of self can be placed into the context of human social evolution. The extremes of the self—absolute selflessness and absolute selfishness—are opposites, and they are also the corresponding vices of great excess and deficiency. They are the poles on a continuum of virtue called Social Oneness. As Aristotle taught us, first, the Golden Mean of this virtue depends on practical circumstances. Second, the Golden Mean lies between the two vices. Third, we need wisdom to identify where the Golden Mean lies for any set of circumstances.

This Social Oneness Virtue can and should be taught in schools and our religious institutions. Believing there is just one path to Social Oneness for all people in all circumstances does not lead to their making effective choices or decisions. Societies need to teach people not only to adapt themselves to their conditions but also to compensate for dysfunctional tendencies in their social behavior, such as becoming enraged or crying when disagreeing with others. Typically, the use of meditation helps a person calm his or her emotions and is an excellent means to help deal with dysfunctional tendencies.

Societies also need to teach its members how to apply practical wisdom to sort out the correct course of action in the most common situations. Above all, societies need to stress that Social Oneness is a virtue we can, and should, cultivate within ourselves. Teaching wisdom is a matter of exposing societies' members to wisdom literature and then asking them to apply that wisdom to practical case examples.

Chapter 4

The Omega Interpretation

We point out in Chapter 1 that many Christians who adhere to the Alpha Interpretation see God as an automatic teller machine. Just swipe a prayer in a machine, possibly called "church," and punch in your "secret code" that says Jesus is God. Then enter your material wish for the moment, or ask for forgiveness for your sins so you will get into a place called heaven. Instantly out pops your money or other wish. Alternatively, Jesus grants your request to forgive your bad behavior, and you are free to do whatever you want again, without the risk of losing your place in heaven as long as you again go to the ATM after any subsequent bad behavior.

Some examples might clarify this point. Praying that your football or basketball team will win the next game is a common ATM request. Praying that God will forgive you for sleeping with someone other than your spouse and then continuing the same infidelity is another example. Praying every Sunday for material prosperity is a common practice in some churches. Praying that God will forgive you for sins that are a repeated part of your daily existence is also a regular request. Asking God to admit you to heaven as you approach death is not an unusual last-minute request at the ATM.

This commonly held view of Jesus as an ATM is a terrible misunderstanding of Jesus' message and its importance for humankind. As we state earlier, Jesus was a sage and maybe even a prophet, but He was not God. Nevertheless, a proper understanding of His message is important for humankind, which increasingly finds itself in a complex and dangerous world of its own making. If we are to create for ourselves a better world, we need to learn and appreciate what He really taught us rather than accept literally as gospel this ATM understanding of Jesus.

Where Did Jesus Get His Remarkable Ideas?

For those who believe in the Alpha Interpretation, the answer to the question of where Jesus got His ideas is that His ideas came directly from God, given that He was the Son of God. In our Omega Interpretation, the answer is that Jesus got His ideas from the same place we all do, for Jesus was a human being.

Each of us is a product of our DNA and environment. Our ideas come from cumulative experiences that are mixed in the pot of our individual lives. We gain new knowledge, experience new things, and adapt our thoughts and behavior based on that learning, our DNA, and those experiences. Then we repeat the process over and over again. Our experiences lead us to embrace, or reject, the ideas of those around us. Thus our ideas result at least partly from a reaction to our environment, our level of awareness or discernment, and our ability to process information.

If our statements in the preceding paragraph are correct, then one would expect that Jesus should have been against the Roman occupation of Jewish land, have accepted the religious leadership of the temple in Jerusalem, and measured according to our modern standards, have been very sexist. However, if we consider the New Testament and what we know about the Galilee region, as well as the whole Jewish area of the Roman Empire in His time, such a statement about where Jesus got His ideas does not match the views Jesus advocated in His teachings.

Yet, if we make a few assumptions that are not commonly made by the institution we call "the church," we believe Jesus does fit this hypothesis concerning the impact of environment and experiences on our ideas and beliefs. We argue that our alternative view of where Jesus got His ideas is more probable than that offered in the Alpha Interpretation.

Historically, there are very few undisputed facts about Jesus' life. Clearly, His life, or what people believe was His life, has had a remarkable influence for the past 2,000 years on humankind. H. G. Wells, the English author and social commentator in the first half of the twentieth century, noted that this penniless preacher from Nazareth is irrevocably at the very center of history. In fact, Wells stated, Jesus Christ is easily the most dominant figure in all history (Wells).

Although Jesus is one of the most dominant figures in history, if not the most dominant, only one historical document exists that even mentions Him by name. That work is *Jewish Antiquities and the Jewish War*, by Josephus, a Jewish general who took part in the Jewish War (66-73 CE) and also wrote about it.

Josephus' history contains a brief one-paragraph reference to Jesus. The first sentence of that paragraph says, "Now, there was about this time Jesus, a wise man, if it be lawful to call him a man, for he was a doer of wonderful works—a teacher of such men as receive the truth with pleasure" (*The Antiquities of the Jews*, Book 18, Chapter 3, third paragraph). Some scholars even argue that someone other than Josephus inserted this reference to Jesus into the history and did so many years after Josephus wrote his work. As of today, there is no undisputed documented evidence, historical or archeological, that Jesus even existed. However, He clearly could have existed. For the inquiring and skeptical mind, the question about His existence remains unanswered.

We make this point to stress that our work here is speculative, as is the work of *all* others who comment on the life of the historical Jesus. However, we think by the time you finish this chapter, you will agree that our speculation is reasonable. You may even conclude that our version is more likely and logical than the speculation Christians use to argue for the Alpha Interpretation and what many treat as literal gospel today.

The Temple of Onias

The New Testament says very little about the background of Jesus. It tells us He was born in Bethlehem, which was then in the Judah portion of Israel. He was illegitimate, and He was born into a poor working-class family. The Gospel of Matthew tells us that He and His family moved to Egypt very early in His life and then eventually moved back to Israel. The other New Testament gospels imply by silence on these matters that nothing like that happened.

The Gospel of Luke (2: 46-49) tells us that as a young boy Jesus had an exceptional experience in the Jewish Temple of Jerusalem. Jesus went missing from his parents and after three days his parents found Him in the Temple conversing with learned men who were astonished at His understanding and answers. That is about all we know from the New Testament about the young Jesus until the story picks up again when He was a grown man in the Galilee, beginning His brief but amazingly effective ministry.

Now, for reasons that will become apparent later, let us take a few liberties in our speculation. Let us accept that He was born in Israel and that He and His family did move to Egypt. However, our speculation is that He remained in Egypt until He was mature, and He did not return to Israel until He visited His mother, possibly to attend an important family wedding.

We also speculate that the Jewish Temple He attended as a boy was the Jewish Temple of Onias in Egypt, which was the only temple outside Jerusalem that conducted religious sacrifices.

This speculation is based on a number of historical facts about the temple and the Jewish community in Egypt. During the Assyrian occupation of Jerusalem in 732-627 BCE, the Assyrian King appointed his own men to the priestly leadership of the Jerusalem Temple. Those appointed were not descendants of Aaron, in spite of the fact that the Torah requires Temple priests be descendants of Aaron, brother of Moses. The Kadokite priests, who had served as priests of the Temple before the Assyrian occupation, were direct descendants of Aaron. They fled occupied Jerusalem to Egypt. The pharaoh of Egypt not only accepted them but also allowed them to build a new Jewish temple—the Temple of Onias—at a location near what is the Cairo airport today ("Leontopolis").

As we indicate earlier, we speculate that the Temple of Onias, hundreds of years old by the time of Jesus, is where Jesus worshiped as a young boy. We can logically assume that the Kadokite priests claimed the priests in the Jerusalem Temple were not legitimate under Jewish law because they were not descendants of Aaron as commanded by God in the Torah.

Therapeutae Education

Besides the association of Jesus with the Temple of Onias, we also speculate that the Therapeutae Jewish community based in Alexandria trained Him during many of His most formative years. How He became a part of that community is impossible to say. Possibly He ran away from home. Possibly His parents realized He was highly intelligent and that giving their son to the Therapeutae community was a way Jesus could get a proper Jewish education. Certainly, this community was the most outstanding Jewish intellectual center outside of Israel and possibly anywhere in the known world, given the presence of Philo of Alexandria (30 BCE to 50 CE), who to this day is considered one of the greatest Jewish intellectuals of all times.

We cannot know for sure if the Therapeutae community educated Jesus because no record of the community's membership exists. In fact, all we know about this community comes from the writings of Philo of Alexandria who was somehow affiliated with that community and probably was one of its teachers and leaders (see Philo reference in Appendix A) during the time of Jesus. It was a community that many scholars at first thought was Christian until historical information clearly proved it was not only Jewish but its origins pre-dated Jesus by several centuries.

By Jewish standards, the Therapeutae community was unique. It was a cloistered Jewish community centered very near Alexandria but had smaller centers in every district throughout Egypt. Jewish monasteries are almost non-existent in Jewish history. However, they existed in Egypt centuries prior to the time of Jesus and may have even been influenced by Buddhist missionaries of India's Emperor Ashoka's (304 BCE—232 BCE).

The Edicts of Ashoka indicate there was Buddhist missionary activity around 250 BCE in the city of Alexandria, Egypt. Another example of the possible influence of Buddhist missionaries is the striking similarity between the Therapeutae and Buddhist religious communities in their use of monasteries and the focus on learning. Furthermore, the name Therapeutae could easily be a Hellenization, by the Greek ruling class of Egypt, of the Indian Pali language's term for the traditional Buddhist faith—*Theravada* ("Therapeutae" in *Webster's New World Encyclopedia*).

These Jewish communities were a contemplative order where individuals not only prayed according to Jewish practices but also studied in individual isolation for much of their time. Philo tells us that the members would come together once a week in a joint session, with the men and women separated by a small waist-high wall, and where joint singing, study, and religious services would take place. The efforts of the community focused on Torah studies, but many individuals also became expert in medicine, Greek philosophy, and Egyptian mystical knowledge that possibly included magic.

Some communities consisted primarily of retired Jewish

men and women who turned over their worldly assets to the communities when they joined the group. In some ways they approached what in the 1980s and 1990s were called in south Florida "Century Villages." These more contemporary communities in Palm Beach and Broward Counties were housed in condos bought primarily by retired New York and New Jersey Jews seeking an active and inexpensive retirement with like-minded people.

Although our lives are quite different from theirs, we find what occurs in the community in which we live—San Miguel de Allende, in the state of Guanajuato, Mexico—to be somewhat parallel to what occurred near Alexandria more than two millennia ago. In San Miguel, although we are not Jewish, we have spent a great deal of time with our Jewish friends studying the Torah, Talmud, and Kabala. At one time, we volunteered with Dr. Haywood Hall, an American emergency physician, to help make his training program for emergency physicians in Mexico a successful venture. In addition, one of us has volunteered as a spiritual counselor with Hospice, and another helps various nonprofit organizations better manage themselves. We are regular participants in a philosophy discussion group, where we learn a great deal more about Greek and Roman philosophers, as well as other great philosophers of the world. In other words, San Miguel is a modern day center for seeking, learning, and service to others.

Thus, what happened in the Therapeutae community so many hundreds of years ago is understandable to us. Indeed, we can envision a very bright Jewish boy being brought to such a community to learn and grow in knowledge of the Torah. We know the love and joy with which our Jewish friends learn, teach, and share knowledge.

We can easily see this community taking responsibility for the education of such a boy, just as our San Miguel Jewish community did for a young woman who wished to formally become Jewish. The ancient community in Egypt would teach such a boy its understanding of what it meant to be Jewish and what it meant to be in a relationship with God.

We can envision how a Jewish community in Egypt would teach Jesus its understanding of what it meant to be Jewish, the art of healing as the Greeks and others knew it, the mysteries of Egyptian magic, and the great works of the Greek philosophers. In this way Jesus would become a very educated man for His, or any, era.

Jesus in India

Jesus, while a young man, possibly took the Silk Road to India, as is argued by Nicholas Notovitch in the *Unknown Life of Jesus Christ* (1890). He states that Jesus was known there by the proper name Issa, which is the Arabic version of His name, and He visited the Lamasery Monastery in Hemis, India, where there still exists a scroll telling about His visit. Notovitch saw that scroll, as did several others at later times.

Figure 1 is a photo owned by Dr. Luis Rey Casillas Celis and taken by his father, who was a Mexican colonel in the late 1940s and later was promoted to the rank of general. The then colonel was attached to a United Nations peacekeeping mission, and he was trying to see if Indian troops were moving toward Pakistan in Northern India. He and his soldiers were caught in the Himalayan Mountains in a snowstorm during which many of his men died. He and the remainder of his men were rescued and taken to the Lamasery Monastery in Hemis.

After he recovered, the head of the monastery took him into a room and showed him a painting. The head of the monastery said, "That is your man, Jesus, when he was here many centuries ago." The general took the photo shown in *Figure 1*, which is a painting of the young Jesus.

Figure 1

A remarkable man

When Jesus eventually went back to His homeland in the Galilee as a mature man, He would appear highly unusual to His many brothers, cousins and fellow Galileans. His knowledge of His religion would be equal to, and even beyond, that of the most religiously informed people in Israel. Although very devout, He would focus not on the letter of Jewish law, as was common in Israel, but rather on the spirit of that law, which was more consistent with Alexandrian Jewish thinking. He would have unique knowledge of the healing arts both from Alexandria and India. In addition, the teachings of men such as Philo would have influenced Him, but also He would have learned important concepts from his travels that He would have integrated into His understanding of theology.

At the time, Israel, like other nations in the region, was a very male-centered society, but, like the Greek philosopher Plato, Jesus would believe women quite capable of the rigors of intellectual thought, and He would treat them accordingly. When He saw people in want of healing, He would heal them. Although Jewish thought instructed Jews not to engage in magic, He would consider it quite natural because of His Alexandrian and Indian background and would use it when appropriate.

More significantly, He would think differently and even talk differently than His peers. He would think on a much deeper philosophical level, and then He would speak in a way that expressed the differences between His thought processes and those of His listeners. To explain His philosophical points, He would follow, for instance, the Greek practice of speaking in stories and parables, given His education in Greek.

He would realize He had far greater knowledge than His listeners or "students," who had almost no education. As a result, He would explain His lessons only in ways His "students" could understand, and He would wait to teach them more advanced lessons until He felt they were ready. He would also impart more advanced lessons to those students close to Him, while providing simpler and more general lessons to those unfamiliar with His teachings.

Jesus would also hold different political views than the

average person from the Galilee. But He would have enough sense not to create hostility in those around Him by asserting His pro-Roman thoughts. He would have realized that the typical Galileans had experienced remarkable hardship under Roman occupation and their Jewish pride made most of them anti-Roman. He would not embrace the ideas of a large set of hawkish anti-Roman Jews called Zealots. Jesus would be pro-Roman because of His association with the Therapeutae community in Roman-controlled Egypt.

That community would have been pro-Roman because of several significant influences. Philo of Alexandria, a probable leader in that Therapeutae community, was also very much part of the Roman establishment in Egypt. His brother was the wealthy treasurer of the Roman province, and his nephew was one of the Roman generals who later served in the destruction of Jerusalem in 70 CE.

As we note earlier, we believe Jesus spent some of His youth at the Temple of Onias. So Jesus would naturally think the temple leaders in Jerusalem were fundamentally wrong. He would be against their religious leadership and disagree with their point of view, while also not advocating rebellion against Roman rule. This assumption that Jesus was pro-Roman allows for a fuller understanding of Jesus' pronouncement in the Gospel of Matthew: "Render therefore unto Caesar the things that are Caesar's, and unto God the things that are God's" (Mark 12:17).

We know from the gospels that Jesus was a teacher of spiritual wisdom but He did not engage in open discussions about theology. First and foremost, Jesus was Jewish, and we can say that He was perhaps the first "Reform Jew," well before such a group came into existence in Germany many centuries later. He was reform in that He focused on the spirit of Jewish law rather than on the *dicta*, or the letter, of Jewish Law. He might have been an unusual Jew for His time, but His message was truly Jewish in character, as our Chapters 9 and 10 demonstrate.

What Was the Message of Jesus?

When Jesus went to Israel, He would have been profoundly impressed with the devotion and religious practice of His less educated first cousin John. Jesus was not seeking any political power, but He was disgusted with the treatment of His cousin by the then Jewish King who ordered the beheading of John. Jesus was also appalled by the improper use of power by the Jewish religious leaders who were not descendants of Aaron. He had no fundamental quarrel with Roman rule because He saw flawed Jewish leadership in Israel and He had seen the value of the Roman peace in Egypt.

Rather then rebel against the Roman Empire, as many of His countrymen wanted to do, Jesus wanted to reform how His fellow Jews approached their religion. Everything He said was addressed to matters of religion and faith rather than politics. He was a Reform Jew who brought a remarkable message directly to His people and indirectly to humankind.

As we mention in earlier chapters, we call our understanding of the New Testament and related documents the Omega Interpretation. This interpretation consists of our ideas based on our own inquiries. Our studies tell us that the spiritual wisdom taught by Jesus was not new and, in fact, was quite analogous to the teachings of the Axial Period's other great religious thinkers throughout the world. To our minds, this synchronicity does not lessen the importance of the message Jesus brought to the world, but instead makes it even more important for us to learn and follow.

Jesus argued that goodness can exist in each of us and that we need to develop our inner love in order to deeply care for everyone and everything. In the Aramaic language of His time with its extreme use of idioms (Lamsa), His concepts were difficult to explain. His solution to this communication problem was to speak idiomatically and in parables. His simple and concrete stories helped His listeners understand abstract concepts such as the Kindom of Heaven, and thereby develop their spirituality.

He then argued that as individuals develop their inner goodness, their subsequent actions toward others bring still more goodness into the world. In the Jewish tradition, a kind act toward others is called a *mitzvot*. When we perform a *mitzvot*, we help create the Kindom of Heaven outside us as our goodness comes back to us in the positive actions and reactions from others and even ourselves.

This concept of a present-day heaven within and outside us is the central message in the spiritual wisdom of Jesus. It has nothing to do with heaven as a place to go after death, but it has everything to do with creating a state of consciousness here and now. Jesus was just trying to get His profound concepts across to His listeners.

Unfortunately, few understood His message of kindness toward others then, as evidenced by the subsequent Jewish War that sought independence through violence from Roman authority (66—73 CE); and few understand now, as evidenced by current religious tensions and wars. His message had nothing to do with His experience on the cross or even whether or not He died on that cross. His message also had nothing to do with His being some sort of human sacrifice offered by God, nor His being God's Son sent for the redemption of humankind's original sin.

Heaven consists of you growing into the best inner person you can be. It is you helping others grow into the best persons they can be. It is your gift of yourself to others, such as playing beautiful music for others or making someone laugh. It is helping a child learn and grow in spirituality. It is making peace and protecting the environment.

Heaven is first and foremost a process of giving yourself to others because of the love that extends to everything around you and beyond. Because heaven is a process, your love returns many times over and in ways you cannot imagine. However, you should never give your love with anticipation of reward; it must always be a pure and unconditional gift of yourself.

Heaven is always in the present, and only the present exists in heaven. That is the message of Jesus. It is sufficiently complex that many of us do not understand it, and fewer of us put it into regular practice. Although His Axial period teachings were not new, His teachings remain universally profound and timeless.

The message of Jesus was so simple: Develop your inner spirituality. Then let that spirituality, with its wisdom, guide your actions throughout life.

The Story of the Crucifixion

As we explain in more detail in Chapter 11, Jesus' views were unfortunately misunderstood. Later, Roman Christian theologians interpreted them to mean that people can find salvation and have a wonderful afterlife by merely accepting Jesus as their God and Savior. The cross came to symbolize that Jesus died for the sins of only those who accepted Him as God. Hence the story of His time on the cross became a critical part of why His message was so misunderstood and later reinterpreted. This misinterpretation continues, in spite of the fact that early Christianity did not focus on, nor subscribe to, the story about Jesus rising from the dead (Scott 215).

The uncomfortable question is, "What really happened that brought Jesus to the situation that He was tried and placed on the cross to die?" After coming to Jerusalem for the Passover, Jesus assembled His disciples for the Passover Seder. The New Testament gospels tell us that at the dinner, He announced that one among the twelve would betray Him. Soon afterward He blessed the bread, broke it as is done at all Passover Seders, and instructed His disciples to eat it, telling them, "This is my body" (Matthew 26:26).

He then took a cup of wine, gave thanks, as is also the Jewish custom, and passed it to the disciples with the instructions to drink it all. Later He announced He would be killed, they would be scattered, He would rise again, and He would go before them to the Galilee (Matthew 26: 29-32). Assuming that Jesus could not foresee the future, this tells us that Jesus was aware of the plan to turn Him over to authorities, and possibly He even created the plan. Or perhaps this statement detailing Jesus' predictions was created after the fact. Alternatively, the statement tells us that the authors who wrote the gospels had wonderful imaginations and took remarkable poetic license with the facts; they included what they thought happened, basing their versions on later word-of-mouth stories.

After the supper, Jesus then went to the Garden of Gethsemane with His disciples. He separated Himself from them and prayed. He then returned to find them all asleep, and Judas came with an armed group of the chief priests and elders. Judas kissed Him as a signal to tell the guards who was Jesus. Jesus surrendered to them while His disciples fled. Jesus was brought to the house of the chief priest where the scribes and elders were assembled.

They charged Him with blasphemy. Jesus replied, "You have said: nevertheless I say to you, Hereafter shall you see the Son of Man sitting on the right hand of power, and coming in the clouds of heaven" (Matthew 26: 64). The scribes and elders declared Jesus guilty. They spat in His face and abused Him.

The next morning Jesus was taken before Pontius Pilate, the Roman governor in the province of Judea. As the highest Roman official, he had to determine whether Jesus was guilty and to what extent He would be punished. Pilate asked Jesus if He was the King of the Jews. Jesus replied, "So you say" (Matthew 27: 11). This probably means, "I have never said such a thing." The chief Jewish priests and elders accused Him of crimes, but He said nothing more in His defense. This weak defense may have been part of His plan because otherwise it is hard to understand His behavior, except as part of a plan to somehow gain favor with the Jewish crowd.

The custom at Passover was for the governor to release a prisoner according to the recommendation of the Jewish crowd.

Pilate let the crowd decide if the person to be released should be Jesus or Barabbas, a notorious thief and criminal. The Jewish chief priests and elders persuaded the crowd to save Barabbas and not Jesus. When Pilate asked the crowd what to do with Jesus, the crowd said, "Let Him be crucified" (Matthew 27: 23). Maybe this is where the plan of Jesus to gain popular support among the people and impress His disciples went wrong, as Jesus might have assumed that the crowd would support Him.

Crucifixion made little sense in this case. It was a severe form of Roman punishment used to shame the reputation of the person as well as subdue a population. The prisoner's hand and legs were nailed or lashed to a cross. After days on the cross, the person's legs were broken so that they could no longer support the weight of the upper body, and the result would be suffocation. This long and very painful death sentence was usually reserved for crimes of treason and other major crimes against the empire. Almost always the bodies were left to rot on the cross to send a public message that would instill fear and compliance within the population.

Jesus may have thought He was going to be freed by vote of the crowd and would therefore gain positive publicity for His bravery in the face of the Roman authorities and the Jewish religious leadership. Or, it could have been part of what would have been a very bold and dangerous plan, that of faking His death on the cross.

Pilate washed his hands in front of the crowd and declared he was abstaining in this decision but wanted to abide by the wishes of the crowd. The custom of accepting the decision of the crowd was similar to the custom in the Roman arena where gladiators fought and the crowd decided the fate of the loser. Once Jesus was found guilty, Pilate had to turn Him over to his soldiers. However, Pilate's delivery of Jesus to the soldiers could, ironically, have been a key event in Jesus' eventual survival. There is also the possibility that Pilate was part of the plan all along to fake the death of Jesus.

The soldiers took Jesus to the common hall, stripped Him, and dressed Him in a scarlet robe. Scarlet was then, and is still, the symbol of royalty, and placing a scarlet robe on Jesus was a way to mock Him as King of the Jews. They put on His head a crown of thorns, placed a reed in His hand, bowed before Him, and further mocked Him by saying, "Hail, King of the Jews!" (Matthew 27: 29). These actions were essential preliminaries if people, especially the priests, were to believe Jesus died on the cross.

The soldiers then took the robe off, scourged and beat Him, put His own clothes back on, and led Him away. They compelled Simon of Cyrene to carry the cross for Jesus, and they took Jesus to Golgotha. They gave Him vinegar mixed with gall to drink. This drink was commonly given to criminals so that their suffering would be less intense while they were on the cross. That mix, which possibly included other drugs, acted as a narcotic and helped deaden awareness.

After tasting it, Jesus did not drink. The soldiers then placed Him on the cross Simon had carried, and they stationed His upright cross between two thieves. The gospels do not reveal all the details of the crucifixion, but do tell us that the soldiers placed over Jesus' head a sign reading: "This is Jesus, The King of the Jews," and the chief priests, scribes, and elders mocked Him.

In the ninth hour on the cross, we are told that Jesus cried loudly, "My God, my God, why hast thou forsaken me?" (Matthew 27: 46). These words are probably a poor translation because Near Eastern martyrs do not speak of God's desertion in the hour of suffering. A more likely translation is "My God, my God, for this you have kept me." In other words, He fulfilled His destiny (Errico and Lamsa 346—352). Regardless of the words, His comments could have been a signal to His plotters that it was time to take Him off the cross.

Someone immediately took a sponge and filled it with vinegar, placed it on a reed, and gave it to Jesus to drink (Matthew 27: 48). Then Jesus "yielded up the ghost" (Matthew 27: 50). John adds that the soldiers were about to break His legs, as they had for the two thieves, when they decided He was dead. So they did not break his legs, but one of them did push a spear into His side, and out came blood and water (John 20: 32-34). Notice how close the time was between Jesus drinking from the sponge and His "death."

Because of the late hour, Jesus could not be buried before the beginning of Sabbath (begins at Friday sundown and ends at Saturday sundown). Joseph of Arimathaea asked Pilate for the body of Jesus, and Pilate commanded the body be given to Joseph. He took the body and wrapped it in a clean linen cloth. Nicodemus arrived that night with a mixture of myrrh and aloe.

Nicodemus and unnamed others placed the body in Joseph's own tomb and had a great stone rolled to close the door of the sepulcher. They departed, while Mary Magdalene and Mary, the wife of Cleophas, sat against the sepulcher that night, but apparently left Saturday morning. That Romans would allow such noble treatment for a convicted dead "political criminal" was extraordinary, as were the decisions of Pilate.

The next day (Saturday) the chief priests and the Pharisees met with Pilate. They asked that soldiers watch the sepulcher because Jesus had foretold He would arise on the third day. They suspected the disciples would take His body and claim Jesus' words were validated. Pilate told them to do as they wished, so they sealed the stone in front of the tomb and guarded the sepulcher. The lapse of one full day seems odd, given the stated concern of the Pharisees.

At the end of the Sabbath (sundown on Saturday), Mary Magdalene and the other Mary went back to the sepulcher. The New Testament tells us that an angel clothed in white rolled the stone away. The guards (in the New Testament called keepers, the watch, and later soldiers) froze at seeing the angel and his action. The angel then announced to the two women that Jesus was not there and that He had arisen. The angel asked them to tell the twelve disciples that Jesus had arisen and would meet them in Galilee.

As they departed, Jesus met the women on the path. He told them He would meet his brothers in Galilee. Some of the sepulcher watchers told the chief priests what they knew. The priests gave money to the soldiers (Matthew 28:12) and told them to say that the disciples had taken the body of Jesus from the sepulcher. The soldiers did as instructed. The Gospel of Matthew does not tell us if the soldiers were or were not the same ones that conducted the crucifixion. What is important at this point is that Jesus was alive. Apparently a plan had existed to save Him, and the plan was working.

The eleven disciples eventually saw Jesus in the mountains of the Galilee as was prophesied (Matthew 28:16). Luke adds to the story by saying that the disciples were terrified and thought they were seeing a spirit. Jesus said to them: "Look at my hands and feet, that it is I myself; handle me, and see; for a spirit does not have flesh and bones, as you see me have" (Luke 24: 39). He asked for some food and ate what they gave Him.

Given these elements of the story, we can conclude that the disciples were not part of the plan to save Jesus and that He was indeed very much alive.

The Gospel of John tells us that eight days later Jesus again came to His disciples, and this time Thomas was present. Jesus said to Thomas, "Reach your finger, and hold my hands; and reach your hand, and thrust it into my side: and be not faithless, but believe" (Luke 20:27). Without any question, Jesus was alive after His experience on the cross, if you believe the New Testament gospels.

Analyzing the Alpha Story

We must recognize that there is no way to substantiate the account given in the gospels. As mentioned before, the only piece of supporting evidence that Jesus even existed as a historical figure is in the history of Josephus. We must proceed on the basis of what was written. In doing so, we argue for an explanation of the events that does not require us to completely suspend all rational thought and believe in a series of very grand and amazing miracles.

Certain troubling aspects of the standard story of Jesus' crucifixion deserve closer consideration:.

First, based on what was written, Jesus clearly knew He was going to be arrested because He told his disciples as much, especially at the end of the famous story involving the bread and wine.

Second, there is another story that also tends to confirm this conclusion. The story is told by Eusebius, the first Christian historian, who wrote his account in 300 CE. That story concerns the King of the Osrhoenians, whose kingdom was outside the Roman Empire in the Parthian Empire. The king fell sick, and he wrote Jesus, saying, "That thou wilt come to me, who adore Thee, and heal all the ill that I suffer, according to the faith I have in Thee. I also learn that the Jews murmur against Thee, and persecute Thee, that they seek to crucify Thee, and to destroy Thee. I possess but one small city, but it is beautiful, and large enough for us two to live in peace" (Eusebius 1, 12).

Jesus replied to the letter by telling Hannan, the secretary to the Osrhoenian king, "Go thou, and say to thy master, who hath sent thee to Me: 'Happy are thou who has believed in Me, not having seen Me, for it is written of Me that those who shall see Me shall not believe in Me, and that those who shall not see Me shall believe in Me. As to that which thou hast written, that I should come to thee,[behold] all that for which I was sent here below is finished, and I ascend again to My father who sent Me, and when I shall [be] ascended to Him I will send thee one of My disciples, who shall heal all thy sufferings, and shall give thee health again, and shall convert all who are with thee unto life eternal and the city shall be blessed forever, and the enemy shall never overcome it." Eusebius tells us that Jesus Himself wrote the letter (Eusebius 1, 12).

Third, the chief priests in Jerusalem were clearly enemies of Jesus, and Jesus correctly thought they wanted to harm Him. Pilate was neither friend nor foe of Jesus, but the priests and the crowd influenced Pilate to rule against Him. As noted earlier, the Torah tells us the priests of the Temple had to be descendants of Aaron (brother of Moses). In fact, they were not, as they were merely appointees of Rome and served at the pleasure of Rome. For example, the Roman Prefect Valerius Gratus appointed the High Priest Calaphas in 18 CE (Josephus 262 and 266). Thus Jesus, as a Jew who knew the Torah, would not feel the priests had any authority over him.

Fourth, the trial and crucifixion story of Jesus is very odd. The chief priests' charges against Jesus would have made little sense to Pilate. Being designated "the Son of God" was an accepted status in the Roman Empire. However, only the Roman Senate determined, by vote, if someone, such as the Emperor, was the Son of God. In this case, Jesus did not claim to Pilate He was the Son of God. The matter would seem really quite silly to Pilate. He probably merely went along with the wishes of the priests to calm them and the crowd.

The claim that Jesus was the King of the Jews was also very strange. That claim was mentioned only as a question in the trial, and the kingship of the Jews was a matter for the Romans alone to decide. At the time of the trial there was no King of the Jews, but Rome always had given that title to someone in the Herodian family.

In fact, from 41 to 100 CE, the approximate area of present day Israel was sometimes under the nominal autonomy of the

Herodian family, who were designated Kings of the Jews, but actually under Roman control. However, the area was sometimes under direct Roman control, just as it was in the time of Pilate. Pontius Pilate was the Roman prefect of Judea from 16 to 36 CE during the reign of Emperor Tiberius (14 to 37 CE). For Pilate to agree with the priests and elders about the guilt of Jesus was politically smart because if unrest in the region persisted, there was always the possibility that his job could be given back to a member of the Herodian family.

Sixth, the fact that Jesus was taken to the common hall, stripped, scourged, and beaten was not unexpected, but that Simon of Cyrene bore the cross is most unusual because the Romans commonly made the condemned carry their own crosses. The fact that the chief priests, scribes, and elders mocked Jesus as "the King of the Jews" while He was on the cross is not surprising. They probably had strong political loyalties to the Herodian family, and to mock someone else as a King of the Jews was to their political advantage.

The accounts in the gospels tell us Jesus was crucified, but they do not provide any details of how He was bound to the cross, such as whether His hands and feet were nailed. Such details were added by later speculation, as well as portrayed in artistic renderings and by Hollywood moviemakers. Historically, the Roman custom was to bind the outstretched arms at the wrist with ropes or strings of hide and then bind the feet at the ankles.

Seventh, from the gospels, we do know that Jesus was on the cross for only three to six hours and possibly as long as nine. The Gospel of Mark says, "And Pilate marveled if He were already dead . . ." (15: 44) as it was such a short period of time before Jesus died. Romans used crucifixion as a form of public execution. It was a long slow death by asphyxiation as the weight of the body caused the lungs to collapse. This asphyxiation was particularly intensified after the legs were broken and the victim became unable to support the weight of his body on the cross. Often birds came and ate portions of the body while it hung on the cross. We suggest that the Jewish Sabbath would not be reason enough for the Romans to act more quickly, but it would influence the behavior of the Jews once the Romans made their decision.

Eighth, while he was on the cross, Jesus seemed to give a signal, and someone immediately took a sponge and filled it with "vinegar." Commonly, such sponges were known to contain a narcotic to ease pain. He drank it and then appeared to be dead. Of note is that the soldier who was breaking the legs of those on the cross did not break Jesus' legs because he concluded Jesus was already dead. A soldier did stab Jesus with a spear, but a well-trained Roman soldier would know where to place a spear stab to kill and where to place a spear to avoid a critical organ. In addition, water and blood flowed from the side of Jesus, and that suggests His heart was still beating.

Ninth, the account of what happened after the crucifixion holds contradictions. For Romans, crucifixion was a sign of strong disrespect. Nevertheless, Pontius Pilate, who had only a few hours before ordered the crucifixion of Jesus, allowed Joseph of Arimathaea to treat the body of Jesus with the highest respect. The preparation of the body is not surprising, but it is worth noting that aloes and myrrh are healing agents and the official watchers, who were soldiers, arrived well after the body was treated. The watchers could have been the same, or some of the same, soldiers that conducted the crucifixion.

Tenth, even the gospels' accounts of Jesus after the crucifixion clearly tell us He was alive. As we point out earlier in this chapter, the story of Jesus with Thomas made it particularly clear Jesus was alive—walking, talking, and eating—after the crucifixion. To draw any other conclusion than He was alive seems impossible. The only questions are whether He survived the ordeal on the cross, possibly with the help of several people, or whether a remarkable miracle occurred in which He died and then was brought back to life. The former option is much more likely, and the latter option sounds like a creative cover story (a lie) to discourage a manhunt for Jesus that could put Him back on the cross. To Jews, telling a lie to save a life, such as the life of Jesus, is not only acceptable but also appropriate.

Alpha or Omega

Over time the essential spiritual message that Jesus preached both before and after His ordeal on the cross was mostly forgotten or ignored, but the more dramatic miracle story, of Jesus dying on the cross and His resurrection, was not. As a result, a different set of ideas (the Alpha Interpretation) replaced His spiritual message (the Omega Interpretation). Eventually, over several centuries, that new theology became a dogmatic loyalty oath and a religious practice designed to politically support the Roman Empire, and later, the royalty of Europe. Today, long after the fall of the Roman Empire, this Alpha Interpretation continues and still defines what the world calls Christianity.

Why do we think the Omega Interpretation is superior to the Alpha Interpretation? There is a rule in logic called Occam's, or Ockham's Razor: it says we should use the simplest explanation that requires the fewest significant assumptions when we select a theory or interpretation. A fourteenth century logician and Franciscan friar, William of Ockham, developed this principle. Many scientists, such as Isaac Newton and Stephen Hawking, adopted and used it in their works (Hiroshi).

To accept the Alpha Interpretation, we must accept some far-fetched and stunning miracles, such as an angel helping Jesus, but no miracles need be accepted if we use the Omega Interpretation. In addition, we must believe some even more remarkable miracles took place, such as the ascent of Jesus into a place called heaven that Jesus Himself asserted did not exist as a *place* (Luke 17: 20-21). The simpler explanation is the Omega Interpretation.

We need to emphasize the point about heaven not being a physical place. The Gospel of Luke clearly quotes Jesus as saying that heaven was *not* a place. It says, "Neither shall they say, Lo here! Or, lo there! For, behold, the kingdom of God [heaven] is within you" (17: 21). The fact that heaven is not a place is particularly made clear in the Gospel of Thomas, Saying 3. Of note is that the Gospel of Luke (24: 51) later says that Jesus ascended to a place called heaven. Either Jesus was wrong about heaven, or some one making up or repeating the cover story did not understand the teachings of Jesus. Either way, the Alpha Interpretation is logically an absurdity.

We believe that Jesus got His idea of the soul / body dualism from Plato and His concept for the form of the soul from Aristotle. These are ideas and concepts he would have been exposed to in the Therapeutae community in Alexandria. Like Plato, Jesus believed each living human has a body and also a soul. Plato is considered the father of psychology because of his views on the soul; many of the views of Jesus about the soul are also of a similar psychological nature. Again like Plato, and also Socrates, Jesus apparently believed the soul was immortal and at death the soul was released from the body. But this is not the view taken by Paul (5—66 CE), the early Christian leader and writer of epistles. Paul was influenced by a parallel example from the Book of Daniel, found in the Jewish Bible (Old Testament). It was from Paul's view that the notion of resurrection originated in Christian theology (Scott 34-36).

We also suspect that Jesus may have believed in reincarnation, as did Plato, and that is why one reads of so many references to rebirth in the New Testament. From Aristotle, Jesus got the idea that when the soul was in the body—and only when it was in the body — only then could the soul, with conscious effort, actually grow and mature. For both Aristotle and Jesus, the souls of persons who were spiritually mature inspired higher reasoning ability.

The Omega Interpretation assumes that Jesus was brought-up in a Jewish community in Egypt to be a well-educated Jew and that He somehow survived His ordeal on the cross. Given the few facts we know, our assumptions do not require us to take leaps of faith grounded in miracle stories. The conclusion to our argument is that the Omega Interpretation is more parsimonious—and in the mathematical sense, more elegant—than the dominant and widely accepted Alpha Interpretation. Given the principle of Ockham's Razor, the Omega Interpretation is superior to the Alpha Interpretation, and the Omega Interpretation is the one we should use.

Which version—Alpha or Omega—is likely to be more useful to our world? Consider these differences:

- If we accept the *Alpha version*, we are told merely to accept Jesus as our God and Savior and then we can go to the ATM with our prayer card any old time and request our favors and gifts and God's forgiveness for our sins. If we accept the *Omega version*, we are told that if we want salvation, we must do the work of developing our inner self, our spirituality, and move away from being ego-centered and unbalanced in our desires for material goods.
- In the *Alpha version*, we are told we must separate ourselves from the rest of humanity who are, by definition, inferior people, unsaved. In the *Omega version*, we are told we are part of the larger Oneness that we must always love and accept.
- In the *Alpha version*, we will find heaven tomorrow if we espouse our faith today. In the *Omega version*, we can find heaven now because of our active effort to create and show rather than hid to others our inner spiritual self.

The Omega Interpretation does not call on us to convert others to Christianity; each of us is on our own path called life. However, it does encourage us to help others who wish and seek our help. The Omega Interpretation tells us that God gives everyone two important gifts: life and free choice. We are not to subvert those gifts of God, either for ourselves or for others. As we move along the path called life, each must make his or her choices, and, when made with spiritual wisdom, they will always include being willing to help others.

Not only is the Omega Interpretation simpler and more reasonable than the Alpha Interpretation, but it is also puts the emphasis on Jesus' call to develop our spirituality.

Chapter 5

Jesus and Process Theology

In this chapter we argue that Jesus of Nazareth used what today is called process philosophy and process theology in shaping His teachings. We contend that the Gospel of Thomas, the Gospel of Mary, and the teachings of Jesus found in the New Testament all reflect process philosophy and theology. Of course, the process philosophy and theology of Jesus were of His time and based on earlier Greek versions of the subjects, which we believe He learned as boy and young adult in Egypt. Unfortunately, people today have an incomplete understanding of those earlier treatments, so to fill the gap, we use the process philosophy and theology of our time to help us grasp what Jesus understood as the process philosophy and theology of His time.

Process Philosophy: In the Beginning

Process philosophy concerns metaphysics, that is, the general theory of reality. The two approaches to metaphysics relative to this chapter are *traditional* and *process*. In the traditional approach, primary reality consists of static substances, such as a chair, a person, a river, a stone, and so on. In contrast, the process approach defines and sees reality as changing and dynamic. In the process approach, as the name suggests, the process of change is the foremost and primary focus.

Process is the becoming and perishing of actual events. Sometimes the process consists of successive stages, that is, a sequence of definable phases focusing on what happened before and what happens next ("Process Philosophy," *Stanford*

Encyclopedia of Philosophy). For example, a seed becomes a tree; a tree becomes a log; a log becomes lumber; lumber becomes a chair; a chair becomes trash; and trash becomes fertilizer. Another example is the preparing of a research paper for class. A student picks a topic; she researches the topic; she writes the paper; and she submits it to the teacher.

Of the two approaches to metaphysics, we argue that the process approach is superior to the traditional. Metaphysics is about what exists; it asks how we should go about understanding and explaining reality. We can judge if one approach is superior to another by applying a pragmatic test of usefulness. For a metaphysical understanding and explanation to be useful, it should provide a cogent and plausible account of reality. These qualities let its users characterize, describe, clarify and explain the most general features of that reality.

For a metaphysical explanation to be considered useful and even powerful, it should facilitate the development of theories that can explain a large set of events and other phenomena, as well as their causes and effects. For example, the theoretical statement that for every action there is an equal and positive reaction covers the broad range of phenomena where action occurs and explains an important cause and effect associated with those phenomena. Thus it is a powerful and useful metaphysical explanation ("Process Philosophy," *Stanford*).

This standard to judge metaphysical explanations leads us to conclude that the process approach is superior to the traditional approach. Why? The process approach leads one to develop theoretical statements concerning why the process changes as it does over time. The traditional approach, on the other hand, leads one to describe the objects rather than what causes the object to change due to some outside effect. Thus the theoretical statements associated with the process approach tend to be about a more comprehensive and broad range of phenomena than those addressed in the traditional approach.

In recent times, the most notable advocate of process philosophy with its process approach to metaphysics was the philosopher and mathematician Alfred North Whitehead (1861-1947). However, the Greek philosopher Heraclitus (537-475 BCE) of Ephesus first articulated process philosophy. Later, other Greek philosophers, such as Parmenides, Zeno, the Atomists of pre-Socratic Greece, as well as Plato and Aristotle, built on the work of Heraclitus.

We argue that Heraclitus and those subsequent philosophers significantly influenced Jesus when He was a student in Egypt. Other Greek philosophers described Heraclitus as an obscure philosopher because of the difficulty they had in understanding his works. Process philosophy is difficult for many to understand because it is sometimes counterintuitive and uses words in unique ways.

Unfortunately the passage of time resulted in almost all of Heraclitus' work being lost, but fortunately fragments survive in quotations and references by other writers, such as Plato. From these pieces, we can derive an approximate explanation of his process philosophy. An example of such a reference occurs in Plato's work titled *Cratylus* (402a=A6, quoted in "Process Philosophy," *Stanford*), where Plato says: "Heraclitus, you know, says that everything moves on and that nothing is at rest; and, comparing existing things to the flow of a river, he says that you could not step into the same river twice" ("Heraclitus," *Stanford*).

Heraclitus was from the Greek city of Ephesus in Asia Minor, so he would have had first-hand knowledge of a river's nature because Ephesus is on the Aegean Sea (Mediterranean) at the mouth of the Cayster River (meaning "Little Meander"). Today Ephesus is famous as an archeological site and for the claim that the Apostle John (John the Evangelist) and Mary, the mother of Jesus, lived there. (We visited the House of Mary in 2005.) Ephesus is also where Paul was driven out of town for preaching against the making and selling of statues of Artemis, a famous local goddess and an important Greek goddess.

A curious twist of irony is associated with Heraclitus' famous metaphor of a river to explain how life constantly changes. With the passage of time, the mouth of the Cayster River eventually silted over, and natural changes in the landscape moved its mouth five miles westward. Ephesus lost its status as an emporium situated at the junction of the Silk Road's terminus and the Mediterranean Sea. As a result, this second largest city of the Roman Empire was eventually abandoned ("Process Philosophy," *Stanford*).

In developing his view about the nature of reality, Heraclitus reacted to the arguments of the earlier Greek philosophers Anaximander (612-545 BCE) and Anaximenes (585-524 BCE), who were from nearby Greek cities. Anaximander argued that the world is composed of pairs of opposites that are in continual tension. Anaximenes argued that the world is not so much a war of opposites but rather a continuum of change.

Heraclitus disagreed with both. He argued that what we normally call reality, such as a river, is a process of change caused by divine universal laws that transcend the physical reality of flowing water. Those laws cause the physical river to flow as it does, and those laws explain why all rivers flow as they do. To Heraclitus, the "river" was not only the physical flowing water but also the divine laws that explain the flow.

Heraclitus used the Greek word *logos* (meaning "word") to represent the concept of divine law. Today, instead of using the word *logos* and mentioning the divine, we commonly use the term "scientific law" or "laws of nature" (e.g., "law of gravity"), and we do not refer to the divine in our explanations. Nevertheless, the concepts are similar ("Process Philosophy," *Stanford*). Heraclitus noted that humans, because our minds interpret our senses incorrectly, commonly understand what we call reality as being a thing or substance. He asserted that we do not easily "see" reality, but instead we see an illusion of it and consider the illusion real.

One common illusion we see consists of separate dualistic things or concepts. Heraclitus said the true reality we should sense and our minds should interpret is actually a unity, a Oneness. He called such an illusion a "unity of opposites." For example, most of us sense light and dark as two separate and unique qualities. Our minds interpret our sense of sight as telling us there is light or dark, and thus we think of those qualities as separate rather than as two aspects of the same thing. Heraclitus tells us our minds are fooled because we cannot easily conceptualize that what we are really seeing are different aspects of the same Oneness of light and dark. Therefore, our mental ability to discriminate light from dark leads us to interpret an illusion as reality.

To Heraclitus, our belief that this perceived duality is reality means our minds are undeveloped. To transcend the illusion, we must first acknowledge that the unity of opposites should structure our consciousness. Our minds can perceive what we think of as reality with different levels of cognition, but our mental ability, or inability, determines which level of cognition we use when we think we perceive reality.

Therefore, reality for us is a function of what our senses tell us. However, it is also the concepts that structure our thinking process as we use those senses. Without the "unity of opposites" shaping our thinking process, our minds see things only as discrete items, as dualities not unities. Once equipped with the knowledge of the "unity of opposites," our minds transcend seeing things in pairs, and in their place we see unities. Seeing a "unity of opposites" makes it easier to conceptualize the causal or functional relationship within the unity. For example, we can more easily understand that we can decrease the darkness by increasing the light.

Heraclitus believed that both the observable finite material and the non-material *logos* should be thought of as a "unity of opposites." For example, the flowing water of a river (the finite material) and the *logos* that we now call the law of gravity (the infinite non-material) together form a unity of opposites. Both the material and the non-material are one.

In sum, Heraclitus concluded that all material substances are in this process of change. Almost all of us perceive the material substance, such as flowing water, without realizing that the material and the ever-present non-material make a "unity of opposites," which is the true reality. What we think is a river—moving water—is an illusion. The true reality is the unity of opposites consisting of material substance—in this case, the moving water—plus its salient non-material opposite, the law of gravity ("Process Philosophy," *Stanford*).

Heraclitus and Jesus believed that when we consider the nature of reality, we should transcend the illusion of separateness and perceive the world in "unities of opposites." To transcend illusion, we must comprehend and see at deeper, more profound, and more subtle levels of our senses and mind. This concept that Heraclitus called "unity of opposites" was, and is, truly profound, but what is even more remarkable is that Heraclitus took this notion of "unity of opposites" to a still more sophisticated and powerful level of understanding ("Process Philosophy," *Stanford*). Jesus then used that understanding in creating His message, as we show in later chapters.

Process Theology

We cannot explain how Heraclitus developed his process philosophy, which includes process theology, because little historical information is available. However, we can infer what would logically make sense concerning his process theology by drawing upon more contemporary process philosophers, such as Alfred North Whitehead, C. Robert Mesle and John B. Cobb, Jr.

Process theology and traditional Christian theology differ significantly. Christian theology invokes theism, which says that God is completely transcendent, supernatural, and unchanging. While God is beyond time and space, God is also personal, present, and active in the governance and organization of the world and universe. Process theology builds not on theism but on pantheism: the universe and God are identical. But process theology goes one step further than pantheism and invokes panentheism: all is in God and God is immanent everywhere in the universe, but adds that God is also more than the universe. To help conceptualize this difference between the two, for panentheism think of the universe as a sub-set of God.

Another important difference between process theology and theism is that in process theology God is dynamic, whereas God is unchanging in theism. Process theology tells us God is not an unchanging static entity but rather is ever expanding, dynamic and interactive with the world in reference to movement, change, and development ("Process Philosophy," *Stanford*). In process theology God manifests both the primordial *logos*, such as the law of gravity, and knowledge that results from God's interacting with His ever-growing creation process, the universe, which includes humans. Thus, for humans, God is a co-creator with them. The following excerpts, selected from Whitehead (158) with some minor editing, point out that God is the binding element that gives us direction and purpose.

> *God is the function in the world by reason of which our purposes are directed to ends, which in our own consciousness are impartial as to our own interests. God is that in life in virtue of which judgment stretches beyond facts of existence to values of existence. God is that element in virtue of which the attainment of such a value for others transforms itself into values for us.*

> *God is the binding element in the world. The consciousness, which is individual in us, is universal in God: the love, which is partial in us, is all embracing in God. Apart from God there could be no world, because there could be no adjustment of individuality. God's purpose in the world is quality of attainment. God's purpose is always embodied in the particular ideal relevant to the actual state of the world. Thus all attainment is immortal in that it fashions the actual ideals, which are God in the world as it is now. Every act leaves the world with a deeper or a fainter impression of God. God then passes into God's next relation to the world with enlarged, or diminished, presentations of ideal values.*

> *God is not the world, but the valuation of the world. In abstraction from the course of events, this valuation is a necessary meta-physical function. Apart for it, there would be no definite determination of limitations required for attainment. But in the actual world, God confronts what is actual in it with what is possible for it. Thus, God solves all indeterminations.*

In process theology, a person believes that God does not actually control the world in the usual way we understand the word "control," but does persuasively influence the world.

Process theology tells us that God encompasses processes as a salient aspect of divine nature. Divine love motivates and guides the course of life toward a new and better world. God is the focal source of creative intelligence, which engenders and sustains the world and endows it with law, beauty, harmony, order, value, and meaning. The divine-to-people relationship is a reciprocity that can be characterized as a union or Oneness. By analogy, the universe is God's body, and God is the consciousness that directs and interacts with that body ("Process Philosophy," *Stanford*, and "Process Philosophy," *The Internet Encyclopedia of Philosophy*).

In process theology, *freewill*—self-determination—is essential. God is either incapable of overriding human self-determination or, more likely, simply honors its necessary existence. "Omnipotence" means the ability to perform *any* conceivable actions. Because people have self-determination, God does not perform certain conceivable actions, and so, from a practical perspective, God is not omnipotent. God's power is persuasive rather than coercive because God does not force humans to make any particular decision and does not, or rarely does, supernaturally intervene in natural processes ("Process Philosophy," *Internet Encyclopedia*). In this way, God's relationship to the world is diffused, indirect, and limited.

Creation of the New Testament

Most Christians consider the writings in the New Testament to be the complete and true information about Jesus Christ. But the New Testament is only a limited collection of early Christian books and letters that consists of perhaps one-third of what could have been included when the New Testament was first assembled and distributed. Eusebius of Caesarea, who was the first person to write the history of Christianity (*Ecclesiastical History*) in 300 CE, tells us that the New Testament gospels were written several decades after the crucifixion of Jesus. Christianity started as the Jesus Movement within the Jewish communities but soon spread to the Greek communities, particularly in Asia Minor (Robinson).

In its first 300 years, each Christian community in and outside the Roman Empire had its own favored gospel or gospels because there was no central church authority. No one common set of writings delineated what was Christianity until the Roman Emperor Constantine required one version of Christianity after the Council of Nicaea (also spelled Nicea) in 325 CE.

Decades later, Father Jerome (347-420 CE), a Roman theologian, and others over many years selected a particular set of gospels and scriptures, and the result is what we call the Bible. Some gospels, such as the Gospel of Thomas and the Gospel of Mary, were not included in the New Testament. The long story of how the New Testament came together and was accepted over centuries is told by Professor Bart D. Ehrman in his book *Lost Christianities*. In brief, he argues that there were at least four versions of the New Testament, with the "Orthodox" version, which was championed primarily from the city of Rome, eventually winning the dispute.

With significant implications, many biblical scholars today argue that the Gospel of Thomas was the one written closest to the time when Jesus was still alive. It was probably compiled when He was alive or soon after His experience on the cross and before the gospels that are included in the New Testament (Robinson).

The Gospel of Thomas and the New Testament

The Gospel of Thomas was among the early Christian cache of documents found in 1945, near Nag Hammadi in Egypt. Biblical scholars believe someone at a nearby religious community buried the documents after the Council of Nicaea in 325 CE, because the cache was inconsistent with the decided upon religious dogma (the Alpha Interpretation) of Nicaea. The Gospel of Thomas consists of 144 sayings that are mostly concise direct quotes of Jesus' words, and at first appearance the sayings seem to be without order (Lynch and Lynch).

We argue that these sayings reflect the process philosophy and theology of Heraclitus, who lived about five centuries before Jesus. We limit our argument to the first five sayings of the Gospel of Thomas *and* related parallel quotes in the New

Testament. In the following cited sayings, we capitalize *He* and *His* because they refer to Jesus.

The five quotes, although referring to the words of Jesus, make points that are relevant to Heraclitus: (1) interpretations cannot die; (2) process is becoming; (3) His theology was pantheism or panentheism; (4) Jesus used obscure wording; and (5) metaphysical reality is a process and not substance.

Interpretations Cannot Die, Saying 1
And He said, "Whoever discovers the interpretations of these sayings will not taste death."

Starting with Saying 1 of the Gospel of Thomas, we immediately see evidence of process metaphysics. Process philosophy argues that concepts such as numbers, facts, and generalizations about relationships exist neither in space nor in time and therefore cannot die ("Process Theology," *Stanford*). Knowledge, including concepts, can be lost but cannot die as animate things do. This quotation states that interpretations of the sayings of Jesus from the Gospel of Thomas cannot die because they exist neither in space nor time; however, access to them can cease to exist for various peoples at different times and places.

The Gospel of John presents a quotation similar to Jesus' words in Saying 1: "If man keeps my saying, he shall never taste of death" (John 8:52). But there is a difference between the quotes from Thomas and John. One can interpret the version in the Gospel of Thomas to mean that when someone has a sufficiently developed consciousness to comprehend the deeper meaning of His sayings, then that one tastes the immortal.

In contrast, one can interpret the Gospel of John's version to mean that when someone puts the sayings of Jesus into action in his or her life, then that one tastes the immortal. With Thomas the stress is on comprehending, and with John the stress is on putting the sayings into action. Both versions are consistent with process philosophy by maintaining that concepts cannot die.

Process of Becoming, Saying 2

> Jesus said, "Let one who seeks not stop seeking until one finds; and upon finding, the person will be disturbed; and being disturbed, will be astounded, will reign and will reign over the entirety."

Again, process philosophy is not about static things but about becoming, which is a continuing process. Once we comprehend reality as a process, that understanding brings powerful insight, which, for example, explains what we now call scientific laws about the universe. The message of Jesus in Saying 2 from The Gospel of Thomas is a persuasive argument for process philosophy because it reflects an in-depth understanding of process metaphysics.

The saying's stress on the importance of seeking until one finds implies that the seeker must look past the illusion with its incomplete and inadequate observation made without wisdom. One must get past, for instance, seeing dark and light as separate qualities. "Being disturbed" and being "astounded" imply that the conclusions resulting from reflection with wisdom are unexpectedly insightful, much like the ones that result from process philosophy. Or, to return to our previous example about dark and light, we learn to see dark and light as a "unity of opposites." The phrase "reign over the entirety" tells us we are dealing with universal scientific laws or principles.

A parallel quote in the New Testament is "Ask, and it shall be given you; seek, and you shall find; knock, and it shall be opened to you: For every one that asks receives; and he that seeks finds; and to him that knocks it shall be opened" (Matthew 7:7-8). Notice the three stages of first asking, then seeking, and finally knocking. The Matthew quote is similar to the one in Thomas, but there is a difference: the stress for Thomas is on seeking, and that implies searching with some individual effort, whereas for Matthew the stress is on asking and very little on individual effort. The Thomas quote clearly reflects process philosophy, and the Matthew quote could possibly reflect process philosophy.

His Theology was Pantheism or Panentheism, Saying 3:
Jesus said, "If those who attack you, say to you, 'See, the kingdom is in heaven,' then the birds of heaven will precede you. If they say to you, 'It is in the sea,' then the fish will precede you. But the kingdom of God is inside you. And it is outside you. When you become acquainted with yourselves, then you will be recognized. And you will understand that it is you who are children of the living father. But if you do not become acquainted with yourselves, then you are in poverty, and it is you who are the poverty."

For Jesus, the Kingdom of Heaven / God is not a place but rather a state of consciousness that is evolving as one interacts with his or her environment and reflects on the deeper meanings that can be understood from those interactions. This saying is pantheistic, or even panentheistic, and clearly is not consistent with the notion of the contemporary Christian churches that God resides in a place called heaven. God is not in one place but rather everywhere and also maybe even beyond the universe.

Although not as clear an example of process theology as the Gospel of Thomas, the Gospel of Luke also does not have the standard Christian perspective of God. Luke's quotation of Jesus makes the point: "And when he was demanded of the Pharisees, when the Kingdom of God should come, he answered them and said, The Kingdom of God comes not with observation: Neither shall they say, Lo here! or, lo there! for, behold, the Kingdom of God is within you" (Luke 17:20-21). Again note that the Kingdom of God is not a place but an evolving higher consciousness.

The statements that "the Kingdom of God comes not with observation" and "God is within you" are consistent with process theology and not common Christian theology. But considering both Thomas and Luke's versions of Jesus' words, a conclusion difficult to ignore is that either the New Testament is wrong or the common Christian teachings concerning a theistic God who lives in a place called heaven is wrong.

Jesus Used Obscure Wording, Saying 4:
Jesus said, "The person advanced in days will not hesitate to ask a little child seven days old about the place of life. And that person will live. For many of the first will be last, and they will become one."

The 114 sayings of Jesus are remarkably obscure, as were the sayings and writings of Heraclitus some 500 years before him. Saying 4 is a good example of that obscurity. Our interpretation of this saying is based on our conclusion that a seven-day-old child is open, innocent, and pure of heart. The child's openness to learn is an important factor in the process that leads to the child learning quickly. The person advanced in days can learn innocence, purity of heart, and openness from the seven-day-old. These are essential attributes for a spiritual person to acquire to order to eventually be One with the universe.

This saying reflects process philosophy and theology, especially where Thomas cites the phrase "will become one." Process philosophy and theology tell us that we are all part of the unity that is the universe, God, and the divine laws that guide everything ("Process Philosophy," *Stanford*). In the yoking of the young and the old, and then the first and the last, the saying also illustrates the continuum in "the unity of opposites."

The Gospel of Luke presents a similar theme: "In that hour Jesus rejoiced in spirit, and said, I thank you, O Father, Lord of heaven and earth, that you have hid these things from the wise and prudent, and have revealed them to babes; even so, Father, for so it seemed good in your sight" (Luke 10:21). The meaning of this quote from Luke is also obscure. However, its obscurity disappears once we adopt the perspective of process philosophy.

The phrase "wise and prudent" uses irony to refer to being engrossed in a materially-oriented intellect. In contrast, the word "babes" connotes innocence and purity of heart. Great Greek philosophers, such as Plato and Aristotle, rejected the process metaphysics of Heraclitus; its wisdom was hidden from them and those who contemplated traditional metaphysics. In contrast, babes are aware of the processes about them and learn remarkably fast as they mature.

Only an understanding of process philosophy and its historical context permits one to grasp the meaning of the Luke quote. The words in the quotation demonstrate a depth of education and sophistication that few have attributed to Jesus.

Metaphysical Reality Is Process and Not Substances, Saying 5:
Jesus said, "Recognize what is before your face, and what is hidden to you will become disclosed unto you. For there is nothing hidden unto you. For there is nothing obscure that will not become shown forth and nothing buried that will not be raised."

For most of us, reality is a substance we call river, but what is in front of our face is moving water. What is hidden is the force that moves the water, but once understood it is no longer hidden. The metaphysical reality is hidden until we grasp the Oneness of the material, the moving water, with the nonmaterial force that moves the water. We need to learn to ignore our mental illusions and see what is truly in front of us. This important understanding can be gained if we see through the lens of process philosophy.

Saying 5 contains philosophical irony when it states, "and nothing buried that will not be raised." To understand the humor, you need to know that the Roman authorities and the Christian church leaders created the circumstances that led to the burial of the Gospel of Thomas and the rest of the Nag Hammadi collection for centuries in Egypt. Those Roman leaders often used force and the threat of force to define the teachings of Jesus, based on their selected Alpha Interpretation and the political needs of the Emperor.

The irony is that Saying 5 predicted what would happen. In 1945, a poor illiterate discovered the Gospel of Thomas and other works while searching for fertilizer. In doing so, his actions became an ironic example of the suppressed and hidden earliest teachings of Jesus, buried and now raised.

Luke and Matthew say something similar to Thomas 5: "For nothing is secret, that shall not be made manifest; neither anything hid, that shall not be known and come abroad" (Luke 8:17 and similar wording in Matthew 10:26). In Luke, Jesus says, "For there is nothing covered, that shall not be revealed; neither hid, that shall not be known. Therefore whatsoever you have spoken in darkness shall be heard in the light; and that which you have spoken in the ear of closets shall be proclaimed upon the house tops" (Luke 12:2).

Proponents of process philosophy argue that traditional metaphysics defines reality incorrectly, and because of that, important truths are hidden from us. Contemporary research in physics and social sciences that results from using process philosophy seems to verify that argument. Once the research inspired by process philosophy was publicly circulated, important theoretical advances became known to the world, and scientific discoveries and practical insights were no longer covered or hidden ("Process Theology," *Stanford*). For example, social science developed Program Evaluation Review Technique (PERT) to help managers comprehend how projects should evolve and what phases (processes) were particularly important if the projects were to be timely. The value of PERT is that it exposes the hidden—that is, what must be done in a timely manner—that normally is overlooked due to the complexity of a large project.

We could continue through all the 114 sayings of the Gospel of Thomas to make our argument. However, with just the first five sayings, we think our argument is sufficiently demonstrated.

Saying 111 is relevant in closing this section:
"Jesus said, 'The heavens and the earth will roll-up in your presence. And the living from the living will not see death.'"

Process theology understands reality as a moving or rolling process in which you understand reality not only differently but also more deeply and fully. Living is a process, and through that process, we can understand that which will never die, specifically, scientific knowledge or what can be called divine truths. They are the "living from the living" in Saying 111.

The term "roll-up" bears contemplating. The mind goes to a scroll rather than a book, which did not exist at the time of Jesus. A scroll was often a formal written communication, which sometimes contained scientific knowledge. Because a scroll is rolled up when not in use, "roll-up" metaphorically indicates all creation is unfurled as an ever-expanding universe. In physics, the term implies all creation is at its point before the big bang.

Reshaping Our Understanding

If our argument is correct—that the Gospel of Thomas and to a lesser extent other writings in the New Testament demonstrate Jesus using the process philosophy and process theology of Heraclitus in His teaching—then what are the ramifications? Many in Christianity like to think of themselves as orthodox, that is, believers in the true teaching of Jesus. Almost all Christians who think they are following the teachings of Jesus are not totally wrong but are significantly misled. We argue with a sense of paradoxical humor that if you wish to be a true orthodox and conservative Christian, then you need to become a "liberal" Christian.

In addition, we believe our argument shows Jesus was aware of some of the greatest philosophical thinking before His time. His profound teachings enlighten us to the process philosophy and theology of our own time. Only since the 1940s have process philosophy and theology been rediscovered. In that brief time, process philosophy has significantly reshaped modern science and revolutionized human understanding. It will continue to do so in the future.

We suspect that process theology will also reshape our understanding of God and help us understand how God and science are a "unity of opposites." In other words, Jesus' teachings are valid, and many people since His time have just not been able to understand His brilliance and the remarkable gift He gave humankind.

Finally, if we are correct that the teachings of Jesus are best comprehended using process theology, then His teachings are essentially interfaith in nature and should not be considered the sole purview of one particular religion. There are many religions in the world, and almost all of them have developed an orthodox, conservative wing as well as a mystical, spiritual wing. The teachings of the orthodox, conservative wings differ greatly from religion to religion. But the teachings of the mystical and spiritual wings are remarkably similar. Process theology reflects the teachings of the mystical and spiritual wings, and thus it is interfaith in its scope.

Chapter 6

The First Interfaith Theologian

Philo of Alexandria could have been a teacher of Jesus. He was born in 20 BCE, 20 years before Jesus, and he died in 50 CE, about 20 years after Jesus was placed on the cross. In Chapter 4, we explain that we believe Jesus' parents took Him to Egypt at a very early age and He lived there until He was a mature adult. We also note He might have even traveled extensively after His education and before what we know of His life in Israel.

We speculate that the Jewish group called Therapeutae, of which Philo was a leading member, could have educated Him in the most advanced knowledge of the Greek, Egyptian, and Jewish cultures of the day. In other words, Philo could have been one of Jesus' teachers when Philo was 30 to 50 years old and Jesus somewhere between 10 and 30. Such an education would be like receiving a combined Ph.D. and M.D. today.

This chapter elaborates on the theme of Philo's probable influence on Jesus by examining Philo's theology. The careful reader will note that Philo's thinking is quite similar to the teachings of Jesus. Interestingly, early scholars thought that Jesus had influenced Philo and the Therapeutae—until their discoveries showed the Therapeutae existed centuries before Jesus and that Philo developed his theology just before and at the same time as Jesus existed. We suggest the influence of the teachings ran primarily from Philo and the Therapeutae to Jesus; but if Jesus was a student of Philo, Jesus might also have had some influence on Philo and later teachings of the Therapeutae.

In writing this chapter, we found Chapters 8 and 9 of Robert Wright's *The Evolution of God* particularly useful and recommend the entire book to readers.

Philo And Tolerance

Philo was devoted to Yahweh, but unlike many other Jews in his time, he was also tolerant and accepting of other religions. In contemporary versions of Exodus (22:28), the Torah reads, "You shall not revile *God*." (The emphasis is ours.) However the Septuagint version, a third and second century BCE Greek translation of that same verse, reads, "You shall not revile *gods*."

Philo did not believe in the existence of other people's gods because he was a devout Jew and fervent monotheist. Nevertheless, Philo took very seriously God's commandment from the Septuagint version of the Torah that said one should "not revile gods." He also adhered to the Jewish admonishment that a Jew may interpret the words of the Torah but he cannot change those words.

Therefore, as possibly the first interfaith theologian and clearly the first known theologian, Philo accepted, tolerated, and honored other faith traditions while maintaining a deep commitment to his own (Wright 189). One can easily conclude that Philo would accept the contemporary Interfaith motto: "Never instead of, Always in Addition to . . . " of the first Interfaith seminary, The New Seminary in New York City, started by Rabbi Joseph H. Gelberman in 1979 (New Seminary).

Philo says that God's law "muzzles and restrains its own disciples, not permitting them to revile these (gods) with a loose tongue, for it believes that well-spoken praise is better" (Philo, 1929, supp. II, 40-41). This statement was part of his sermon about the preservation of peace and dignity among faith traditions.

Philo believed the commandment of God demanded that Jews show respect for the religious opinion of others. As an interfaith theologian, Philo spoke to a higher purpose for religion. The divine to him was quite abstract and essentially unknowable, but the divine supported moral uplifting and must be in harmony with science and philosophy.

Was Philo incorrect in using the Septuagint translation of the Hebrew into Greek, especially given that he was literate in Hebrew? The Hebrew word *Elohim* in that key quote from Exodus means "god," but the word could be either singular or plural. When *Elohim* is the subject of a sentence, the verb in the sentence, just as in English, tells the reader if the subject is singular or plural. When *Elohim* is the object of the verb, it could be either singular or plural.

Thus any Septuagint translator must decide whether to use the plural or singular. Third and second century BCE translators chose the plural, whereas later translators picked the singular. Which is chosen does make a difference. The use of the plural encourages Jews, Christians, and Muslims, who all consider the Torah as sacred, to have an interfaith perspective of tolerance. The use of the singular encourages them to have an insular perspective.

The twenty-first century needs strong tolerance among faith traditions to lessen the likelihood of interfaith conflict. Selecting the insular perspective is, unfortunately, dysfunctional for our era. Fortunately, the Jews in Alexandria in the third and second century BCE chose the plural translation. This choice made it easier for Philo and others to diplomatically challenge the anti-Semitism of their day.

Philo's tolerance was wisely practical in the Greek, Roman, and Egyptian crossroads where he lived. He was born rich to a very influential Jewish family in the Roman province of Egypt. For a person with such a background to stay on good terms with other rich and powerful people was particularly delicate. Polytheistic Roman emperors deemed themselves gods, and they required all citizens and non-citizens of the empire to worship them publicly. As a result, Roman officials and citizens confronted monotheistic Jews and demanded they also worship the Roman Emperor as a god in their synagogues. Devout Jews, including Philo, refused, and this refusal led to anti-Semitic riots in Egypt.

At one point in his life, Philo led a delegation of Jews to Rome to plead their case to Emperor Caligula, who was a narcissistic absolute ruler. In the chamber with the Jewish delegation, Caligula asked why Jews refused to eat pork. Philo answered, "Different people have different customs and the use of some things is forbidden to us as others are to our opponents" (Philo, 1929, 181).

Caligula said to the delegation that though the Jews are "foolish in refusing to believe that I have got the nature of god," they are, at bottom, "unfortunate rather than wicked" (Philo, 1929, 183). At this meeting, possibly because of his religious tolerance, Philo was successful in his diplomacy. The Emperor ruled that the Jews of Alexandria did not have to worship Caligula's statute in their synagogues and were allowed to maintain their lives with their Jewish religion.

Athens Versus Jerusalem

The modern conflict of philosophy and its outgrowth—secular science—versus biblical religion already existed in the Roman Empire. The conflict was best illustrated in the tension between Athens, known as the center of secular philosophy, and Jerusalem, known as the center of revealed religious truth. During the lifetime of Jesus, Philo was tied to both cultures, and he became famous as a philosopher for seeking and finding a synthesis of Jewish biblical theology and Greek philosophy.

He felt that a revealed religion could not only withstand

any challenge from educated and thoughtful people of reason but that, in the process of such challenges, reason would nourish religion, and vice versa. Philo's perception of the interdependence of Jewish religious thought and Greek philosophy would lead him to fuse the two viewpoints into a new theology. We argue in this book that Philo's fused interfaith theology informed Jesus and served as the basis for His teaching.

The interfaith aspect of Philo's theology led him to develop close Greek friends and to engage with them in their cultural activities, such as the theater, horse racing, and boxing. In Philo's view, the closer the friends were, the stronger the need to share a common worldview.

Philo came to believe that Judaism and large parts of Greek philosophy were not only true but also consistent with each other. Thus he read Plato in terms of Moses and Moses in terms of Plato. To him, they said essentially the same thing but each from its unique perspective. As a result of this fusion, the historian of religion Edwin Goodenough (10) declared Philo to be one of antiquity's most important thinkers.

Jews, Christians, and Muslims can find in Philo an ancient Abrahamic theologian whose language lends itself to modern sensibility. Parts of his writings remind us and other students of comparative religion of Buddhism and later Judaism, Christianity, and the mystical writings of Islam. Philo was a remarkable man in that he created for knowledgeable and thoughtful people a conceptual bridge between the secular and the spiritual.

The concept of an anthropomorphic god fell out of favor among Greek philosophers five centuries before Philo noted its arbitrariness and foolishness. One can note in the Hebrew Bible and the Old Testament that God sits on a throne and exhibits human traits like jealousy and rage. Philo thought this understanding of God absurd.

Philo said that if horses and cattle created theology, then horses would draw the forms of gods like horses and cattle like cattle (1983, 61). Further, he said the Torah's anthropomorphic depictions of God were merely allegory. To Philo, God was personal, but "no name nor utterance nor conception of any sort is adequate" in any attempt to describe God (1929, 5: 331). God is beyond the mere material because God is ineffable and transcendent.

Philo also wrote that God related to humans, and his one word explanation for that relationship was the Greek word *logos*. To Philo, the *logos* was the reasoning principle in the universe and the natural law for all humans and matter (Goodenough 108). The word *logos* included what modern science calls the basic laws of physics, chemistry, biology, and so on.

The *logos* is the set of divine rules and laws that keep the world operating and intact. It exists in both the material aspects of the universe but also in human behavior. Philo says, "The logos was such a Bond of the Universe as nothing can break" (1929, 3: 217).

With its divine laws and the influence of those laws on humankind, the *logos* gives history a direction and even a purpose (*telos*). This purpose includes a moral direction, insofar as history influences the movement of thoughtful and reflective humankind toward the good. Philo noted that the *logos*-driven history would work "to the end that the whole of our world should be as a single state, enjoying the best of constitutions, a democracy" (1929, 3: 97). For Philo, the *logos* existed before the universe and what we call matter. Prior to the universe, God formulated the *logos* much like a computer programmer designs an algorithm to run a computer. To Philo, the six-day creation was allegorical and certainly not literal. The *logos* is the divine algorithm. It brought into the material universe what we think of as existence, and thus ultimately created earth and all life forms, including humans.

According to Goodenough (108), Philo said, "The logos was conceived in God's mind before all things and is manifested in connection with all things." Heraclitus, whom we discuss in Chapter 5, clearly influenced Philo in that Philo's conceptualization of the *logos* appears to be the one Heraclitus developed several centuries before. The *logos* consists of the divine laws and principles that govern such things as human behavior and natural phenomena, like the law of gravity. Heraclitus and Philo believed that the *logos* was humankind's primary contact with the divine.

In Philo's theology, God is both beyond the material universe but yet, in an important sense, is also the material universe. In part, God is like a video game designer in that the designer is outside the game, but nevertheless the game is an extension of the designer and reflects the designer's mind, imagination and creativity. However, in part, God is also the substance of the universe. The label for this view is not theism but rather panentheism.

The *logos* reconciles the transcendence of God with what is also the divine presence in the world. The logos is imbued with God's spirit and values, so that if one knows the *logos*, one knows the divine intention and God's presence and purpose.

Humankind, collectively and individually, co-creates with God's immanent presence, and the co-creation process can best be accomplished if humankind senses God's presence and purpose. Like two people working together efficiently, their harmony is largely dependent on each knowing the presence and purpose of the other.

For each human, the first step in co-creation with God is to try to understand God, especially God's purpose. The *logos* is the key to that understanding. Science is often the vehicle for advancing human knowledge about nature and, therefore, for understanding the divine laws called *logos*. With greater knowledge continually developed through science, we can better decipher the *logos* and bring ourselves closer to spirituality and enlightenment. Ultimately, the *logos* is the guide to the realm of the divine, including our understanding of the human soul.

Contemporary epistemology (the branch of philosophy that studies the nature of knowledge, its limits and justification) tells us that although science is a process to ever increase knowledge concerning scientific laws, inherently humans can never obtain final or definite conclusions about those laws. The process is always ongoing and the knowledge itself infinite in character.

With almost parallel logic, Philo two thousand years ago said that final and definite conclusions concerning the *logos* do not, and never will, exist. Humans cannot obtain perfect knowledge about a transcendent and ineffable God. The process of discovery is always on-going, and potential knowledge to be discovered is infinite in character. The best we can do is continually grow our cumulative knowledge and attempt to find harmony with the *logos* in our daily lives.

The *Logos*

Certainly, science can help us decipher the enigma called the *logos*, but religions' Holy Scriptures, such as the Torah, can also. Philo, as a Jew, observed that the Torah reflected, and helped Jews understand, the *logos*. The Torah set out the rules of living in community. To him, the Torah was also the law of nature and the divine law for living in harmony with nature. Therefore, Philo felt both kinds of law were part of the *logos*.

Philo's concept is also very similar to the Buddhist notion of *dharma*. It is both the truth about how the universe works as well as how one should live in harmony with that universe. Philo believed there is an intimate unity between scientific laws and the prescriptions of moral laws.

Influential philosophers of the twentieth century, such as Bertram Russell, have told us the two kinds of law do not relate to each other. In contrast, ancient thought tells us scientific laws and the proper understandings of virtue are God's creation, and both are parts of the *logos*. The ancients believed we should act in harmony with both because by acting in harmony with both, we further bring them about. We should do this because humanity should strive to fulfill God's *telos*.

But what is God's *telos*? The Holy Scriptures of the Jews and other groups tell us that the *telos* of these faith traditions includes living increasingly in greater harmony with other people. Philo says, "This is what our most holy prophet through all his regulations especially desires to create, unanimity, neighborliness, fellowship, reciprocity of feeling, whereby houses and cities and nations and countries and the whole human race may advance to supreme happiness" (1929, 8: 235). In other words, loving God is important, but we also should love our neighbors and even our enemies.

Because the *logos* is something everyone can understand by seeking to do so, the ability to decipher its enigma is not limited to one group of people, such as the Jews. Deciphering is an empirical activity that can eventually lead to the discovery of knowledge. The seekers of such knowledge must transcend their material observations to grasp the immaterial divine laws that cause the material to act as it does.

Philo feels that the Greek philosophers did well in their seeking without the advantage of being Jewish. Philo says, "What the disciples of the most excellent philosophy gain from its teaching, the Jews gain from their customs and laws, that is to know the highest, the most ancient Cause of all things . . ." (1929, 8: 235). If someone is a seeker, that person can eventually determine what it takes to achieve harmony with God.

Anyone, through observation and reflection, can fathom the *logos*. However, that fathoming can be done well or poorly, which will lead either to proper or wrong conclusions. Doing it well, so that one moves beyond the material world with its illusions and ultimately reaches proper conclusions, requires wisdom, especially spiritual wisdom. Wisdom alone provides the means to escape the illusions of the material world and for us to transcend thereby to the immaterial divine laws. The *logos* is the path to the divine, but one can travel that path successfully only with wisdom as the guide.

Wisdom

As a Jew, Philo found the literature of spiritual wisdom in books such as Psalms, Proverbs, the Song of Solomon, and the Book of Sirach. In other religious traditions, similar literature exists and is of equal importance in understanding the divine law behind what happens and does not happen in the material world (Lynch and Lynch).

Writers often present wisdom through poetry and depict wisdom as a woman, such as Yahweh's daughter, who is sometimes called Sophia. In many ancient writings, Wisdom is commonly represented by the feminine pronoun. "Happy are those who find wisdom," for "Her income is better than silver, and Her revenues better than gold . . . nothing you desire can compare with Her . . . . Her ways are ways of pleasantness, and all Her paths are peace. She is a tree of life to those who lay hold of Her; those who hold Her fast are called happy" (Proverbs 3: 13-18).

Another way to understand *logos* is to observe that there is not only a physical version of a law such as gravity, but there is also a social version that we can call "social gravity." Learning social gravity and its negative effects is also learning what is meant by the expression "fear of the Lord." The saying in Proverbs (1:7), that "The fear of the Lord is the beginning of knowledge," presents Wisdom. Proverbs also tells us that Wisdom, meaning Sophia, says, "My child, if you accept My words and treasure up My commandments within you . . . if you indeed cry out for insight, and raise your voice for understanding . . . then you will understand the fear of the Lord and find the knowledge of God" (Proverbs 2:1-5).

Because the *logos* exists, the earnest seeker can find spiritual wisdom by following Her back to the divine. The seeker can then understand how God created the universe. This understanding allows the seeker to achieve harmony with God's *telos* by co-creating with the divine in daily life. Spiritual wisdom is the transportation and the guide that allows seekers to transcend the material world. Hence Sophia—Wisdom—plays two interlocking roles: She helps God create the universe, and She is the means for the earnest seeker to transcend to the divine.

Part of Her purpose is to impart a sense of integrity, justice, caring, and honesty to the seeker. Her purpose includes "teaching shrewdness to the simple" and "prudence to the young" (Proverbs 1:3; 1:4). To Wisdom, there is no difference between learning virtue and learning self-interest.

She teaches you to watch life as it evolves around you and to keep your eyes and ears open as you later reflect on what you saw and heard. She tells you your purpose is to understand which behaviors bear fruit and which lead to sorrow. Finding fruitful behaviors helps you determine what is divine law, and that, in turn, helps you understand what the *logos* is.

Holy Scriptures present the wisdom of the sages and are an incredible time saver for sincere seekers. One can and should simply watch the consequences of one's behavior. However, seekers with a greater or more urgent desire for wisdom can gain insight faster by studying their and other Holy Scriptures. If the potential seeker is too proud and haughty to study or even simply watch what life teaches, then that person's knowledge of what is truly valuable is small. This lack of knowledge leaves a person too vulnerable and open to disaster. Proverbs tells us that "pride goes before destruction, and a haughty spirit before a fall" (16:18).

The wisdom literature parallels what insightful science of human behavior tells us. The Book of Sirach says, "Many a man is prevented from sinning by poverty, and when he rests he is not tempted." Furthermore, the Book of Sirach tells us,

"The rich man's sleeplessness wastes away his flesh, and his anxiety drives away sleep. " Sirach states, "Jealousy and anger shorten life, and worry ages a man prematurely" and adds, "A glad heart is good for the body" (Rad, 1972, 125-127).

Like the literature of human behavior, the general rules for living, guided by wisdom literature, deal with cause and effect. However, they are not absolute but rather probabilistic divine rules. For example, Proverbs warns young adults to avoid the company of murderous thieves because "people who live by the sword die by it." Proverbs also tells men not to sleep with another's wife because the betrayed husband loses honor and more: "For jealousy arouses a husband's fury, and he shows no restraint when he takes revenge"(1:18-19; 6:34).

The *logos* allows those willing to search and learn to discover that life steers them to virtue. If people want happy lives, and if they carefully look around for the causes and effects of human behavior, they will see the value in virtue. They will come to understand that divine law includes social gravity and that everything is under God's control.

Life continually teaches the more thoughtful and perceptive seekers among us that divine law also includes virtue, which ultimately derives from the original and continuing *logos*. To the extent we can see and hear the thoughtful seekers, leaders who articulate those virtues and show us how to make them a part of our lives, social harmony will exist with its dividend of pleasantness and peace among us. Conversely, to the extent we ignore those thoughtful seekers who bring us the divine laws from the *logos*, pain and suffering from lack of social harmony shall exist among us.

God created the *logos* so that those who pursue life and rationally act in their self-interest, in its deepest sense, will find Wisdom. This attainment occurs regardless of where or when they live. Spiritual wisdom is both God's eternal Wisdom and the means by which seekers come to acquire it. The genius of the design of the universe is that it leads seekers toward, and eventually to, spiritual wisdom.

Wisdom is God's mind. When we learn deeper lessons from observing social phenomena, we learn Wisdom and follow it back to its source, which is *logos* and is God. Philo says, "And it is when the mind's course is guided along that road that it reaches the goal which is the recognition and knowledge of God" (1929, 3: 82-83).

Adherence to virtue is merely being in harmony with the *logos* and thus with God. Philo says, "For the *logos* of God, when it arrives at our earthy composition, in the case of those who are akin to virtue and turn away to Her, gives help and succor, thus affording them a refuge and perfect safety, but sends upon Her adversaries irreparable ruin" (1929, 5: 343).

In summary, seeking to attain spiritual wisdom leads to communicating with the divine. It is a means to understand the *logos* and transcend the material world while being in the material world. It is you merging with the *logos*, and you permitting spiritual Wisdom (Sophia) to guide your daily actions. Once you know spiritual Wisdom, then with your *freewill* you must travel the next step by allowing Her to guide you as you proceed down the path of life. Proverbs (4:6) tells us, "Love Her, and She will guard you."

Linking The Material And The Immaterial

Philo points out that the human mind has a twofold relationship with the *logos* (Runia 65-67). First, the human mind is to the body as the *logos* is to the material world. The relationship is the reasoning principle of each, as it *can* govern humans and *does* govern the universe. Second, each person is born with the *logos* already in his or her mind. Although this *logos* to mind relationship exists, individually we must recognize, acknowledge, and use our *freewill* to activate and grow that relationship.

Just as we are born with intelligence to think and muscles

to move, we are also born with a spark of the *logos* within us so that we *can be* in a spiritual relationship with God. We must develop our intelligence and muscles as we mature so we can optimize our functionality in life. We must also develop our relationship with God by seeking and growing within us spiritual wisdom. If we do that, we can let Her, Sofia, guide our daily actions and optimize our spiritual functionality.

Bringing spiritual wisdom into our lives can be done only with the rational mind. However, we must understand that the rational mind exists in the same mind that also houses baser animal impulses, which can distort visions and corrupt motivations.

If base impulses dominate you, then your relationship with the *logos* is overwhelmed, and you are not in union with the divine. Jesus called this situation living in the Kingdom of Man. In contrast, if your rational mind dominates and uses spiritual wisdom as a guide, then your *logos* relationship grows stronger, as does your union with the divine. Jesus called this situation living in the Kingdom (Kindom) of God.

Therefore, if you wish union with the divine, seek out and develop within you the purest wisdom possible, as well as the most spiritual. Do this with your rational mind fully in charge, and do not allow your passions and temptations to control you. Realize that this endeavor is often hard work. In addition, few others will choose to follow such a path in their lives, and so few will actually achieve living in the Kindom of Heaven.

Doing so is co-creation with God. Your rational mind, using your *freewill* to overcome the pleasures of the flesh, works *with* spiritual Wisdom (Sophia) as a guide to live your life. Philo says, "Every comrade of the flesh hates and rejects this path and seeks to corrupt it. For there are no two things so utterly opposed as knowledge and pleasures of the flesh" (1929, 3: 82-83).

Philo notes our senses lead us to false opinions, our egoistic biases corrupt our cognition, and our language does not capture the true texture of reality. Thus each is an impediment to understanding spiritual wisdom, the *logos*, and ultimately God. According to Philo, the path to the divine is "not that way of thinking which abides in the prison of the body of its own *freewill*, but that which released from its fetters into liberty has come forth outside the prison walls, and if we may so say, left behind its own self" (1929, 4: 317-318).

The irrational will channel the senses and rouse the passions, resulting in cravings. With our rational mind, we must transcend those cravings so that only the divine within us gives direction to our actions. If we are to act in harmony with the divine, we must rid our minds of ego and desires so that pure reason and spiritual wisdom will guide us. If a person accomplishes that, then that person daily co-creates with God. Philo says, "So if you wish to have God as the portion of your heart, first you yourself become a portion worthy of Him" (1929, 5: 157).

Becoming The *Logos*

Spiritual wisdom, with its connection to *logos*, is the necessary key if the Omega Interpretation discussed in Chapters 4, 9 and 10 is to be understood and acted upon correctly. The New Testament's Gospel of John opens with the words, "In the beginning was the Word (*logos*), and the Word (*logos*) was with God, and the Word (*logos*) was God." This Gospel tells us Jesus taught and lived the *logos*. The gospel (1: 14) says, "And the Word (*logos*) became flesh and lived among us, and we have seen His glory, the glory as of a father's only son, full of grace and truth."

Any person who fully understands and lives the theology of Philo becomes the *logos*, as did Jesus. When a person does that, he or she becomes the son or daughter of God, just as did Jesus. Such a person is full of grace and truth. Philo refers to the *logos* as "the son of God" because a person who seeks, discovers, and becomes the *logos* is the true prodigy of God. That Jesus alone, in and before His time, reached that status is possible but not likely. We believe that everyone has the potential to reach that status, and we hope many more will and then properly be recognized as sons and daughters of God.

Our argument in this chapter is that Philo's theology influenced Jesus, who preached generosity, tolerance, and universal love. The Gospel of John (1:9) says Jesus is "the true light, which enlightens everyone." Our conclusion is that Philo influenced the message of Jesus, who lived what Philo taught. Philo was a worthy and remarkable theologian, and Jesus improved his message of spirituality and brought it to the world. That message is what we call the Omega Interpretation.

Chapter 7

The Gospel of Mary

This chapter is about the remarkable and little known Gospel of Mary, whose authorship is attributed to Mary Magdalene. Unfortunately only portions of it survive. The insights found in the Gospel of Mary are sociologically and psychologically astute, and we only wish more of the original text were available to our contemporary world.

We feel this gospel is important for anyone trying to understand the male-female relationship, whether it is between two people or the male-female relationship within a single person. First, whether the two people are married or not, or of the same sex or not, a relationship involves the appropriateness of male and female power within that couple. The second understanding of relationship is even more primary and insightful. It involves the unity of opposites within each person's soul. It addresses how to let the male and female parts of the soul reach equal status and fullness and thus move the person closer to attaining the Kindom of Heaven.

In this second and more abstract relationship, "male" and "female" are words representing qualities and powers within the soul. Whether between two people or within the soul of an individual, these relationships are not distinct but rather are symbiotically linked, as will become more obvious as we progress through this chapter.

In Chapter 5, we explain how we believe Heraclitus, the Greek philosopher, had an enormous influence on Jesus, and we discuss Jesus' use of the concepts of material and non-material "unity of opposites" in His teachings. The Gospel of

Mary can be read as a good illustration of the "unity of opposites" in action. For example, the *unity* of the partners in a male-female relationship transcends both individuals, and in the process of their entering into a relationship together, they develop into something more than they were as individuals.

If a couple is to have a wholesome union, Divine Law, meaning the *logos* governing the process, requires them to establish a deep relationship of mutual love and respect. Without the observance of this Divine Law, which each partner must freely choose to honor and adhere to, the partners do not treat each other correctly. In other words, the relationship is just not healthy and appropriate. In observing this Divine Law, each partner expects, desires, and works to create a relationship of love and respect, and doesn't take advantage of the other.

Love based on the Divine Law is reciprocal. It requires giving of oneself to one's partner but also mutual respect and honor for the well-being and happiness of the other. As the reader considers the sayings in the Gospel of Mary, this "unity of opposites" should be kept firmly in mind.

We present the "chapters" of sayings in their reverse numerical order than in the original Gospel of Mary. Our reason is simple: the information and context in the gospel is easier to understand when working from the end of the gospel toward the beginning.

Background Facts

The Gospel of Mary is not part of the New Testament, and only portions of it have been found. The first segments of the gospel were discovered in 1896, when a German scholar, Dr. Carl Reinhardt, acquired them in Cairo. This version is called the Papyrus Beronlinensis 8502, and it is also known as the Berlin Gnostic Codex, PB 8502, BG 8502. Because of various wars and other factors, it was not translated and published in English until 1955 (Leloup 5; King 9).

Another discovery, made 49 years later, augmented and supported the discovery of 1896. This discovery was written in the Coptic language and found, along with many other ancient Christian documents, including the Gospel of Thomas, in the Nag Hammadi discovery in 1945. In addition, two other very small fragments of the Gospel of Mary have been found written in the Greek language. We use primarily the Nag Hammadi version for our analysis in this chapter.

By far the most complete version is that of the Nag Hammadi discovery, which is commonly called the Nag Hammadi Library. As mentioned in other chapters, an illiterate Muslim camel driver found a collection of documents near the Nile River in December 1945, not far from the small Egyptian town of Nag Hammadi. The camel driver was looking for bat fertilizer near a cave, and instead he found an old jar full of manuscripts. One story is that he used pages of the manuscripts to light a fire that night to stay warm. An alternative story is that he took the manuscripts home and that night his mother used several pages to kindle the fire in her stove (Ehrman 21). Possibly that is how many of the pages of the Gospel of Mary were lost.

The camel driver's find is still the most complete version of the Gospel of Mary known to exist. The major missing portions are (a) all of Chapters 1, 2 and 3; (b) parts of Chapter 4; (c) Chapters 6 and 7; and (d) parts of Chapter 8.

Our analysis of the Gospel of Mary is necessarily incomplete because of the missing portions, but the followings points can be made with some certainty:

- The gospel tells us that Jesus held Mary Magdalene in high regard.
- Jesus apparently taught Mary many lessons *after* His time on the cross.
- Mary was with a number of the disciples, and they asked her what Jesus had exclusively taught her.

- Andrew and Peter were very sexist in their relationship with Mary.

Some biblical scholars discount the Gospel of Mary because they consider it to be a Gnostic gospel, and Gnosticism is a version of early Christianity that mainstream Christian churches deem heretical. From an orthodox Christian perspective, if it is Gnostic, it logically should have not been included in the New Testament. The gospel was found with many Gnostic documents, and although some ideas, such as the stress on gaining knowledge, are Gnostic in tone, we do not see many of the themes typically associated with Gnostic thinking, such as the mention of a Demiurge and an addition to the creation story.

Thus we conclude that the Gospel of Mary is, at most, only influenced by the Gnostics. But for several other reasons we can understand why it was not included in the canon of the New Testament. First, the text diminishes the importance of Peter. Given Peter's standing as the founder of the Catholic Church, the "official" church would not want the Gospel of Mary included in the New Testament.

Second, clearly the anti-sexist tone of the Gospel of Mary would hurt the strongly male-oriented institution of the church then, and even now. Third, and more significantly, the Gospel takes a very strong position against the concept of original sin, a position that would destroy the Alpha theological argument of the church, as we discuss in Chapter 4 of this book. In addition, the Gospel of Mary clearly states that Jesus admonished His followers not to develop any additional rules or laws beyond the ones He developed and taught. Recognizing this prohibition would subvert the policy and practice of the church to create new rules and laws for itself.

A comment on sexism is needed at this point. The reader must remember that in the time of Jesus, Jewish society and, in fact, most of the world was highly biased against women.

Both in the New Testament and the Gospel of Thomas, we can observe that Jesus was far less sexist than other Jews of His period. But even His approach, liberal for the time, could make many in our contemporary Western society uncomfortable. The words of Simon Peter in Saying 114 from the Gospel of Thomas (cited in Lynch and Lynch) illustrate the inequality of the sexes at that time; many in our era would consider the words of Jesus also to be sexist:

> **Simon Peter said to them, "Mary should leave us, for females are not worthy of life." Jesus said, "Look I shall guide her to make her male, so that she too may also become a living spirit resembling you males. For every female who makes herself male will enter heaven's kingdom."**

Modern thinkers on gender might ask why Jesus would say a woman should have to make herself into a man in order to enter Heaven's Kindom. We interpret Jesus' words as referring not to the physical body of the person but rather to the unity of male-female consciousness. When the two opposites join spiritually and enter the same consciousness, they create a unified spiritual vision. Our point regarding the meaning of "male' in this passage becomes more evident later in the chapter.

Gospel of Mary, Chapter 9

Lines 1 and 2
> **When Mary had said this, she fell silent, since it was to this point that the Savior had spoken to her. But Andrew answered and said to the brethren, "Say what you wish to say about what she has said, I at least do not believe that the Savior said this. For certainly these teachings are strange ideas."**

Lines 1 and 2 indicate that Mary is in the company of many of the most important disciples of Jesus and they are listening to her. Andrew directly challenges the veracity of her message and her truthfulness in delivering it.

Lines 3, 4, and 5

Peter answered and spoke concerning these same things. He questioned them about the Savior: "Did he really speak privately with a woman and not openly to us? Are we to turn about and all listen to her? Did he prefer her to us?" Then Mary wept and said to Peter, "My brother Peter, what do you think? Do you think that I have thought this up myself in my heart, or that I am lying about the Savior?"

Here Peter, the brother of Andrew, goes even further, making the argument that Mary is *unworthy* of this knowledge. He feels that women should not be considered the intellectual equals of men. In his mind, therefore, the man he admires and loves most in life could not possibly have chosen her over him to receive these teachings. In a most pleasant manner, Mary challenges Peter and keeps the discussion focused on her truthfulness while ignoring his demeaning comment.

Lines 6, 7, 8, and 9

Levi answered and said to Peter, "Peter you have always been hot tempered. Now I see you contending against the woman like the adversaries. But if the Savior made her worthy, who are you indeed to reject her? Surely the Savior knows her very well. That is why He loved her more than us. Rather let us be ashamed and put on the perfect Man, and separate as He commanded us and preach the gospel, not laying down any other rule or other law beyond what the Savior said."

Mary Magdalene clearly has a defender in the person of Levi. Because Peter had a reputation as a hothead, his emotionalism is given as the reason for his clouded judgment. Levi notes that Jesus did indeed consider Mary worthy, and, therefore, how could any of them doubt His judgment and say differently? He even notes that Jesus loved her more. Levi adds the point that they (who became the church) should not make rules or laws beyond those already made by Jesus. We say more about this later.

Given that the Apostle Peter is considered the founder of the Catholic Church, should anyone be surprised that this gospel was suppressed? Prior to the establishment of the Catholic Church as an *official* church of the Roman Empire by Emperor Constantine in 325 CE, many house churches were organized and run by women. Jesus had female followers who clearly were important to Him in terms of supporting and spreading His teachings.

What is particularly important about Chapter 9 in this gospel? First, it illustrates a significant example of the bias against women at that time. Second, clearly Jesus took a strong position against the demeaning and devaluing of women. Third, confronting sexism is a matter for both men and women. Both sexes must understand that the female role also includes seeking God, and by implication, both sexes are equal in terms of loving, serving and representing the Divine. And last, we should note that despite this gospel, which tells us that sexism runs counter to the teachings of Jesus, many in the modern Christian communities continue to follow the Alpha Interpretation with its sexist policies.

Gospel of Mary, Chapter 8

Chapter 8 starts on line 10 because lines 1 through 9 are missing.

Line 10

And Desire said, "I did not see you descending, but now I see you ascending. Why did you lie since you belong to me?"

Notice that a person is not speaking. The Gospel of Mary anthropomorphizes "Desire" as a male to help the reader understand the male-female relationship. Jesus considers desire to be the controlling agent in the Kingdom of Man. Recall that Mary Magdalene was known as a prostitute who was controlled by male desires until Jesus showed her how to change her life. In these words, the primary force in the Kingdom of Man notices that "he" (Desire) is losing her. Desire admits that "he" did not even notice her when "he" controlled her.

Line 11

The soul answered and said, "I saw you. You did not see me nor recognize me. I served you as a garment and you did not know me."

Mary's soul is anthropomorphized as a female. When the male controlled her, her soul notes that the male (Desire) did not even know her. The male treated her merely as something he owned or as a point of pride for his ego. Her true self meant nothing to him, and there was no mutual love or respect.

These words reflect remarkable insight into what was often the male-female relationship at the time of Jesus and is still too often the norm in our time. In startlingly brief language, the connection is made between the mind-set that belongs to the Kingdom of Man—desire—and what is often the worst aspect of the male-to-female relationship, the inability to truly "see" and value the object of desire as more than a mere object. Note that Peter, Andrew, and other male disciples have totally missed the message of Jesus. We think this fact is revealing. Only Levi has grasped Jesus' intent.

Line 12
When it said this, it (the soul) went away rejoicing greatly.

We interpret "soul" to constitute her inner self. Why is her soul rejoicing? Maybe her rejoicing occurs because her soul at that moment has gained insight and the deeper knowledge called wisdom. That insight sets her soul free, and she is exhilarated with knowledge and freedom. She realizes the chains of Desire are broken, and from this moment on, her soul will no longer be associated with this very un-evolved form of male desire.

We believe these words reflect the influence of Heraclitus, with his stress on the "unity of opposites" (explained in Chapter 5 of this book) but in a negative dysfunctional manner. Desire that arises within the Kingdom of Man represents a regressive driving force in the male-female relationship, one that should be positive, functional and ever-evolving.

Once her soul transcends and she understands that Desire is negative and exerts an inappropriate controlling force on her, then the soul (the female) can be in command of her life. Through that realization the woman becomes free of the negative force. Wisdom (Sophia) sets her free, hence the comment that "the soul went away rejoicing greatly."

Line 13
Again it came to the third power, which is ignorance.

We believe Line 13 implies that not being aware of this male-female relationship involving desire means being ignorant or being unaware. In other words, Mary or the soul's ignorance of the power in the relationship and of the "unity of opposites" gave unequal power to the male (Desire). Thus the male controlled her in a relationship that did *not* constitute a unity of opposites.

Line 14

The power questioned the soul, saying, "Where are you going? In wickedness are you bound? But you are bound; do not judge!"

Notice that the "power" called "Ignorance" thinks of Mary as bound in wickedness. We see irony. If this "power" is "ignorance," then how can its judgment be correct? Are we who succumb to this power also wrong in our judgment of others? Are not the implications of this statement by Ignorance significant?

Notice that Ignorance demands she not judge others, but at the same time binds her with his judgment of her wickedness. Line 14 reflects amazing insight. Don't we bind others in the same way when we say others are at fault and then declare that they cannot be judgmental of anyone else? This behavior exhibits a type of ignorance.

Line 15

And the soul said, "Why do you judge me, although I have not judged?"

Notice that her soul, which is *not* ignorant, challenges the power of Ignorance. Where is the fairness? Ignorance is judging her when she has not judged Ignorance. Does this unfairness make sense? Yet, this pattern is common in many dysfunctional relationships. Note also the courage it takes to call Ignorance to account.

Line 16

"I was bound though I have not bound."

This line marks the point of realization and understanding. This is her soul's "aha!" moment when transcendence occurs and the relationship, one of being bound, is understood as only an illusion. Without this remarkable moment, she could not understand her situation or circumstance. Her soul's "aha" moment is the result of transcendence and not its cause. The "aha" occurs when she transcends, and once that occurs, she understands.

She comes to realize that she has allowed herself to be bound! She is as much the problem as is the male. Unless there is mutual binding in the male-female relationship, then the relationship is not one of equals; nor is it one of unity. Such an unequal relationship is not fair to either partner. We consider her realization to be another insight into a dysfunctional male-female relationship.

Line 17
> "I was not recognized. But I have recognized that the All is being dissolved, both the earthly things and the heavenly."

We need to see that the person who binds another person with his or her judgment does not recognize the other person as a perfect and complete soul. When this denial of another person's soul occurs, the Kindom of Heaven as a mind-set for both the male and the female is being destroyed.

Whether through ignorance or non-recognition of the other's soul, the action is destroying the possibility of attaining the Kindom of Heaven. The complying person's non-action and nonresistance to such ignorance is also destroying the Kindom of Heaven for both of them. Certainly, the offending person's actions are wrong, but it is significant that Jesus is calling on the complying persons to assert themselves in these circumstances as well.

Line 18
> When the soul had overcome the third power, it went upwards and saw the fourth power, which took seven forms.

Life is a process that should be about continually learning and growing in spirituality. In the process, we overcome all of the powers in their various forms. Once you have learned to overcome something like ignorance in your life, the challenge continues with even greater multiple challenges. The way ignorance manifests itself in our lives becomes more and more subtle with each layer that is exposed, making it ever more difficult to detect.

Line 19
> **The first form is darkness, the second desire, the third ignorance, the fourth is the excitement of death, the fifth is the kingdom of the flesh, and the sixth is the foolish wisdom of flesh, the seventh is the wrathful wisdom. These are the seven powers of Wrath.**

The Gospel of Mary tells us that Wrath appears in seven forms. Each form exerts a power over us, in the way gravity causes water to flow, but each is a power our *will-power* can transcend. Wrath must be understood as a power in the male-female relationship, and each of us must transcend all seven forms in order to be free. Those powers that constitute the Kingdom of Man must not control us.

Line 20
> **They asked the soul, "Whence do you come, slayer of men, or where are you going, conqueror of space?"**

Until now, the Gospel of Mary discusses primarily how males abuse the male-female relationship. At this point, the discussion shifts. Here the power of Wrath seeks to understand how this female, who has destroyed the material man of the Kingdom of Man, intends to proceed.

The use of the term "space" tells us we are dealing with the material Kingdom of Man rather than the non-material Kindom of Heaven because God and Heaven are always about the permanent that transcends space. With the knowledge gained, the female has gained power, but what shall she do with that power in the male-female relationship?

She has choices. She can use this new power within her, and her acquired freedom, for gains in the Kingdom of Man (e.g., gaining wealth and political power) or for spiritual gains. With newly acquired freedom come newfound choices, which can either help her on her spiritual path or allow her to regress into the Kingdom of Man.

Line 21

The soul answered and said, "What binds me has been slain and what turns me about has been overcome [. . .]."

She has already made her choice. The soul has transcended, and the earlier bonds do not hold her any longer. She has chosen the Kindom of Heaven. Her soul has overcome the past forces, and now she is free.

Line 22

"[. . .] and my desire has been ended, and ignorance has died."

Now that her soul has transcended Desire, no one can tell her what to do or not do. When she transcended, Ignorance or Wrath no longer controlled her life, and she became free to make her own choices instead of letting Ignorance or Wrath make choices for her.

Line 23

"In an aeon I was released from a world, and in a type from a type, and from the fetter of oblivion, which is transient."

It took thousands of years, but she released her soul from the consciousness belonging to the Kingdom of Man. Her soul and fate are no longer predetermined and controlled. Instead, she has become her own person who freely decides what she wants to be. Her soul was bound to oblivion, but now it has transcended to the Kindom of Heaven.

Line 24

"From this time on will I attain to the rest of time, of the season, of the aeon, in silence."

With this impressive success over the negative powers, her soul will continue to the end of time through its many seasons or lives in the millennia ahead. As she proceeds though time, she will no longer need to argue and fight the powers because she has conquered them all by transcending them. This is the ultimate success for everyone and the Gospel of Mary's way of explaining that success.

We have several observations about Chapter 8 of the gospel. Each line of the chapter is, in its implications, a paragraph that the serious reader must contemplate and understand with care. The Gospel of Mary, like most of what Jesus said and did, is obtuse, meaning it is abstract, layered and sometimes nuanced. It is, therefore, easily misunderstood. Nevertheless, we can gain remarkable and useful insights from this gospel once we understand the philosophy and theology Jesus embraced.

We have found that reading Chapter 9 of this gospel—with its admonition to recognize the equality of women—before reading 8 helps in understanding the deep message Chapter 8 provides: The soul can cast off the destructive powers of desire and ignorance that prevent it from attaining the Kindom of God. Similarly, the male-female relationship can reach its fullness when unfettered from negative powers and instead is bound with equal respect.

The Gospel of Mary

Gospel of Mary, Chapter 5

Chapter 5 deals with Mary's role of leadership. Note that part of this chapter is missing, as well as all of Chapters 6 and 7.

Line 1

But they were grieved. They wept greatly, saying, "How shall we go to the Gentiles and preach the gospel of the Kingdom of the Son of Man? If they did not spare Him, How will they spare us?"

Jesus has told His disciples to go out into the world with His teachings, but they are afraid for their lives. Notice that the gospel says His disciples should go forth to the Gentiles. It does not mention the Jews. Before His time on the cross, Jesus addressed His efforts to only the Jews and not to the Gentiles. Focusing on the Gentiles starts with the conversion of Paul. (See Chapter 11 of this book for details concerning when the ministry focused on the Gentiles.) This additional focus of His ministry indicates that the Gospel of Mary was written after His time on the cross and after Paul joined the Jesus Movement. Also note that Paul is not part of this discussion.

Line 2

Then Mary stood up, greeted them all, and said to her brethren, "Do not weep and do not grieve nor be irresolute, for His Grace will be entirely with you and will protect you."

With these words, Mary Magdalene takes a leadership role among the disciples to comfort and encourage them to do the needful. She tells them their protection is the message of His teaching.

Line 3

> "But rather, let us praise His greatness, for He has prepared us and made us into Men."

In this statement Mary includes herself as being made "male," meaning "made whole," incorporating both aspects of the "unity of opposites," female and male. Mary has not become a man but rather has achieved the balanced male and female unity that goes beyond the separate opposites.

Given the Gospel of Thomas Saying 114, which refers to making females male, we believe this line in the Gospel of Mary makes a significant statement about women and indirectly about men. Mary's argument is that the disciples' gratitude for what He taught them and their desire to share it with others should replace their emotion of fear. She points out that they have all, herself included, become "Men"—become male—in the true sense of growing in spirituality through the teachings of Jesus.

Line 4

When Mary said this, she turned their hearts to the Good, and they began to discuss the words of the Savior.

The Gospel of Mary helps us understand that Mary was an effective leader; she turns the hearts of the group away from fear and focuses them on the work to be done. Such an achievement is a remarkable act of leadership, all the more so for those times. In fact, she not only turns the disciples away from their fear, she replaces it with appreciation for what they have gained from the good that Jesus taught them. She tells the disciples that by discussing the words of Jesus, they reinforce His teachings and prepare themselves to preach His message.

Line 5

Peter said to Mary, "Sister, we know that the Savior loved you more than the rest of the women."

We notice the sexism of Peter, who nevertheless presents his comment as a backhanded compliment. With these few words, he acknowledges her leadership, but still derides and challenges her.

Line 6
"Tell us the words of the Savior which you remember which you know, but we do not, nor have we heard them."

Peter is challenging her, and in the next line she accepts and responds.

Line 7
Mary answered and said, "What is hidden from you I will proclaim to you."

Yet, in spite of Mary's repeated explanations, what was hidden from Peter remains hidden—because of his engrained sexism.

Lines 8 and 9
And she began to speak to them these words: "I," she said, "I saw the Lord in a vision and I said to Him, 'Lord I saw you today in a vision.' He answered and said to me, 'Blessed are you that you did not waver at the sight of Me. For where the mind is there is the treasure.'"

These lines report a vision within a vision in which Jesus and Mary had a discussion. At the time of Jesus, visions were considered highly significant. Also the fact that Mary looked at Jesus directly is noteworthy because Jesus awed many and they looked away. Her being able to hold her gaze is important in the context of the times. This incident makes an important statement about Mary as a strong and equal person in Jesus' group.

Line 10

I said to Him, "Lord, how does he who sees the vision see it, through the soul or through the spirit?"

In a vision, you are not physically seeing with your eyes or other senses. The spirit brings that vision directly to your mental consciousness, which then allows your inner self, or what some call the soul, to see the vision. Mary's question is especially sophisticated.

Line 11

The Savior answered and said, "He does not see through the soul nor through the spirit, but the mind that is between the two that is what sees the vision and it is [. . .]."

Note that portions of line 11 are missing, as is the rest of Chapter 5. What we have of His answer is what an educated person today might expect, in that it places the mind between spirit and soul. This reply shows a subtle understanding that scientists today would certainly grasp, given the advances in the study of the brain, but is an unexpected answer coming from the time of Jesus.

Our observations of the gospel's Chapter 5 underscore the importance of Jesus' position on the value of women. Mary is a leader. Peter challenges that leadership, but she clearly is not upset by the challenge. She deals with it directly, and with respect and dignity. Jesus treats her like an equal, and this treatment confirms her status as someone important in His eyes. In addition, she asks a profound question of Jesus, a question that shows her acute awareness and depth of knowledge.

Gospel of Mary, Chapter 4

The fragment of Chapter 4 that survived the passage of time starts on line 21. All of Chapters 1, 2, and 3 are missing.

Line 21 of Chapter 4 starts in mid-sentence.
   . . . will matter then be destroyed or not?

Line 22
   The Savior said, "All nature, all formations, all creatures exist with one another, and they will be resolved again into their own roots. When everything is 'destroyed,' each is not destroyed but only returned to 'its own roots.'"

Line 23
   "For the nature of matter is resolved into the roots of its own nature alone."

Line 24
   "He who has ears to hear, let him hear."

We really have little to work with, but we can determine that Jesus is describing the nature of matter consistent with what current science tells us. For example, if you burn something, the material changes into its basic elements.
   Starting with line 25, we have a new topic, but we shall see there is a linkage to the previous topic.

Line 25
   Peter said to Him, "Since you have explained everything to us, tell us this also: What is the sin of the world?"

Jesus, who used the word "sin" in the context of His Aramaic language and the teachings of Plato, translates the word as "missed the mark" or "unripe," meaning the person's consciousness is not sufficiently developed. From the Aramaic of that time, "sin" refers to an effort against the natural flow of evolution and done because of a person's ego-identification. In this meaning, "sin" is a violation of natural law, and it is anti-evolutionary behavior, whether in thought, speech, or action. In contrast, the meaning of "sin" in the Greek language is similar to English, which connotes a wrong has been done.

Line 26
The Savior said "There is no sin, but it is you who make sin when you do the things that are like the nature of adultery, which is called sin."

You can almost hear the frustration in His words to Peter. Jesus is saying that sin is not a wrong but rather a description of an action. A sin occurs because a person missed the mark of what they should do or because he or she has a consciousness that is not sufficiently developed. The sin lies in the act, not the person. In the case of adultery, the individual creates the sin precisely because the person missed the mark by being insufficiently developed spiritually.

Once the consciousness is more developed, the behavior will change, and "sin" will cease to exist. Sin is a comment about the development of a person's spirituality. It is not a wrong, but rather the actions of an undeveloped or non-spiritual person. Peter just did not understand what Jesus meant by the word "sin," and that misunderstanding was important.

The implication of Jesus' words is that the term "original sin" is a misnomer because the whole concept is foolishness. If sin does not mean a wrong, as one would expect from the Greek meaning but rather "unripe" or "miss the mark," then a reasonable translation is that "original sin" means "the first unripe act" or "the first time missing the mark." This understanding of original sin is similar to a situation in which a toddler misses his mouth with his food when first learning to eat with a spoon. The toddler does not commit a wrong but simply misses the mark, as a parent should expect from a toddler.

Would God logically curse the whole human species because Adam and Eve in Genesis did not have a sufficiently developed consciousness shortly after God created them? Realistically, from the story, Adam and Eve were toddlers! To go further and say that only the sacrifice of God's Son by crucifixion could remove the curse is just nonsensical. In what way is the crucifixion of God's Son a proper atonement for the mistakes of two toddlers?

Given that these assumptions are central to the Alpha Interpretation, which is used almost exclusively by Christianity today, the Alpha Interpretation should be disregarded as illogical. If one believes that the Gospel of Mary reflects the thoughts of Jesus, then the Alpha Interpretation misunderstands His message.

Line 27
"That is why the Good came into your midst, to the essence of every nature in order to restore it to its root."

"The Good" in the statement refers to Jesus and His spiritual message He brought to the world. His purpose is to teach others the fundamentals of being a spiritual person so that they can actualize them with other individuals through all living their goodness.

Line 28
Then He continued and said, "That is why you become sick and die, for you are deprived of the one who can heal you."

Becoming sick and dying is a manifestation of the material world. To transcend it and reach the everlasting, you need spiritual teachings. These teachings allow you to move from being an unripe material person living in the Kingdom of Man to being a developed spiritual person living in the Kindom of

Heaven. What is important to notice in this dialogue is that the topic continues to be sin, and this continued discussion provides us with an insight about sin's nature. Jesus ended with a favorite expression of His.

Line 29
"He, who has a mind to understand, let him understand."

In other words, "Did you get it?" Are you even smart enough or open enough to get it? By Jesus using the word "understand" in His concluding expression, His conclusion becomes an even stronger statement than His usual conclusion, which uses the words, "Those who have ears to hear." Jesus is saying that this is a profound idea and requires deep insight if the meaning is to be fully understood.

Line 30
"Matter gave birth to a passion that has no equal, which proceeded from something contrary to nature. Then there arises a disturbance in its whole body."

Jesus tells us that the materialistic world births a passion or a wanting that is a strong magnet. He declares that this yearning is contrary to nature and disturbs the Oneness. Thus, for each of us, the challenge is to not allow the desire that comes from materialism to control us and to not allow the controlling passion of wanting or yearning to exist within us.

Line 31:
"That is why I say to you, 'Be of good courage, and if you are discouraged be encouraged in the presences of the different forms of nature.'"

Jesus tells us that a person's attitude is important. Keeping a positive outlook is essential if materialism with its ego-driven consciousness is to be confronted successfully. Your confrontations require great courage and sustained effort.

Lines 32 and 33
> "He who has ears to hear, let him hear." When the Blessed One had said this, He greeted them all saying, "Peace be with you. Receive my peace unto yourselves."

Line 34
> "Beware that no one leads you astray saying 'Lo here or lo there! For the Son of Man is within you.'"

If you follow His message, then Jesus is within you. This wording is similar to the Gospel of Thomas Saying 3 about the location of heaven. These statements clearly do not reflect theism but rather do reflect pantheism, or panentheism, because heaven is not a place as it is in theism. These words suggest that Jesus used process theology to present His message, as noted in Chapter 5 of this book. The key words are "Lo here or lo there," which reflect thinking that is "astray" when it comes to pinpointing the location of heaven. Even more significant are the words "is within you."

Lines 35 and 36
> "Follow after Him! Follow His message by living it. Those who seek Him will find Him."

Notice that the word "seek" is used rather than "ask." This use of "seek" is similar to the wording in Saying 2 of the Gospel of Thomas. There the words "Let one who seeks not stop seeking . . ." are used instead of "Let one who asks not stop asking. . . ."

Line 37

"Go then and preach the gospel of the Kingdom."

This statement is similar to Saying 33 in the Gospel of Thomas where you are admonished not to keep your light under a cover.

Line 38

"Do not lay down any rules beyond what I appointed you, and do not give a law like the lawgiver lest you be constrained by it."

This sentence presents an unmistakable commandment from Jesus. It is very much a statement addressed to His group of followers. He was not trying to establish a new religion but rather reform an existing one. Jesus wanted His followers *not* to add rules, laws or conditions to what He had already said. What is alarming is that those who have issued church rules on many subjects—such as homosexuals not being allowed to marry, priests not being allowed to marry, priests being only male, and so on—are violating this very direct and clear commandment.

Line 39

When He said this He departed.

As we finish reading what is left of Chapter 4 of the Gospel of Mary, we can recapitulate some significant observations. This chapter does not appear to be addressed solely to women, and we think this inclusion of men is important: Jesus' thoughts in this gospel apply equally to men and women.

The subject of sin is particularly important to Mary, who is identified as being a sinner. The gospel is saying that sin is only a matter of the individual not being developed enough spiritually. It says we are all works in progress and that is the nature of this God-given process called life.

Why Not Included

The gospel clearly addresses Mary in particular but also addresses matters of interest to women in general. Ironically, the message of Jesus in this gospel is also addressed to men in that it largely concerns the very nature of sexism with its negative implications for the male gender as well as the female.

This gospel says that women must define their roles in life in much broader terms to make themselves equal partners and achieve a unity of opposites with men. Being equal is particularly necessary when it comes to donning the mantel of spiritual leadership. The insights of the gospel relate to the root causes of poor male-female relationships. This gospel challenges the important misunderstanding that sin is something that should be characterized in terms of wrongs; instead, sin should be thought of in terms of developing individual spirituality.

Given the assumed equality of women, the indirect criticism of Peter, the position taken against original sin, the injunction against the church issuing any new laws, and the concept that sin is not about wrongs but rather about an individual's undeveloped spirituality, we are not surprised that the Gospel of Mary was not included in the canon of the New Testament. Fortunately, the Gospel of Mary is available today for those who seek a fuller understanding of Jesus' message. This gospel adds strength to our thesis that Christianity needs to abandon the Alpha interpretation, which we think is a mistake, and adopt the Omega Interpretation, which we argue is what Jesus meant in the message He preached.

Chapter 8

The Issue of a Personal God

Does God get involved directly in our lives? In other words, does God care about each person as an individual and interact with that person on a constant basis? For atheists, that question is pure foolishness, and therefore their response is simply to challenge the premise of the question and ask whether a God even exists.

We argue that Jesus was very aware of this question about the role of God and reached His own conclusion, a conclusion reflected in the Omega Interpretation but not the Alpha Interpretation. For people of faith who follow the Alpha Interpretation, the question about God's level of concern and involvement is difficult to address, as we explain later in this chapter. If the answer to the question about whether God directly intervenes is "yes", then God is what is called "a personal God." If the answer is "no", then God is "an impersonal God." But we argue that Jesus thought the answer was much more complex than a simple "yes" or "no."

Most who have faith in an impersonal God believe that God created the universe but after that God let humans determine their own destiny. At the beginning of the American republic, leaders such as John Adams and Thomas Jefferson confronted the question of how God could let bad things happen to good people by reasoning that God was not a personal God. To Adams and Jefferson and other founding fathers who thought as they did, God created the universe, and except for very unusual circumstances, God merely allowed that creation to operate on its own. They believed that God gave humans the important gift of *freewill*, as well as the resulting good and bad consequences that stem from their *freewill* choices. People with such a faith believe God rarely interacts with individual persons because such interventions would negate God's all-important gift to us of *freewill*.

One reason this approach to religion has lost favor is because of the difficult questions the concept of *freewill* poses for those accepting the Alpha Interpretation. Those who dislike the concept of an impersonal God often note that people, including the Nazis, have made abhorrent *freewill* choices. They note the death of millions of Jews and others that have resulted from those choices. Versed in the Alpha Interpretation, they conclude that God could have prevented the Holocaust and stopped those horrible deaths but valued *freewill* more than His chosen people.

Those who follow the Alpha Interpretation find the *freewill* argument to be an unsatisfactory excuse for God's inaction. For them, this is a remarkably emotional matter, and they ask how a so-called loving God could permit such horrible consequences to take place and use *freewill* as an excuse for doing so. They reason that if God were perfect, especially in all He does, then He would not create or allow terrible events to occur. To many people, worshipping such a God is unacceptable. It is no surprise many people who ask these questions have lost their faith.

Those who think in this manner might argue that the Good Samaritan law requires a stranger who comes upon an accident to provide assistance to the victim. They also note that if you know a crime is going to be committed, that same law requires you to report the potential crime. They then reason that because we hold ourselves to such a standard, should not that standard also apply to God?

They claim that God's wish to allow *freewill* to operate is an absurd reason for God allowing terrible things to take place. If your friend is drunk, should you not intervene against his or her *freewill* and take the car keys so that your friend cannot drive? Should not a loving God do at least as much?

Most people of faith today reject the concept of a non-personal God. Many even believe God sends His angels to watch over them. Their Alpha Interpretation leads them to conclude that God does care about each person as an individual. The Religious Second Awakening, with its use of the Golden Rule, influences them. If they were *not* so influenced, they would conclude that God is essentially impersonal and, not illogically, neutral to what the Nazis did; after all, that was a matter for humans and not God.

However, some individuals, who once accepted the Alpha Interpretation and do accept the Golden Rule of conduct, reject God. They reason that if God is all-powerful and the Golden Rule is the correct standard of conduct for humans and God, then there are many occasions when God violates that standard of conduct. In fact some of those occasions would be considered criminal neglect or worse if a human acted as God acts. Their logic ultimately brings them to the conclusion that God just does not exist.

People of faith today find themselves either ignoring thoughtful arguments or struggling to make sense of their faith because of those arguments. We make a case later in this chapter that if someone adheres to the Omega Interpretation rather than the Alpha Interpretation, those thoughtful arguments no longer present a problem in logic.

For those who subscribe to the Alpha Interpretation, there is yet another problem in logic. If God does intervene frequently, thereby indicating God is personal, the argument that the greatest gift God gives humankind is *freewill* then becomes empty. If a parent tells an adult child he is responsible for his life and yet daily intervenes to give the "child" additional money when requested, then does the parent's declaration of the child's individual responsibility mean anything?

The God of the Torah

The God in the Jewish Torah is depicted quite differently from the God of the Christian New Testament and even from the later portions of the Jewish Bible. The God of the Torah focuses on creating the Jewish nation, including an ethic and religious observance for a people. The God of the Torah is essentially impersonal toward individuals except as they relate to the establishing of a nation. In contrast, the God of the New Testament seems very personal and can be described as even loving toward individuals.

To compound these contrasting portraits, one need only look at the varying treatments of God in other faith traditions. For example, God plays virtually no role in the Buddhist faith. The Buddha, to emphasize self-responsibility, would not even discuss the subject of God. For the Buddha to introduce God into his philosophy would dilute or confuse his message of self-reliance. But in other faith traditions, God is of central importance. In Islam, for example, God is very personal.

The Torah (the first five books of the Jewish Bible) tells the story of how God selected a particular person—**Abraham**—and over many years shaped his descendants into not only a distinctive people but also a "chosen people." Looking at the history of the Jews, we can easily see that being God's chosen people does not mean living in great material splendor or having ultimate political power. In fact, being a "chosen people," in the Jewish understanding, is more a responsibility than an honor or reason to be considered an elite group.

Jews individually over the centuries have made a remarkable contribution to Western civilizations in such fields as music, art, philosophy, science, entertainment, and business. In addition, their Torah has created a tradition of living righteously; and that tradition has served as an example to other peoples, has helped shaped the concept of justice, and has contributed significantly to a model of how society can be built upon law. Clearly, their impact has enriched modern societies.

The God of the Torah is interested in a people and their evolution as a people. Although, with some notable exceptions, God is not shown as concerned with particular persons, God is very much concerned that the Jewish people observe rules of moral conduct, that they worship in a particular manner, and that they follow unique practices that set them apart from other peoples. God helps them win battles, but His concern for the individual development of individual Jews is not immediately evident in the Torah.

This God of the Torah is willing to kill and murder many enemies of the Jews, but also many Jews who do not follow His word. Although this God includes in His moral code a clear statement against murder, He actively and commonly murders and sometimes demonstratively approves those who kill and even murder to further His agenda (Deuteronomy Chapters 2, 3, 4, 7, 8, 9, 13, and 20).

In ancient times, the gods of the Greeks, Romans, Vikings, and other groups were not personally involved with humans, with only a few exceptions. Gods had their "lives" and normally had little interest in the affairs of humans. However, if humans begged and implored them enough with the proper prayers and offerings, sometimes one or more gods did affirmatively answer human prayers, such as allowing them an advantage in battle. However, the Hebrew God and the other gods did expect people to help themselves, as well as remain loyal to their respective gods.

The Hebrew God was different from the Greek and Roman gods, but some similarities are important. Jealousy was a noticeable trait. Killing and war were common activities. They expected worship from the mortals. Nevertheless, the Hebrew God was significantly different from the other deities in aspects apart from being worshiped in a monotheistic way.

The Hebrew God was a shepherd and teacher of a people. The Torah tells us that the Hebrew God tended His "sheep." Clearly, God had favorite sheep among His flock, such as Jacob, but God also taught all of the flock to be good and moral. He did so in the context of making the sheep function as a flock. In addition, God taught them to identify themselves as a distinct people.

Sheep in a flock often go astray, and, as is common among sheep, many are stubborn and difficult to shepherd. However, God did shepherd the chosen people and cull some of the more dysfunctional ones from the flock, as we note in Chapter 3. As God helped the Jews grow into a nation after their period of slavery in Egypt, God shepherded, with the help of Moses, the flock to what we today call Israel.

God As a Teacher

In the Omega Interpretation, God is a teacher, and every person is a student in God's learning laboratory called life. In the Torah, God is a shepherd and in some important respects is also a teacher. In the view of Jesus, God is a teacher who is focused on the individual; we no longer see an emphasis on God as shepherd of a flock. However, we do believe that Jesus still considered God as a shepherd even though Jesus did not stress this aspect in His teachings.

With the *logos* (such as the guiding laws of nature) as explained by Heraclitus and Philo, God sets the circumstances in motion so that we *can* grow spiritually in life's teaching and learning laboratory. However, just as in any learning situation, Jesus stresses that the students of spirituality must actively engage and wish to learn through using their *freewill*. As in the Alpha Interpretation, *freewill* is also important in the Omega Interpretation.

According to the Omega Interpretation, individual *will power* to grow and learn becomes essential. The individual's exercise of *freewill* by deciding to engage in the learning process is vital. Students must be seekers of knowledge and wisdom if they are to be good students. Learning is a process of co-creation, involving effort on the part of both teacher and student. In the Omega Interpretation, God creates the learning situations in our lives, but we must *want* to learn from those situations in order for the learning to take place.

Normally, learning occurs only with some, if not a lot of, individual effort. Some people find such an effort unpleasant, especially as it takes them away from fulfilling their worldly desires. In addition, at times learning occurs only through a degree of pain and suffering.

The act of teaching is personal for the teacher because the teacher is concerned with the students' well being. In the Omega Interpretation, God's focus as a teacher is on individual spiritual growth and the individual's development through acquiring and then living spiritual wisdom. However, God does not have the goal of providing for human enjoyment or pleasure, as would an ATM god. The focus of God is limited to the teaching and shepherding roles. In other respects, God is primarily impersonal.

In the Omega Interpretation, God wishes every individual to be successful at achieving spiritual growth but realizes that will not always happen. God knows that some people just will not use their *freewill* to engage in spiritual growth and His lessons will fall on deaf ears. Learning is a cumulative process, and some students will at times be engaged in learning and at times be overtaken by worldly concerns. There will not always be steady progress.

God also knows that some individuals will easily grow spiritually and that others will find spiritual growth to be difficult. Like any good teacher, God is available to all individuals and wishes the best for each. However, God is particularly pleased with progress and works harder for those He finds have potential or who can benefit from extra help.

Bad Things Happen to Good People
We all notice bad things happen to good people, such as

failing a test or having an accident, even to those who put a great deal of time into religious activities. We also notice the opposite is true: bad people, who, for example, cheat in business, become wealthy. In other words, good things happen to bad people.

Observers of both situations often employ a common rationalization for these occurrences: some things are just beyond their understanding as humans. Other people are frustrated by what they believe is unfairness; they put a great deal of effort into believing in God, and still bad things happen to them or those close to them. Hard working individuals who wish for what they consider fairness are disappointed and, as a result, may even abandon their belief in God.

A factor that needs consideration is the deeper meaning of the word "good." Most people who question why bad things happen to good people are like most students; they misunderstand the meaning of the word "good" in the learning process. For students, the problem lies in their understanding of what they consider as "good" and "bad" when they get a grade from their teacher. For them, what is good is only a teacher's positive assessment of their work, such as a grade of A+.

Speaking as educators, we believe that those students are wrong. What is "good" is a teacher's assessment of their work that allows them to understand how they can improve in learning the assigned material. What is "bad" is information that does not contribute to an awareness of how to improve. For people who wish to be more spiritual, a good lesson is one that provides them the necessary information to grow spiritually. After all, the person ultimately responsible for a student's learning is the student and not the teacher.

As college professors, we tell students we do not grade based on the intensity of their studying or the effort they apply but rather we grade on their performance. This is not a pleasing answer for most students who receive a poor grade, but it is the right answer. Especially at the college level, a teacher's job is to provide honest evaluations of students' performances so that students can better assess what they still need to learn.

Without such an accurate evaluation from the teacher, students are seriously handicapped in their part of the co-creation we call the teacher-guided learning process. In the learning laboratory of life, God also provides sometimes brutally hard but honest assessments that allow individuals to realize whether they are learning their spiritual lessons.

In other words, individuals are mistaken about what they think is the unfairness of life. They are receiving valuable information to reflect upon, and they can use it to improve themselves. They may not "get" the lesson, but they get the needed feedback. Just as teaching is not about rewarding hard work with a high grade, life is not about rewarding highly religious people with material wealth or power. It is about performance, which, in the case of spirituality, means learning spiritual wisdom and applying it.

Although many people of faith accept that God lets bad things happen to good people, how they rationalize it varies. Some, like Job in the Book of Job, acknowledge that the reason is unclear and probably beyond human understanding. Others, such as the Jewish leaders in the time of the Babylonian exile, conclude that bad things are God's punishment for past misdeeds of the Jewish people, that is, for breaking the covenant. For Jesus, bad things happen to good people to help individuals learn spiritual lessons that then allow them to transcend into more deeply spiritual persons.

Another obstacle to learning that people often encounter is their lack of reflection on themselves and what occurs to them in life. The individuals who learn and grow the best try to understand what situations such as test results tell them about what they have and have not learned. This self-reflection is critical for their intellectual growth. Poor learners typically look at the life situation as they do test results; they complain about the grade rather than try to understand what they still need to learn.

What happens to you in life is a means for God to communicate what you have learned but also what you still need to learn. Sometimes hardships are the best communication possible to allow people to understand where they have gone amiss or are lacking in their process of spiritual growth. Sometimes material success is the worst communication possible if an individual does not learn from that "success" where he or she has fallen short in spiritual growth.

The values of the Omega Interpretation are similar to those of Aristotle who said that "the good" is a life worthy of being lived. To Jesus the purpose (what the Ancient Greeks called *telos*) of life is for one to grow into a well-rounded spiritual person. To that end, God is our teacher, but we are the ones who must do the learning.

Understanding God as impersonal has powerful positive consequences for humankind. Like Buddhist teachings, this understanding of God encourages people to take charge of their lives. It encourages them to create good with their lives by working positively with others rather than expecting an ATM god to deliver. It also teaches people they must take responsibility for the collective of which all are part.

Although we find this impersonal perspective of God appealing, we believe the Omega Interpretation achieves the same positive outcome of encouraging people to take charge and be responsible for their lives. In the Omega Interpretation, God is a personal God, that is, personal in the same way an outstanding teacher is personal, but only in that role of teacher and guide. God is actively involved in our lives on a daily basis, but that does not mean God should furnish us enjoyment and pleasure or keep us from pain or discomfort. Rather God teaches spirituality to those of us who wish to learn, and with it we *co-create* with God our own enjoyment and pleasure as we experience life.

Misunderstanding What Is God's Help

When we ask for help from God, the answer can come in many ways. The story of a man trapped in a flooded house is relevant here. He is in his house, and the river near his home floods. He is trapped. He prays for God's help. A man, in a truck with high clearance on the road outside the trapped man's house, sees the situation and offers to take him to high ground. The trapped man refuses, saying he has already asked for God's help and is just waiting for God to answer. The floodwater rises more, and now a man in a boat offers to take the trapped man to high ground. He refuses, saying he has already asked for God's help and he is confident that God will provide. The floodwater rises significantly, forcing him to flee to his roof. A helicopter pilot sees his danger and offers him a ride. He refuses, saying he is waiting for God's help.

The waters rise again. This time the trapped man dies in the flood. He goes to heaven. He asks God, "Why didn't You answer my prayers?" God says, "I sent you a truck, a boat, and a helicopter. You refused each time. How many times must I answer before you accept?" As we ask for help, we tend to assume we know the answer God should give us. What we assume the answer will be might not be the answer we get from God. As a result, we are often angry or disappointed when we do not get what we want in exactly the form we want it.

An illustration from our experiences in Mexico might demonstrate this point. Until recently, we had an almost daily group of kids asking for "mo-nee" each time we left our house in a typical working-class neighborhood. When we first moved in, and for a while afterwards, we made the "mistake" of giving some small change to one nine-year-old. In exchange we asked him to perform some small chores, such as helping to walk the dog or carry objects into the house from the car.

After just a few payments of money for "work," we soon had ten kids—ages four to fourteen—asking us for money whenever we went outside our house. In addition, they continually rang the doorbell if they knew we were home. When we answered, they asked for "mo-nee," with or without any work associated with it.

We concluded that if we continued to give one or more kids "mo-nee," we would soon have a hundred or more asking for handouts. Regarding the one kid whom we had given money for "work," we noticed he used his earnings to buy candy, cokes, and other immediately consumable junk foods. We assumed the other kids would do the same because when they asked for "mo-nee," they said it was to buy a coke or potato chips.

Like God in the flood story, we did not necessarily get the answer from those we helped that we thought was appropriate. Because of that, the story about "mo-nee" got us thinking: what if God immediately gave all human beings in the world all the "mo-nee" or gifts they asked for. Given the powers we attribute to God, God could be an unlimited ATM that simply spits out "mo-nee" on request. Our guess is that most of us would use that largess to buy the equivalent of "adult junk food" in the broadest sense of that concept, and we would not advance spiritually.

Let us assume that rampant inflation did not occur and God gave out money like an unlimited ATM. Why would people work? Why should anyone work, especially to better himself or herself spiritually? Ironically, if God were an ATM that provided money on demand, then no one would make the junk food or anything else because that would be work and most people would see no need to work. We thought back to the cargo cult discussed in Chapter 1 of this book. Why work if God provides the cargo?

Unless God provided the goods by some miracle, such as the unlimited ATM, nothing would be available for purchase. Everyone would have the "mo-nee," but no one would be able to buy anything with it. Clearly, God would be self-defeating His plan to be an ATM of any kind, and we do not think God is short-sighted.

So if God is a personal God who cares for the spiritual development of people, what makes sense for God to do? The old adage about teaching a man to fish rather than giving him a fish seems appropriate in such circumstances. If you give people a fish, they have enough for one meal. But if you teach them how to fish, they have food for a lifetime. Therefore, could we say that what makes sense for God to do is to teach us how, metaphorically, to fish?

Unfortunately, the answer to that question is also a problem. For God, something more is needed than merely teaching us "to fish." Consider the over-fishing that currently exists in the world. Clearly, the impact of teaching how to fish, or to fish more efficiently, has been dysfunctional for the environment. In addition, the equivalent of over-fishing is a common problem in other life endeavors.

Based on the Omega Interpretation, the answer for a personal God primarily concerned about our spiritual growth is more than teaching us a useful skill or trade. It is teaching ethics and wisdom through the lessons of life that go well beyond the "me, my, mine" attitude that prevails in much of the world today when we pray and expect God to deliver. It is instilling in our hearts a concern for the metaphorical environment that prevents us collectively from over-fishing the oceans. For God, the teacher, it is *not* giving us what we materially want and *not* even teaching us how to get material goods, but *it is* helping us learn the wisdom of how to live "the good life."

In other words, there is interconnectedness, a Oneness among all peoples, the earth, and even the universe. In being good students of spirituality, we need to learn from life's spiritual lessons, including being concerned for the well-being of the environment. That is what a well-developed spiritual person does.

Yes, learning is important, but learning useful knowledge and skills clearly is not enough. As a person makes daily decisions, each person must think beyond himself or herself to the Oneness of which that person is a part. The fish of the oceans are part of that Oneness, and our "over-fishing," in whatever area of life, does diminish that Oneness and so diminishes us.

Understanding an All-Powerful Personal God

In understanding an all-powerful personal God, we believe that Heraclitus' process philosophy and theology was useful to Jesus. As we note in Chapter 5, we believe Jesus understood reality from His study of Heraclitus, most likely as a youth in Egypt. If we are correct, Jesus thought reality is not a thing but a process consisting of many "unities of opposites."

Jesus also saw good and evil in terms of a "unity of opposites." For Him, there was a Kingdom of Man (evil, meaning missed the mark or unripe spiritually) and a Kindom of God (good, meaning spiritually evolved). Each exists, and each is an aspect of a particularly important "unity of opposites." Similarly, one aspect of the unity cannot be understood without the other because both are essential and are always yoked. Good cannot be fully understood without evil.

In addition, divine laws explain the relationship that exists between the opposites and how one can and should use *freewill to* move from the negative Kingdom of Man to the positive Kindom of God. Those divine laws are captured in spiritual wisdom; learning and living spiritual wisdom is the process called "spirituality."

Jesus, the Teacher, realized, as we mention earlier, that God knows learning can only really occur within the student if the student exercises *freewill* and chooses to learn. A teacher can greatly assist in the learning process, but the learning must take place within the student. Thus learning is a "unity of opposites" consisting of the teacher and the student.

Life is God's most important gift to humankind. But the second most important of God's gifts to humankind is *freewill,* and the giving of *freewill* to humans does limit God's power in this world, as we note in Chapter 5. The gift of *freewill* demonstrates that God freely refrains from the use of His full powers out of a desire for the ultimate betterment of humankind. This refraining reflects God's wisdom.

The Omega Interpretation is built on the understanding that God creates for each of us the circumstances and sometimes the motivation so that we can learn. Our learning must include an ethic and a wisdom that focuses on the Oneness of which we are all a part. At the same time, we must maintain a sense of individuality so that all persons take responsibility for their own actions. In addition, the circumstances must permit an evolutionary learning process because learning is achieved by building upon previous insights.

Learning, including learning spiritual wisdom, often includes trial-and-error that helps us discover more useful knowledge and wisdom. Such learning often includes our appreciating the painful result of doing something in error. Many of us learn more from our mistakes than we do from our successes. At the start of the learning process, each of us is "unripe," and we often "miss the mark." With learning, we mature sometimes easily, but often we feel pain in the process. In our efforts as college teachers, we call painful learning, such as a student receiving a grade of F for a poor performance, the "two-by-four learning experience," meaning it takes a figurative blow on the head with a two-by-four piece of wood to get the attention of some students.

As we note in Chapter 5, ethical divine "laws" exist, and life can teach them to us. Consider the ethical virtue of gratefulness. If we use Aristotle's concept of virtue, virtue is not an on-off switch but rather a rheostat that makes the light brighter or dimmer. Like using a rheostat, we can turn a virtue to low or high. What we need to do is adjust the virtue to the needs of the particular moment.

On either end of a virtue rheostat, there is too little or too much of the virtue, turning it into vice. Both ends are "sins," meaning they "miss the mark" or are spiritually "unripe" for the situation. For the virtue of gratefulness, we shall label the sin of "too little" as "ingratitude" and the other sin of "too much" as "fawning." If a person shows no appreciation for a gift but has the social skills to do so, we can say the person acts with ingratitude. If the person shows excessive appreciation for a trivial gift but has the social skills to do so correctly, we can say the person is fawning or being a sycophant.

The ethical learning challenge for the student is to feel and show the appropriate gratefulness for any given situation—not ingratitude or fawning, but the correct level of appreciation. When our young Mexican friend did some "work" for us, such as walking our dog, and we gave him "mo-nee" for his labor, some small measure of gratefulness from him, such as a smile, was appropriate.

When we gave him a bicycle after an accident that damaged his right leg, a larger display of gratefulness, such as saying "Gracias" and giving a smile of thanks, was appropriate. We did not need or want grand displays of gratefulness, but we did want him to function correctly in a larger society and to learn that the virtue of gratitude is important for his development as a person. Therefore, we taught him to say "Gracias" before he gleefully rode off down the street and, in the process, built up the muscles in his damaged right leg.

The mission that Jesus took upon Himself was to teach spiritual wisdom, which He considered to be food for the soul. Jesus' *telos* (end purpose) was to teach His disciples and, through their efforts, show people how to move from the Kingdom of Man to the Kindom of God. However, Jesus was a realist and did believe that few would make such a choice, in spite of His efforts. Nevertheless, He believed that if even a minority of people moved from the Kingdom of Man to the Kindom of God, then monumental progress would be made in society because their united vision would serve as a significant and positive force in the world.

Possibly God gains additional spiritual wisdom from observing humans attempt to learn and live spiritual wisdom. Maybe that reciprocity is part of the reason God wants us to freely experience spiritual growth. Possibly in such a manner God continually co-creates spiritual wisdom through His process of giving life and our process of learning spirituality.

Lesson Offered

Our parents, partners in life, friends, and even enemies have continually taught us, your authors, spiritual wisdom and ethical lessons. Yes, we also learned lessons from books, teachers, and religious studies, such as going to Torah study. However, we must confess that many times we were blind to certain lessons and did not learn them.

When, with our *freewill*, we opened our senses to see the metaphorical light and hear the metaphorical sound, we did indeed learn. However, too often in our lives our spiritual immaturity left us blind and deaf; and thus we still did not learn many important lessons. Fortunately, lessons are often repeated. Sometimes after many attempts, we finally opened our eyes and ears, and then we learned. We quickly admit that we are still learning, often slowly.

No one should blame a person for being blind or deaf, or a student for being a slow learner. Nevertheless, we need *not* continue to live in the world of the blind and deaf if we can change that situation by merely being willing to open our eyes to the light and our ears to the sound. "Opening our eyes" means we reflect on what has just happened and try to understand the deeper meanings of life's lessons beyond the material illusion called experience.

God (or, if you prefer, "Life") continually creates and then offers events and circumstances so that each of us can grow spiritually. However, we must co-create with God. If we choose to see the light and hear the sound, we grow spiritually. Sometimes we easily learn those lessons. However, too often we learn those lessons the hard way. Sometimes the cost of that education is very high, such as the loss of a friendship or even a spouse. Sadly, although the personal cost is very high, we can forget to use our *freewill* to learn the intended lesson.

In 2005, we were in Louisiana when Hurricane Katrina killed about two thousand people. One of our former universities—Louisiana State University—became at that time the largest field hospital in the history of the United States. For three weeks, Thomas volunteered at that hospital, which treated six thousand patients, and he spoke with over two thousand in that short period of time. It was a remarkable experience for him, and he felt he grew spiritually from it.

Significantly, he saw many others also grow from their horrible experiences. For example, many told him they learned that their previously-valued material possessions were really not important. Although lessons were costly in terms of loss and pain, spiritual growth came directly from that natural disaster.

Jesus taught that God continually gives us lessons. Jesus also believed that the wiser among us reflect on what happens to them and others, and they seek from those experiences to gain personal growth. They look upon those occasions as gifts from a very personal God and realize that each of us is a co-creator with God. The spiritually-wise among us accept each gift from God with gratitude and realize they must also unwrap the gift and apply it to the rest of their lives.

We argue here that because of Philo (see Chapter 6), Jesus believed the God of the Torah is the God of all faith traditions. Jesus knew that God was shepherding the chosen people, but also watching over every person—past, present, and future. Nevertheless, certain sheep are more important to the larger task of getting all the sheep to the correct destination. Shepherding includes trying to help cooperative sheep be the best they can be. The well-being, including the growth, of each is important, but never to the point of endangering the flock or not attaining the ultimate destination for the whole flock.

At one important level, the way each of us understands God as personal or impersonal depends on our perception. If you feel God is in your life, God is personal. If you do not, God is impersonal to you or perhaps God does not exist. However, we think Jesus would say your understanding of God should go beyond the mere perception of what you feel and the resulting illusion.

Perception is important, but it is not sufficient for understanding. Someone can make a remarkable difference in your life, but your awareness of that difference and even your awareness of that person's existence can be totally unknown to you. Nevertheless, that person changed your life. Just because you did not perceive that person does not mean that the person did not change your life. Perception may be absent, but that person was important to you. We think Jesus would say that you might not perceive God, but God is very important in your life.

Considering a larger sense of purpose, we think Jesus would say God is both personal and impersonal. Like a shepherd, God cares for the flock as a whole, and we think Jesus believed God does have a purpose (*telos*) in mind for that flock. Thus Jesus would say that when God is acting in that manner, God is not personal for the individual.

However, when God gives individuals lessons, then God is personal. Like the good shepherd, God *also* does care for each member of the flock, and, in this way, is personal for the individual. The focus of God the Shepherd is on the spiritual growth of the person rather than upon material desires or the material well-being of the person.

What you assume is significant determines how you view God. If you assume that living is in itself the ultimate purpose for existing, then God's impersonal behavior, such as letting a crack baby die after a painful two-week existence, is an emotionally persuasive reason to reject God. However, if you assume that life is primarily a tool or a means to teach larger spiritual lessons, then that argument for rejecting God is not as powerful. Further, if you believe in reincarnation, the argument becomes even less persuasive.

If you assume, as the Omega Interpretation does, that the learning and the living of spiritual lessons are the purpose of life and the ultimate gift from God, then our perceived negative impersonal behavior of God has little significance. Let us assume, as does the Omega Interpretation, that a person is really not his material nature, but rather his eternal soul. Let us also assume, as Jesus did, that life's lessons with their spiritual wisdom are soul food. If that assumption is correct, then there is remarkable meaning and sensibility to the actions of God, and God is truly a loving God in the deepest sense of the word "loving."

The shepherd has paramount concerns for the flock as a whole, but the shepherd does focus concern on individual members of the flock. Given that our Shepherd is an all-powerful God, the Shepherd can do both for His extensive flock and the individual member. Although not understood by the sheep, the Shepherd's plan has a purpose for the flock, as well as for every individual member of the flock.

That plan and purpose include His teaching the sheep they need to become conscious co-creators with God by learning to act in love and harmony with each other and the universe. Each individual is important, but each of us is also a part of a larger Oneness. Jesus felt both opposites are important, and we must treat them as One because they form a "unity of opposites."

According to Jesus, our challenge is to open our eyes and ears, reflect, and gain from each and every such experience as if it were a gift from God—because it is. God is infinite, and our growth potential as a co-creator is also infinite. Jesus tells us we must keep our eyes open for the light and our ears open to the sound while staying eternally grateful for the gifts we are always receiving.

Chapter 9

The Essential Message

This chapter presents the message of Jesus found in the Sermon on the Mount. In December 1999, we visited Israel and went to the likely place that Jesus gave this sermon. Close to the north side of the Sea of Galilee runs a two-lane road that parallels the shoreline. Near the northeast end of the Sea of Galilee is a small park with several springs. This is where the loaves of bread and fish miracle took place, according to Helena, Emperor Constantine's mother. She was in this area over 300 years after Jesus, but she seems to be the accepted authority on where most of the Jesus story took place.

Just immediately north of the park and next to the road is a hill. When you make the easy short climb up that hill, you find a tree with some rocks around it. We imagined that is where Jesus gave His lessons to His first disciples. A few feet from the tree, the hill drops off sharply to the road 20 feet below. It is an ideal place to talk to a group of several hundred followers, who would be listening from the road below. We could almost hear Jesus recite the Sermon on the Mount in that setting.

The Sermon on the Mount was primarily addressed to his newest followers, as it explained the purpose of His ministry, how people should live His message, and His religious and spiritual standards. When we were on that hilltop, we could easily imagine His followers mesmerized, knowing they were witnessing something very important, but also not really understanding the full import of His words.

Food For The Soul—The Purpose Of Jesus' Ministry

The first point He made, after He was baptized by His cousin John, was, "It is written, man shall not live by bread alone, but by every word that proceeds out of the mouth of God" (Matthew 4: 4). Jesus was quoting from Deuteronomy (8:3): "And God humbled you and suffered you to hunger and fed you with manna, which you did not know, neither did your fathers know; that He might make you to understand that *man does not live by bread alone; but by everything that proceeds out of the mouth of the Lord does man live.*" (The emphasis is ours.) When Jesus points out that "everything proceeds out of the mouth of God," He is referring to the *logos*, a concept we discuss in detail in Chapters 5 and 6.

In these words of Jesus, we see the influence of Heraclitus. In particular, we can see Jesus' use of juxtaposition. Juxtaposition is a placing of dissimilar objects or concepts in close proximity to emphasize their differing traits and at the same time to make us think about possible connections or implications.

In this case, the juxtaposition involves the tangible bread and the intangible word of God. In this "unity of opposites," both are food: one is material and finite, while the other is nonmaterial and infinite. Bread represents material food that is essential for life, and the word of God represents what is essential for living the good life.

The word (*logos*) of God is the spiritual food essential for us to grow and transcend our limited material existence. In other words, spiritual food is critical in moving us from the Kingdom of Man to the Kindom of God. Jesus knew He had to remind humankind of the existence of spiritual sustenance, or "soul food," and our need for it. This was His mission and purpose in life.

Sometime after this realization, Jesus was walking on the northwestern shore of the Sea of Galilee when He saw two young men, brothers, who were fishing. He said, "Follow me, and I will make you fishers of men" (Matthew 4:19). Like His words in the Sermon on the Mount, which came later, these words also express a "unity of opposites": (a) being "fishers of fish" and (b) being "fishers of men." In this case, the unity, or parallel, is the harmony of both types of seekers. One seeks material food to feed the body, and the other seeks non-material food to feed the soul.

Jesus' ultimate purpose was to awaken humankind to spiritual food, and He understood that He needed followers to accomplish that purpose. The Sermon on the Mount was His first teaching, which was primarily for His new growing band of followers, those who were now becoming His disciples. His learning in Jewish thought, particularly His admiration of Isaiah, and His education in Greek thought, particularly that of Heraclitus, are evident in those teachings.

Jesus picked up the spirit of Isaiah's message of peace, but He framed His message using the style and philosophy of Heraclitus. For example, He used several "unities of opposites" to express the main themes of His process theology. He explained what was of central importance to Him at this, the beginning of His ministry, namely, spiritual love that had to come from the human heart (See Chapter 15 for more detail.). He also outlined what the disciples must know and apply to their lives, and the challenges they should expect because of their beliefs.

Sermon on the Mount

The sermon focuses on eight central points, often called the beatitudes. Religious scholars believe that they were presented not in a single lesson but rather as a series of lessons.

Jesus began by first explaining that ego and material desires do not drive spiritual persons, and because of that, they are happy and content within themselves. This happiness results from the process in which they move from the Kingdom of Man to the Kindom of God. Next, Jesus wanted His new disciples and others to understand that the process is primarily a matter of seeking, which is always an on-going struggle involving uncomfortable internal change. Third, they had to approach the process of seeking with an open mind but with caution. Fourth, hunger and thirst for righteousness should motivate their process of seeking.

Jesus' fifth point was that the process of seeking should result in one becoming merciful. Sixth, to be successful, the process would require the follower to have a pure heart. Seventh, the process would result in followers becoming peacemakers, and eighth, the process would also result in their being persecuted for their efforts. In other words, they should expect others to revile, persecute, and falsely accuse them because of what they learned in the process of seeking. Finally, Jesus noted that although being persecuted would be painful, it would also be an excellent indicator that they were doing exactly what a good spiritual person should do.

First Beatitude
Jesus said, "Blessed are the poor in spirit: for theirs is the Kingdom of Heaven" (Matthew 5:3).

Similar to the beatitude that Matthew reports, Luke quotes Jesus as saying. "Blessed be you poor: for yours is the Kingdom [Kindom] of God" (6:20). Luke's version of Jesus' words gives the impression to modern readers that we have to be impoverished to be blessed. This was the interpretation for many centuries. It allowed "good" Christian political and business leaders to exploit others as they reasoned that their victims' reward was not necessarily in this lifetime and they would get it later in heaven. This is also the main doctrine that the Central and South American liberation theologians argued against in the 1980s and 1990s. Incidentally, the Pope excommunicated those theologians from the Catholic Church for their efforts.

Jesus spoke in the local language of Aramaic, but His story was first written in the various gospels in ancient Greek. The word "spirit" in Aramaic probably meant "pride" and referred to those who were poor in pride. It could also mean "humble, unassuming, and free from racial prejudice." In other words, "poor in spirit" meant not being driven by the ego. In the last two centuries BCE, the word "poor" became a synonym for "pious" or "saintly." People poor in spirit were humble and relied totally on God, not on material possessions (Errico and Lamsa 58).

Also, the word "blessed" could have been translated as "happy, content, blissful, delighted, and fortunate" (Errico and Lamsa 58). For us the word "blessed" just does not capture the most likely emotion of what was meant. We prefer "happy" and "content." Therefore, the translation would be "Happy and content are those who are not driven by ego or material desires . . . ."

Matthew's gospel uses extensively and exclusively the phrase "Kingdom of Heaven." Mark and Luke use the term "Kingdom of God" (Errico and Lamsa 58). The meaning of the two terms is the same. We believe that Jesus meant we are in the Kindom of Heaven / Kindom of God when we are being spiritual.

Based on the Bible translation from the ancient Greek, many modern readers would disagree with the first beatitude. They would say the opposite: that a lively person who sings out that he loves God is clearly the person rich in spirit, and certainly such a person is the one who has found the Kindom of Heaven. But no, the translation from the ancient Greek tells us that Jesus is saying those *poor in spirit* are the ones who live in the Kindom of Heaven. Jesus is not saying we should be gloomy. Using the ancient Greek version rather than the Aramaic leads us to misunderstand His teaching in this first and important beatitude.

We argue that the proper translation of this beatitude is "Happy and content are those who are not driven by ego or material desires, for they are spiritual persons." Using the "unity of opposites," Jesus is telling us there is a cause and effect linkage between (a) those not driven by ego or material desires and (b) being a spiritual person. Being influenced by Greek philosophers such as Plato, He is also telling us that a person who reaches advanced spirituality will be happy and content.

Second Beatitude
Jesus said, "Blessed are they that mourn: for they shall be comforted" (Matthew 5:4).

The similar version of this beatitude in Luke reads, "Blessed are you that hunger now: for you shall be filled. Blessed are you that weep now, for you shall laugh" (6:21). His version also adds, "But woe to you that are rich! For you have received your consolation" (Luke 6:24). Jesus says, "Woe to you that are full! For you shall hunger. Woe to you that laugh now! For you shall mourn and weep" (Luke 6:25).

Trouble and suffering can be extremely useful for gaining spirituality because many people will not become seekers of spiritual wisdom unless driven to do so by circumstances. At the time of Jesus, the Galilee region was a center of insurrections against the occupation of the Romans. The people of Galilee engaged in many failed attempts to free themselves from the Roman yoke. As a result, Jesus felt that His people would be particularly open to the comfort of His spiritual message. This beatitude offers that comfort.

The Kindom of Heaven as a process is not without struggle, and that struggle will make the person uncomfortable and even sad. However, through that struggle, the person receives a profound feeling of being comforted by what he or she learns.

The process of struggling itself changes you, and being changed, you become comforted. Being meek means being humble, and certainly increased spiritual wisdom brings humility and a sense of awe. With spirituality, you realize your birthright to bring harmony and true inner success to your life.

Third Beatitude
Jesus said, "Blessed are the meek: for they shall inherit the earth" (Matthew 5:5).

This beatitude parallels a common proverb in the Middle East: "The meek shall inherit the earth." The beatitude and proverb are about the type of person who does not retaliate, who believes in nonresistance, and who submits to injustice, even at great inconvenience. Jesus is against chronic restlessness caused by the desire for revenge. Jesus is also against repaying evil with evil. He is for the gentle person who bends like a tree during a heavy storm and thereby survives (Errico and Lamsa 60).

Asserting to others that you are correct and bullying others are the opposite of being meek. "Inherit the earth" is a metaphor saying you will ultimately be successful. For the process of spirituality to work, you must realize that it is a constant process and you always have much more to learn. You should have no desire to expect or force others to accept your point of view. Yours is a path of growth to be traveled with courage, caution and open-mindedness.

Fourth Beatitude
Jesus said, "Blessed are they who do hunger and thirst after righteousness: for they shall be filled" (Matthew 5:6).

Hunger and thirst are basic needs that come with living in a human body. So the desire for righteousness also needs to become basic and fundamental to us. We must be seekers; and if we are patient and persevere, we shall succeed. We must seek righteousness, meaning not only right conduct, but also right thinking. As Emmet Fox, a spiritual leader in the early twentieth century, notes, "What you think in your mind you will produce in your experience" (31).

Righteousness is defined more completely in the rest of this and the next chapter, as well as in Part 2 of this book. The bottom line is that if you hunger and thirst after righteousness, in time you will be filled with inner happiness and the contentment that comes from being spiritual.

Fifth Beatitude
Jesus said, "Blessed are the merciful: for they shall obtain mercy" (Matthew 5:7).

This message is very similar to the concept of karma, meaning in this circumstance that others reflect your thoughts and actions back onto you. Jesus is merely extending the Torah's *mitzvoth* requirement that Jews be merciful in terms of debt forgiveness, freeing of slaves after seven years, leaving portions of a harvest for the poor, and so on. One of the results of achieving spirituality is that individuals become merciful, kind, and forgiving toward others. With being merciful, kind, and forgiving toward others, the recipients of the kindness often treat the original givers as they were treated.

Sixth Beatitude
He said, "Blessed are the pure in heart: for they shall see God" (Matthew 5:8).

"Pure in heart" is an Aramaic idiom to describe a sincere, contrite individual. It also refers to a person with a clear mind (Errico and Lamsa 62). In the Jewish Bible, for someone to see God was unusual; to do so was considered a unique honor. A necessity for spirituality is that one be a sincere, contrite individual; without those qualities, one cannot properly "see" God.

Seventh Beatitude
Jesus said, "Blessed are the peacemakers: for they shall be called the children of God" (Matthew 5:9).

The word "peacemaker" is rarely used in the New Testament. Today, the term is often used in connection with the United Nations and refers to an attempt to keep warring factions from fighting each other. In the Roman context, peace (*Pax Romana*) came only after the Romans had conquered a territory and subjugated the people; in other words, peace was gained through force. This "forced" peace was a form of submission to the might and will of another.

In Aramaic, "peace" means "to surrender." The term carries the message of surrendering your ego to the will of God and thereby "being at peace" and "being in tranquility." In the Jewish context, "peace" means being calm and at ease with yourself. Therefore, a peacemaker would be someone who helps others be calm and at ease with themselves.

In the Middle East, peacemakers were people who sat at the gates of the city without compensation and acted as judges to reconcile people who had grievances with others. Like the modern day mediator, the peacemaker's job was to settle quarrels and calm disputing parties. Typically, the peacemakers admonished people who used force to settle disputes. (Errico and Lamsa 63)

The phrase "children of God" can have many meanings. It can refer alternatively to people who are immature; dependent on God; under the protection of God; in the same image as God; having the same characteristics as God; disengaged from life; or followers of God. We take it to mean "followers of God."

We restate the beatitude in this way: "Blessed are those

who help others to be calm and at ease within themselves by reconciling the grievances among quarreling parties. Others shall think of them as followers of God."

Eighth Beatitude
Jesus said, "Blessed are they who are persecuted for righteousness' sake: for theirs is the Kingdom of Heaven" (Matthew 5:10).

Luke presents a related idea: "Woe to you, when all men shall speak well of you! For so did their fathers to the false prophets" (Luke 6:26).

Jesus elaborated on the eighth beatitude by saying, "Blessed are you, when men shall revile you, and persecute you, and shall say all manner of evil against you falsely, for my sake" (Matthew 5:11). Similarly, Luke reads, "Blessed are you, when men shall hate you, and when they shall separate you from their company, and shall reproach you, and cast out your name as evil for the Son of Man's sake" (6:21). Jesus is clear that following His teachings will not result in everyone loving you and giving you respect. Instead, some will hate, persecute, and falsely say bad things about you. If they do so, then such behavior indicates you understand and live His message. In other words, you are acting righteously.

If you are righteous, meaning following the spirit of the commandments, you will probably live what you believe. However, those around you may not share your sense of righteousness, and they may be so upset with you that they persecute you. Clearly the history of the civil rights movement in America illustrates that reality. This beatitude says that persecuted persons who follow the teachings of Jesus, such as Martin Luther King, Jr. are doing the right thing and acting spiritually.

To Jesus, the ultimate purpose of life is that which the Greek Plato and the Jewish community of His time embraced.

The ultimate purpose for many of the ancient Greeks was being happy by living a good life, but there was a difference of opinion (for example, between Epicurus and Plato) as to what was "a good life." For Plato, "a good life" was a life worthy of being lived, which meant a person contributed to the community. To Epicureans, it was a life properly fulfilling the senses, which for some meant indulgent behavior and others meant moderation. The ultimate purpose for Jews was, and is, to live by following the commandments in the Torah.

The ultimate purpose of life for Jesus is having the Kindom of Heaven mindset and behaving accordingly, but He thought that mindset would result in being happy and living the good life as defined by Plato. To Jesus, the Kindom of Heaven mindset was living the spirit of the Jewish commandments as He interpreted it.

Jesus summarizes the first section of the Sermon on the Mount by saying, "Rejoice, and be exceeding glad; for great is your reward: for so persecuted they the prophets who were before you" (Matthew 5:12). The great Jewish leaders of the past were often persecuted. That your actions raise such a response in peoples is a good indicator that you are doing exactly what a spiritual person should be doing.

Living the Message

The next section of Jesus' famous sermon stresses what it means to live or not live His process theology.

> **Jesus said, "You are the salt of the earth: but if the salt have lost its savor, can it be salted? It is henceforth good for nothing, but to be cast out, and be trodden under the foot of men" (Matthew 5: 13).**

What is salt that it does not taste like salt? It is worth very little and cannot be effective in its purpose of flavoring or preserving food. If you are salt, you must act like salt if you are to be effective. If you are blessed, then you need to act as though you are blessed. If God is within you, then realize this, and reflect it in how you express your thoughts, speech, and actions. This expression goes well beyond just proclaiming your beliefs. It includes how you live and treat others everyday because of those beliefs.

Jesus carries the point further in the following saying:

"You are the light of the world. A city that is set on a hill cannot be hid. Neither do men light a candle, and put it under a bushel, but on a candlestick; and it gives light to all that are in the house" (Matthew 5:14-15).

The word "light" in Aramaic means "teaching, enlightenment, brilliance, and intelligence." At the time of Jesus, "light" also meant "God's word," "the teaching of the prophets," and "God's presence." (Errico and Lamsa 66)

You are enlightened by God's word, and you must act accordingly. You should not hide what you have learned from God's lessons. You should reflect those lessons in your treatment of others. Jesus summarizes His point by saying:

"Let your light so shine before men, that they may see your good works, and glorify your Father who is in heaven" (Matthew 5:16).

When you reflect God's lessons, your *actions* are a silent praise to God that can be heard loudly not only by God by also by those around you.

The process theology of Jesus includes, as it must, a *telos*, or purpose. Jesus announced that His purpose was not to destroy the Jewish law or diminish the Jewish prophets but to accomplish the purpose of Jewish law and the prophets. Jesus was never anything but a Jew. However, being a Jew does not mean that you agree with all Jews or even one other Jew on all things. Jews always reserve their right to think, learn, and disagree. His purpose was not to create a new and separate faith tradition.

Today, Jesus would be called a Reform Jew. He would not accept the Christian Alpha Interpretation of who He was. He was a Reform Jew but also a rabbi, a guru, and an adherent to the Omega Interpretation. He saw himself as a reform advocate of Jewish doctrine, including its simplification, and an advocate for cleaning up the corruption of Temple politics, but He always wanted ultimately to accomplish the purpose of Jewish law and the prophets. He advocated ratcheting up the then current understandings of the Jewish commandments with other interpretations that reflected greater righteousness and thus, He argued, were more valid.

> **Jesus said, "Think not that I am come to destroy the law, or the prophets: I am not come to destroy, but to fulfill. For I say to you, until heaven and earth pass away, one jot or one tittle shall in no wise pass from the law, till all be fulfilled" (Matthew 5:17-18).**

In the Jewish tradition, one cannot change a word of the Torah, but one can interpret those words in such a manner that they mean something quite different from the interpretations of the past. For example, the clear wording of the Torah is very hostile to homosexuals, but the current interpretation by many Jews allows them to accept homosexuality. The Torah is a living and breathing document that reflects the understanding of both today's Jews and those of the past. Without that understanding, one cannot grasp either the dynamic nature of the Jewish tradition or the message of Jesus.

In Matthew 5:19-20, Jesus argued that breaking even one

of the smallest and least of the Torah's 613 *mitzvoths* (commandments to perform good deeds) and then teaching the error to others would make a person one of the least in the Kindom of Heaven. Clearly, Jesus does not feel He was doing that with His ministry. He felt He was not only following the laws (commandments) but also following a more righteous version of those laws.

Jesus argued that breaking a *mitzvoth* and teaching that error did not remove anyone from the Kindom of Heaven entirely, but it did lessen that person in the Kindom. Thus the Kindom of Heaven was not a single consciousness but rather existed on a continuum of least to most. Obviously, He thought that differences of opinion within the Jewish community about the Torah's commandments had to be tolerated, and having those differences did not remove anyone from the Kindom of Heaven. Hence Jesus was not a fundamentalist but a liberal who tolerated, but did not necessarily accept, the religious views of others.

Jesus continues with the argument that someone who lives by example the true meaning of the Torah and teaches others to do the same will be called great in the Kindom of Heaven. Apparently, He felt He was doing that by offering interpretations of commandments that met a higher test of righteousness. In other words, Jesus felt He was among the best of Jews in disagreeing with the interpretation of the Torah made by the more literal scribes and Pharisees.

He also argued that offering more demanding interpretations of commandments was correct only if the reformer's righteousness exceeded the righteousness of the scribes and Pharisees. In other words, He believed His interpretations of the commandments were *more* righteous than those of the then Jewish leadership and therefore superior to the Pharisees' interpretations. Jesus said, "For I say to you, that except your righteousness shall exceed the righteousness of the scribes and

Pharisees, you shall in no case enter in the Kingdom of heaven" (Matthew 5:20).

Matthew 5:21-22 gives an example of how Jesus' teaching exceeds the righteousness of the scribes and Pharisees. In Matthew, Jesus refers to the well-known Jewish commandment, "Thou shall not murder," which Christians misstate, as "Thou shall not kill." Jesus argued that one should go further than simply avoiding the act of murder.

He raised the standard by staying that if you are angry with your brother without cause, even if it does not involve killing him, such feelings are improper and break the commandment of the Torah. In addition, being angry with someone who says you are improper in such matters is also wrong. In other words, He argued for a higher standard of righteousness that extends to feelings and thoughts as well as actions.

In the Jewish custom at the time of Jesus, if you did a wrong, you needed to make an offering to God at the Temple for your poor behavior because your behavior also offended God. The offering was to gain forgiveness from God. Jesus said, "Therefore if you bring the gift to the altar, and there you remember that your brother ought against you; leave there your gift before the altar and go your way; first be reconciled to your brother, and then come and offer our gift" (Matthew 5:23-24).

Jesus is saying that if you bring an offering to God because of your improper attitude toward your brother, you also need to reconcile with your brother. Today, Jewish custom requires that if you do something wrong to someone, you must apologize to that person on at least three separate occasions. If the offended person does not forgive you after the third apology, the wrong shifts to the offended person.

In Matthew 5:25-26, Jesus says that seeking forgiveness is not sufficient, that you should apologize quickly before the person seeks justice from the courts. Part of your apology should be to pay full damages to the aggrieved person for your wrongdoing. Jesus, therefore, is suggesting a higher standard and a different way to atone.

Jesus cites another example to clarify His message about righteousness. Addressing the commandment against adultery, He says that to be righteous a person needs to do more than just not commit the actual act of adultery, but that even looking at a woman with lust is wrong (Matthew 5:25-28). Again, He says the action and the thoughts and feelings are wrong and by implication they are tied together. This admonition went far beyond standard Jewish belief in that only the physical act had been prohibited and not thoughts and feelings.

In Matthew, Jesus goes on to cite other examples of His higher standard of righteousness. One involves divorce. He notes that, under Jewish law, a man could divorce his wife for no cause by giving her a written notice of their divorce. To Jesus, this way of divorcing was wrong unless the wife committed adultery. With just the written notice, the wife had no claim for settlement, as she has in modern day divorces. She was simply left abandoned and without resources to survive. She was undesirable for remarriage, and this unsuitability often left the woman and her children in abject poverty. Jesus thought this situation was cruel. To Jesus, summary divorce by a man was wrong, and He said that if the man were to marry again, he would be guilty of adultery (Matthew 5:31-32).

Another example of His higher standard of righteousness than in traditional Jewish law is a false swearing of an oath to God. For Jews, this meant not swearing an oath or making a promise to God that you could not or would not keep. For Jesus, His standard was not to swear a false oath of any kind to anyone (Matthew 5:34-37).

Other examples of His higher standards address justice and retribution. He cites the then standard of an eye for an eye, and a tooth for a tooth, used to determine proper judgment in a Jewish trial. That standard in the time of Jesus came to be used to settle personal disagreements beyond the courts, regardless of the wording of the Torah. The standard was intended to mean that people could not expect more in compensation than was taken from them.

But Jesus argued for a person to resist demanding and seeking any retribution at all. He said a person should even "turn the other cheek" (Matthew 5:38-39). In matters involving a court settlement, He argued that if the court decides against you and awards damages against you, then you should go beyond the court-awarded damages and pay more to the victim (Matthew 5:40-41).

His last examples of proper righteousness, cited in Matthew Chapter 5, involve human interrelations. If someone asks for help, give it. If someone wishes to borrow from you, do not turn him or her away. You should do more than love your neighbor; you should also love and bless your enemies and those that curse you. Do good to those that hate you. Pray for those who despise and persecute you (Matthew 5:42-48). Jesus argued consistently for higher standards of righteous behavior than what the Pharisees and scribes interpreted as necessary.

His Religious and Spiritual Standards

Jesus also suggested higher standards for personal religious practices. Like Jews before and after Him, charity and prayer were, and are, important personal religious activities. He added that giving should be done in a way that others in the community would not know how much you gave.

"Let not your left hand know what your right hand is doing" is an Aramaic expression. It means that no one should know what you are doing lest you are doing those things to impress others or appear pious. God knows and sees a good deed, but no one else need know. Today non-profit organizations often publish donors' names because some would not give unless they were assured others knew of their generosity to charity. Jesus disapproved of such public display of charitable giving (Errico and Lamsa 91).

Jesus also argued that public displays of praying for the sake of appearing religious were inappropriate. He said one should pray in secret and one should not use rote repetitive prayers (Matthew 6:1-8). In His view, prayer was a person's private conversation with God, not a vulgar public show for others to see.

He even suggested a prayer that we know as the Lord's Prayer. That prayer begins with "Our Father," which is a mistranslation of the Aramaic in that those words were only a term of affection, such as "beloved," without any reference to the male gender. To Jesus, God was not considered to be an almighty awesome deity but rather a loving and respected "parent" (Errico and Lamsa 94).

In that prayer, one can see His use of the "unity of opposites" and a different meaning of "pray" than we use today. The "unity of opposites" occurs three times: (1) done in earth, as it is in heaven, (2) forgive us our debt as we forgive others' debt, and (3) lead us not into temptation but deliver us from evil. Jesus reasoned that if we forgive others, then God will also forgive us (Matthew 6:9-15).

In addition, this prayer gives us a behavioral standard that is easy to understand. It is, therefore, more likely we will apply it in everyday situations. It prepares us to be aware of God's presence, discern what is proper and improper behavior, and be more sensitive to God's spiritual lessons given to us with our daily life. These themes are similar to those in the Gospel of Thomas and are elaborated upon in Part 2 of this book.

The words "pray" and "praying" at the time of Jesus did not mean what they mean today to a Christian. To Jews in Jesus' time, a prayer was *not* a request to God for what we might need or want; nor was it a formal act of outward reverence to impress God, as it often is today. After all, an all-knowing

God knows what we think, want and need without our asking. In addition, there really is nothing we can do as humans in terms of a formal act of reverence that could impress God.

Instead, prayer was a means to prepare us to receive divine messages, lessons, and admonitions. It was to help us be aware of God's presence and discern the appropriate and inappropriate in our lives (Errico and Lamsa 94). Like ritual bathing and deep breathing before meditation, prayer was a form of cleansing and opening up of the heart to receive God.

In the Jewish tradition at the time of Jesus, there were many proscribed fast and feast days. Jesus also had standards regarding fasting. One should not show sadness or complain about having to fast and should not act as if that fasting were a form of martyrdom. Fasting is done as an offering; it is our gift to God to demonstrate our sincere love. Jesus called for us to anoint our heads and wash our faces when fasting. Fasting should be done in secret, just as prayer (Matthew 6:16-18). The common theme in all His standards was to avoid bragging about one's religious practices, to not be a hypocrite, and to avoid being judgmental of others.

The importance of growing in spirituality was central to what Jesus taught. Jesus wanted people to focus not on material treasures but on what He called "treasures in heaven," by which He meant the process of growing one's spirituality. How one defined treasure — as material or heavenly — defined the light that was in the person's heart. Jesus believed that the light in a person's eye indicated light or darkness in that person's heart.

In addition, Jesus said that a person could not serve the material wants of life and at the same time serve God in growing his or her spirituality. In other words, one cannot serve two masters at once. Jesus stressed that we should not worry about material concerns but rather increase our spirituality, including our righteousness (Matthew 6:19-34).

Jesus particularly did not want people to be judgmental of others. He did not like gossip, criticism, and slander. He felt it was wrong to judge the habits, weaknesses, and actions of others. Being judgmental needlessly encouraged others to be judgmental.

What standard you used for judging others would eventually be used to judge you. Instead, people should focus on fixing their own problems rather than judging the problems of others. To be judgmental was to be a hypocrite (Matthew 7:1-5).

In matters of spirituality, Jesus had still more strong suggestions. For example, He said not to give spiritual wisdom to those who cannot appreciate such a gift. Finding the spiritual wisdom necessary for your growth is a matter of seeking it, and you will find it because God wishes you to be spiritually successful. We all need to do our own searching to find wisdom that is appropriate for our individual spiritual path.

Jesus told us to treat others the way we wish to be treated. Realize that few people will be successful in growing spiritually. Being spiritual prepares you for the challenges of life. Those who hear the spiritual lessons and ignore them will find they are not prepared for life's challenges, and their challenges will defeat them (Matthew 7:6-27).

Jesus also warned us to beware of false prophets; they appear innocent but inwardly are ravening wolves. Prophets can be known by their deeds because good people produce virtuous deeds and bad people produce evil deeds. Just because people act religiously does not mean they are spiritual. While not being perfect, our teachers must nevertheless "walk-the-walk," demonstrating with their actions their own spirituality.

His Essential Message

As we mention previously, the Torah focused on taking the descendants of Abraham, Isaac, and Jacob and creating a viable nation consisting of twelve tribes. Part of that nation-building process involved defining ethical standards and expectations about what was righteous behavior for a Jew.

In the Torah, laws on social issues enhance the likelihood that the Jewish people will live together in peace and harmony. In short, the laws of the Torah are to enable the Jewish people to live together in unity. The Torah proscribed a specific sacrifice to God for each offense committed for each offense that challenged or threatened that harmony.

Jesus offered a different interpretation of how to handle offenses such as killing others, adultery, and inappropriate prayers and praying. He also suggested how to properly apologize when you commit a wrong to another, indicated what was an appropriate divorce, and gave instructions for swearing oaths, making proper retribution, and conducting oneself in court.

Our belief is that Jesus wished to reform particular interpretations of Jewish "laws" in the Torah. He wanted a stronger code of conduct that helped each person be a better person. Over all, He focused more on people developing their spirituality than He focused on creating a better social situation that would allow people to live and work together as Jews.

In accordance with Heraclitus' teaching, Jesus saw a "unity of opposites" that consisted of the Kingdom of Man and the Kindom of God. His goal was to move as many people as possible into the process of transcending from the Kingdom of Man to the Kindom of God. Torah law significantly did much of that, but it was limited.

To Jesus, the Divine plan that could move a person from the Kingdom of Man to the Kindom of God was a spirituality based on unconditional love of others, what in Chapter 14 we call spiritual love. From an operational perspective, how could that love be accomplished? His answer was a code of conduct.

If individuals ask for help, Jesus says you are compelled to give it. If individuals wish to borrow from you, do not turn them away. Do more than love your neighbor; also love your enemy. Bless them and do good to those that might wish you harm. Pray for those that despise and persecute you. His answer to the problems of His time was a revolution in personal thought and attitude rather than armed rebellion against the Romans or anyone else.

In matters of religion, His biggest concerns were for one not to be a hypocrite but to be sincere in one's faith practice. People who gave to charity in order to brag about their giving, who prayed to somehow improve their social status, and who fasted for attention disappointed Him. Jesus was not a materialist; instead, He was a strong advocate of growing one's spirituality. He even contended that if you were a materialist, you could not be spiritual. He was strongly negative about judgmental people, whom He felt were commonly found among the weekend religious faithful of His day. To help a person learn to be spiritual, He offered a long list of guidelines. However, the best summary of Jesus' thoughts on spirituality is the Golden Rule: Do unto others as you would have them do unto you.

Chapter 10

The Message Through Parables

A parable is a short moral or religious story that illustrates a point. The ancient Greeks used this approach to teach morality. (Most modern readers know of Aesop's Fables, written over 2,000 years ago.) Jesus used parables to communicate His message, and they were an excellent way of doing so, given that His audience was mostly illiterate. Semites, an indigenous people from the Middle East, of which Jesus was one, used parables for teaching, conversations, debates, songs, speeches, and even bargaining. The parables in the New Testament are poetic and mystical, but they also address social issues. There are forty parables in the Gospels of Matthew, Mark, and Luke.

In this chapter, we focus on selected parables that we group by theme. The first set of stories focuses on the topic of what constitutes the Kindom of Heaven. In this set, Jesus teaches us that the Kindom is a *process*, and He suggests ways to understand, value, and develop the Kindom within us. The second group of parables explains the differences between being wise and being foolish. The parables on the third theme directly address those followers who wish to teach His spiritual lessons.

The Kindom Of Heaven

As we explain in previous chapters, Jesus reasoned using the philosophic tool called "unity of opposites." The most important "unity of opposites" in His message was the paradigm, or consciousness pair, of (a) the Kingdom of Man and (b) the Kindom of Heaven (God). Together they constitute a continuum showing the process of change in consciousness during which a person moves ideally from the Kingdom of Man toward the Kindom of Heaven, with the ultimate goal of merging completely with the Oneness that constitutes the Kindom of Heaven.

The Kingdom of Man consists of our materialistic world in which the ego is dominant and human desire controls our behavior. Jesus believed that His teachings, with the help of His disciples, could inspire a significant number of people to grow in spiritual consciousness and thereby move from the mindset of the Kingdom of Man to that of the Kindom of Heaven.

Jesus used parables to communicate His message to the public about how to accomplish that shift in consciousness. He felt that if even a small number of people acquired the Kindom of Heaven consciousness, it would make a radical and positive difference in world consciousness. The individuals who acquired that consciousness would benefit; but, significantly, humankind as a whole would also benefit.

Jesus used parables because people could not understand a straightforward explanation of the Kindom of Heaven or the concept of consciousness. In Matthew 13:13, Jesus said, "Therefore I speak to them in parables: because they seeing see not; and hearing they hear not, neither do they understand." As teachers with a combined experience of over five decades, we can understand a teacher's frustration with students who just do not comprehend the full extent of the lessons.

One of us had a dramatic frustration in an attempt to teach ethics to masters' level students. Thomas started with a straightforward explanation of an ethical code, but clearly the explanation did not work in that particular class because the students' attention was not focused on the lesson. So he resorted to an entertaining story with an ethical message that explained the essence of the code of ethics. It worked!

Parables are normally short stories that entertain the students but also teach the desired lesson. As a teaching method, they can sometimes be the only means to communicate an important but difficult or dry lesson. As Paulo Frererie demonstrated in his book *Pedagogy of the Oppressed,* the best way to teach an agrarian, illiterate population is with examples drawn from their daily lives. So many of Jesus' parables involved planting crops and cooking—all-important daily activities for his followers.

Jesus used eight parables to explain His understanding of the Kindom of Heaven consciousness.

The first set of eight parables centers on recognizing the process, the nature of that consciousness, its value, and how to develop that consciousness.

In the first parable, found in Matthew 13:18-23, Jesus uncharacteristically explains the parable before He presents it to the disciples. Incidentally, notice how difficult it is to understand the King James version.

The Sower

Hear ye therefore the parable of the sower. When any one heareth the word of the kingdom, and understandeth it not, then cometh the wicked one and catcheth away that which was sown in his heart. This is he who received seed by the way side. But he that received the seed into stony places, the same is he that heareth the word, and anon with joy receiveth it; Yet hath he not root in himself, but dureth for a while: for when tribulation or persecution ariseth because of the word, by and by he is offended. He also that received seed among the thorns is he that heareth the word; and the care of this world, and the deceitfulness of riches, choke the word, and he becometh unfruitful. But he that received seed into the good ground is he that heareth the word, and understandeth it; which also beareth fruit, and bringeth forth, some a hundredfold, some sixty, some thirty.

The point is that where you sow your seed does make a difference in terms of its chances of becoming a viable crop. The wiser person knows this and acts accordingly by planting his or her seeds in well-cultivated ground. Being wise results in a bountiful harvest.

With that explanation, Jesus then presents the second Sower parable (Matthew 13:24-30):

He said, "The Kingdom of Heaven is likened unto a man which sowed good seed in his field: But while men slept, his enemy came and sowed tares among the wheat, and went his way. But when the blade was sprung up and brought forth fruit, then appeared the tares also. So the servant of the householder came and said unto him, 'Sir, didst not thou sow good seed in the field? From whence hath it tares?' He said unto them, 'An enemy hath done this.' The servants said unto him, 'Wilt thou then that we go and gather them up?' But he said, 'Nay, lest while ye gather up the tares, ye root up also the wheat with them. Let both grow together until the harvest: and in the time of harvest I will say to the reapers, "Gather ye together first the tares, and bind them in bundles to burn them: but gather the wheat into my barn."

To explain an abstract and often sophisticated concept, parables need to contrast things one is using everyday. This juxtaposition is essential. Jesus juxtaposes common images from daily life to bring out the underlying philosophical opposites. Those opposites form a unity that becomes the moving path, a *process*. Jesus does this to communicate His lesson in a subtle but effective manner.

The Sower parable tells us that the Kindom of Heaven is about wisdom and applying it to life's challenges. To understand the parable, we need to look at three sets of images to see the underlying "unity of opposites" and the recommended *process* for us to follow. The first juxtaposition presents (a) good seeds and (b) seeds for tares (weeds). The second is (a) wheat (food plants) and (b) tares. The third is (a) a good man and his servant and (b) his enemy. The underlying "unity of opposites" shows (a) the mix of good and bad in life and (b) the harvesting and separating of the good from the evil. The *process* is one of allowing maturation to occur before a person can harvest and separate the good from the bad.

The lesson of this parable is that the spiritual wisdom (the good seed) from the Kindom of Heaven will eventually become spiritual food (wheat plants) as we *process* it within ourselves (the field). However, the material world (tares, a weed) from the Kingdom of Man, which is non-spiritual, results in an indigestible substance (the grown tares). Life consists of both good and bad, and they exist together at the same time. The "unity of opposites" consists of two parallel *processes*: one involving spiritual growth (wheat plants) and the other growing ego identification and desire for material things (tares).

The answer, according to Jesus, is to let both the good and bad seeds grow within us as we mature. If we try to pull the tares too soon, we will harm the young wheat plants. Once the plants reach maturity, meaning once we reach spiritual maturity, we need to reap both crops. Then we can and should separate the two. This *process* makes it possible to destroy the grown tares and take the separated wheat and store it in a safe place. With this *process* in our life, we can move from living in the Kingdom of Man to living in the Kindom of Heaven.

The second parable Jesus chose on this theme to explain the Kindom of Heaven is the analogy of the mustard seed, found in Matthew 13:31-32.

The Mustard Seed
Jesus said, "The Kingdom of Heaven is like to a grain of mustard seed, which a man took, and sowed in his field. Which indeed is the least of all seeds: but when it is grown,

> it is the greatest among herbs, and becometh a tree, so that the birds of the air come and lodge in the branches thereof."

Again, the Kindom of Heaven is a *process*, and it is one that starts very small and grows into something that is large and beneficial. The juxtaposition appears in (a) the tiny mustard seed and (b) the huge tree that it becomes. The "unity of opposites" represented in this parable is (a) the smallness of the seed that is God's spiritual wisdom and (b) the remarkable spiritual growth in both the person and those around that person. The *process* is one of *becoming*, from the least in size to the greatest.

The seed (spiritual wisdom) is the beginning of life, but it is only a potential. The tree (a spiritual person) is the huge mature tree that grows from the tiny seed. Again notice the maturing *Process* of life in which the smallest of seeds becomes the greatest of herbs (a spiritual person) and provides a *Place* for birds (the spirit and soul) to lodge (the spiritual person gives aid and comfort to many). This parable helps us understand the Kindom of Heaven as not a *Place* but as a *Process* in which the spiritual lessons mature in the seeker, who becomes a blessing (happy and content) for everyone.

The Leavened Bread
> Again he said, "To what shall I compare the Kingdom of God? It is like yeast, which a woman took and hid in three measures of flour, until it was all leavened."

The Leavened Bread parable, found in Matthew 13:33 and Luke 13:20-21, stresses how the *process* of the Kindom of Heaven grows from a small "starter." The first juxtaposition of images shows (a) the yeast and (b) the flour. The second is (a) the small yeast starter the woman hid in flour and (b) the final leavened bread. The "unity of opposites" lies in

(a) the spiritual lesson that is the hidden but active substance and (b) the resulting growth made manifest in a spiritual person. The chemical action of yeast starts a *process* in which a small amount of yeast in several measures of flour causes over time the bread to rise.

Jesus is telling us that the spiritual wisdom of the Kindom of Heaven (His lessons) should not be thought of as mere words. Rather, they are the key ingredients in a *process* that raises us up and brings us to spiritual maturity.

Tares of the Field
He answered and said unto them, He that soweth the good seed is the Son of man; The field is the world; the good seed are the children of the kingdom; but the tares are the children of the wicked one; The enemy that sowed them is the devil; the harvest is the end of the world; and the rears are the angels, As therefore the tares are gathered and burned in the fire; so shall it be in the end of this world. The Son of man shall send both his angels, and they shall gather out of his kingdom all things that offend, and which do iniquity; And shall cast them into a furnace of fire; there shall be wailing and gnashing of teeth. Then shall the righteous shine forth in the sun in the kingdom of their Father, Who hath ears to hear, let him hear.

The fourth parable in this set, *The Tares* [weeds] *of the Field*, is presented in Matthew 13:37-43. Briefly summarized, it says Jesus sows the good seed (spiritual wisdom) and the world is His field. The children of the Kindom of Heaven (the disciples of Jesus) sowed the good seeds and the children of the Kingdom of Man (those who are ego-centered and materialistic) sowed the tares. The harvesting *process* separates the tares (the evil) from the righteous. The resulting harvest from good seeds symbolizes the bounty of our spiritual maturity.

The juxtaposed images are (a) the children of the Kindom of Heaven (His disciples and followers), who bring us righteousness and (b) the children of the Kingdom of Man (those who are ego-centered and materialistic), who bring us nothing of real value and, in fact, distract us from what is good. The "unity of opposites" is (a) righteousness and evil and (b) our own *freewill* that must harvest both and separate the distractions from the righteous. The *process* shows the flow of life in which the followers of Jesus play a key role as they distribute the spiritual food. Ultimately, each person must harvest his or her own crop, including separating the good from the bad.

Treasure Hidden in the Field
Again, the Kingdom of Heaven is like unto treasure hid in a field, the which when a man hath found, and hideth, and for joy thereof goeth and selleth all that he hath, and buyeth that field.

This parable, found in Matthew 13:44, points out that the *process* for developing one's spirituality appears hidden but has significant value once discovered. The juxtaposition depicts (a) the treasure hidden in the field and (b) the man selling all that he has so that he can buy the field. The "unity of opposites" lies in (a) the spiritual wisdom, which is infinite, non-material and not readily in view, and (b) the material, which is finite and easily seen. Here there are two *processes*: (a) recognizing what is of value and (b) placing a priority on it.

Jesus is telling us that the Kindom of Heaven is always here, but it is not conspicuously in view. However, it is something we can find if we seek. Furthermore, it is more valuable than all of one's material possessions, and we must recognize its value. The *process* of moving from the Kingdom of Man to the Kindom of God requires us to seek what is most valuable and to rid ourselves of our egocentric ways and desire for the material.

The Pearl of Great Price
Again, the Kingdom of Heaven is like a man who is a merchant seeking fine pearls, who having found one pearl of great price, he went and sold all that he had, and bought it.

The Pearl of Great Price parable, from Matthew 13:45-46, helps us grasp that the Kindom of Heaven is of extreme value. This parable is similar to the previous one. In this parable, the person is a seeker of something highly valued, which is the Kindom of Heaven. Once the seeker finds the pearl of great value, he sells everything, meaning all of his material things, so that he can acquire the pearl, meaning the Kindom of Heaven.

The juxtaposition here is (a) one pearl of great price and (b) the man getting rid of all that he had. The "unity of opposites" involve (a) the infinite and non-material Kindom of Heaven represented by the perfect pearl and (b) finite material possessions. Two *processes* occur in (a) seeking something of great value and (b) ridding oneself of material possessions that hold one back in obtaining the Kindom of Heaven. Jesus is telling us in this parable, as in the former parable, that obtaining the Kindom of Heaven involves realizing its great value, seeking it, and giving up the desire for material possessions.

The Net
Again, the Kingdom of Heaven is like a net, that was cast into the sea, and gathered some fish of every kind, which when it was filled, they drew up on the beach. They sat down, and gathered the good into containers, but the bad they threw away. So will it be in the end of the world. The angels will come forth, and separate the wicked from among the righteous, and will cast them into the furnace for fire. There will be the weeping and the gnashing of teeth.

The Net, found in Matthew 13:47-50, helps us understand

that the *process* of attaining the Kindom of Heaven involves an effort in searching and a choice between what is important and unimportant. The juxtaposition of images shows (a) a net which gathers fish of every kind and (b) the sorting of the good fish from the bad. The Kindom of Heaven involves the following two activities: (a) the gathering of experiences from a broad search, the net of life, but also (b) sorting the lessons that help us learn righteousness from those experiences. While gathering, we broadly search to experience what life can teach us.

The "unity of opposites" lies in (a) the broadly searching and (b) the narrowly searching. The *process* involves searching with two different and opposite types of searches that must be done together as a unity. However, this parable has an added twist because the two required functions are inherently conflicting. Jesus tells us that finding and reaching the Kindom of Heaven involve a two-step process. It consists of gathering life's experiences broadly but also sorting through them to determine what is truly important in those experiences. The processes are thus (a) learning from experience broadly but also (b) sorting narrowly.

With the sorting, you narrow the search, looking for only the lessons that can help you grow as a spiritual person.

The Scribe Like the Householder
Jesus said, "Therefore every scribe who is instructed unto the Kingdom of Heaven is like unto a man that is an householder, which bringeth forth out of his treasure things new and old."

This parable, from Matthew 13:52, tells us that spiritual wisdom, which is the treasure of spirituality (Kindom of Heaven), is both new and old. The juxtaposition depicts (a) scribes who are instructed in the Kindom of Heaven and (b) a householder who brings forth new and old treasures.

The "householder" is the owner of the treasure, meaning the one who has spiritual wisdom. "Bringeth forth" refers to a person manifesting the wisdom with actions. Scribes who are instructed in the Kingdom of Heaven learn spirituality: their learning consists of being guided by the old treasures from the Torah and the new treasures from Jesus' Sermon on the Mount. The "unity of opposites" is in (a) the old spiritual wisdom from the Torah and (b) the new spiritual wisdom from the Sermon on the Mount. The process requires learning both in unity.

In this parable, Jesus says that every person who is instructed in the Kindom of Heaven needs to know both the old and the new. To be knowledgeable about the Kindom of Heaven, a person must be taught the Torah's commandments and Jesus' new commandments as stated in the Sermon on the Mount (which we discuss in Chapter 9, "The Essential Message").

The Wise And The Foolish

The second theme found in the collection of parables concerns recognizing and discerning between the wise and the foolish, which is similar to our theme in Chapter 13, "Practical Spiritual Knowledge." There are five parables in this group, and some are unusually long for parables.

Ten Virgins
Then the Kingdom of Heaven will be like ten virgins, who took their lamps, and went out to meet the bridegroom. Five of them were foolish, and five were wise. Those who were foolish, when they took their lamps, took no oil with them, but the wise took oil in their vessels with their lamps. Now while the bridegroom delayed, they all slumbered and slept. But at midnight there was a cry, "Behold! The bridegroom is coming! Come out to meet him!" Then all those virgins arose, and trimmed their lamps.

> The foolish said to the wise, "Give us some of your oil, for our lamps are going out." But the wise answered, saying, "What if there isn't enough for you and us? You go rather to those who sell, and buy for yourselves." While they went away to buy, the bridegroom came, and those who were ready went in with him to the marriage feast, and the door was shut. Afterward the other virgins also came, saying, "Lord, Lord, open to us." But he answered, "Most assuredly I tell you, I don't know you." Watch therefore, for you don't know the day nor the hour in which the Son of Man is coming.

The parable of *The Ten Virgins*, found in Matthew 25:1-13, helps us understand the difference between being wise and foolish. This parable contains three sets of images in juxtaposition. The first juxtaposition presents (a) the wise virgins and (b) the foolish virgins. The second shows (a) being invited in and (b) being rejected. The third consists of (a) the oil and (b) the light of the lamp. We believe the virgins represent our child-like innocence and an immaturity. Being invited in and then being rejected refers to reaching or not reaching the goal in the Kindom of Heaven *process*.

As we note in Chapter 9, the word "light" in Aramaic means "teaching, enlightenment, brilliance, intelligence, God's word, the teaching of the prophets, and God's presence." In the context of this parable, "light" refers to the enlightenment or realization of a spiritual person, and the oil is fuel that permits the light to exist. The oil represents the accumulated spiritual lessons God gives.

The "unities of opposites" in this parable lie in (a) not being spiritually prepared and (b) being spiritually prepared. There are two *processes* in this parable: the wise ones are invited in, and the foolish ones ultimately are rejected. The wise ones realize that their spiritual lessons fuel their way to realization and enlightenment. Thus those lessons cannot be forgotten or jeopardized by diluting or ignoring them. The foolish ones are neglectful and careless with their spiritual lessons.

Both the wise and foolish exist in the Kindom of Heaven *process* at its beginning. However, being wise and acting wisely means you will progress and finally be invited to the marriage feast (reaching enlightenment and realization). Being foolish means that you may get close to realizing your goal, but ultimately you will be distracted, lose focus, and not do the needful. The marriage feast will be closed to you. Being wise is a matter of seeking out spiritual wisdom, being prepared to use it, and actually using it. Because there is a limit to your physical life, you must be proactive in using your time wisely to make as much progress as you can.

For some who hear this parable, the fact that the wise do not share their oil with the foolish may seem to violate the teachings in the Sermon on the Mount: "Do unto others as you would have them do unto you." Giving to others is important, but you should not give at the cost of sacrificing yourself and thereby not reach your ultimate goal of becoming an enlightened spiritual person.

In learning to be a lifeguard at a beach or pool, one of the first important lessons to follow is not to place your own life in jeopardy to save another. If you do, the result could easily be the loss of two lives rather than one. Our primary responsibility is to our own spiritual development, and our secondary responsibility is to help others. Never neglect your primary responsibility for your secondary responsibility, but realize both are important.

Talents

For the Kingdom of Heaven is as a man, going into another country, who called his own servants, and entrusted his goods to them. To one he gave five talents, to an-

other two, to another one; to each according to his own ability. Then he went on his journey. Immediately he who received the five talents went and traded with them, and made another five talents. In like manner he also who got the two gained another two. But he who received the one went away and dug in the earth, and hid his lord's money. Now after a long time the lord of those servants came, and reconciled accounts with them. He who received the five talents came and brought another five talents, saying, "Lord, you delivered to me five talents. Behold, I have gained another five talents besides them." His lord said to him, "Well-done, good and faithful servant. You have been faithful over a few things; I will set you over many things. Enter into the joy of your lord."

He also who got the two talents came and said, "Lord, you delivered to me two talents. Behold, I have gained another two talents besides them." His lord said to him, "Well-done, good and faithful servant. You have been faithful over a few things; I will set you over many things. Enter into the joy of your lord."

He also who had received the one talent came and said, "Lord, I knew that you are a hard man, reaping where you did not sow, and gathering where you did not scatter. I was afraid, and went away and hid your talent in the earth. Behold, you have what is yours."

But his lord answered him, "You wicked and slothful servant. You knew that I reap where I didn't sow, and gather where I didn't scatter. You ought therefore to have deposited my money with the bankers, and at my coming I should have received back my own with interest. Take away therefore the talent from him, and give it to him who has the ten talents. For to everyone who has will be given, and he will have abundance, but from him who has not, even that which he has will be taken away. Throw out the unprofitable servant into the outer darkness, where there will be weeping and gnashing of teeth."

Talents were units of money in the Roman Empire. The parable of *The Talents*, found in Matthew 25:14-30, points out that a wise person has initiative and does more than only attempt to conserve what he or she has. The juxtaposed images are (a) the two servants who grow their wealth and (b) the one servant who buried his wealth, with the result that it did not grow. The "unity of opposites" concerns spiritual growth: (a) making no progress and (b) making progress.

Movement toward the Kindom of Heaven consciousness is a continuous *process*, like being in a flowing river. If you are not trying to move forward, then the force of the water will take you backward. To make progress, you must always try to move forward against the current of life. You cannot coast upstream, but you can coast backwards. The *process* in this unity occurs with being active in pursuing your duty to grow spiritually, a duty which one servant did not fulfill.

Jesus is telling us that the Kindom of Heaven is about all of us pursuing our duty to God and ourselves. This pursuit means we must grow in our spirituality to the maximum extent of our ability. Not growing results in our lack of progress or even our regression, like muscles that are not exercised. In other words, we atrophy or lose our spirituality. Possibly the adage—use it or lose it—best captures the message of this parable.

Rich Fool
Jesus said, "The ground of a certain rich man brought forth abundantly. He reasoned within himself, saying, 'What will I do, because I don't have room to store my

crops?' He said, 'This is what I will do. I will pull down my barns, and build bigger ones, and there I will store all my grain and my goods. I will tell my soul, "Soul, you have many goods laid up for many years. Take your ease, eat, drink, be merry."

"But God said to him, 'You foolish one, tonight your soul is required of you. The things which you have prepared—whose will they be?' So is he who lays up treasure for himself, and is not rich toward God."

The parable of *The Rich Fool*, found in Luke 12:16-21, teaches us that we should not put off building our spirituality. The first set of juxtaposed images appears in (a) the crops of grain and (b) the goods laid up in storage. The second lies in (a) building a bigger barn for his crops and (b) neglecting to improve his soul. The "unity of opposites" shows (a) focusing on material wealth and (b) focusing on spiritual wealth. The *processes* here are (a) growing and building spiritual wealth and (b) neglecting to do so because you are too focused on growing material wealth.

Negligence is common and unfortunate. Jesus warns that neglecting to grow your spirituality is very foolish because your opportunity ends when your life ends, which can be at any moment. While you are spending time and energy tearing down and rebuilding, you are not spending time on the needful. An underlying lesson here is that we need to be ever diligent and anticipate what we will need in order not to disrupt our progress. If we neglect building spiritual wealth when we have the opportunity, we are *not* rich in what is really important as far as God is concerned.

Faithful and Wise Servant
Let your loins be girded and your lamps burning. Be like men watching for their lord, when he returns from the

marriage feast; that, when he comes and knocks, they may immediately open to him. Blessed are those servants, whom the lord will find watching when he comes. Most assuredly I tell you, that he will dress himself, and make them recline, and will come and serve them. They will be blessed if he comes in the second or third watch, and finds them so.

But know this, that if the master of the house had known in what hour the thief was coming, he would have watched, and not allowed his house to be broken into. Therefore be ready also, for the Son of Man is coming in an hour that you don't expect him.

The parable of *The Wise and Faithful Servant*, found in Luke 12:35-40, tells us that we must always be vigilant and not let our guard down. There are two stories here, one meant for the servant and one for the master. Both are about the necessity of being watchful and prepared. But being watchful for the returning lord, supposedly a positive expectation, is not the same as being watchful for a thief, a negative expectation.

The lesson in spiritual wisdom is the same for each of the stories. The juxtaposition for both servant and master concerns (a) not being prepared and (b) being prepared and watchful. The "unity of opposites" shows in (a) being alert, prepared and watchful for spiritual lessons as they come on God's schedule and (b) being inattentive, neglectful, not watchful, and not prepared to receive the lessons. The *process* is one of actively preparing for whatever lessons may come.

As in the previous parables, Jesus is saying that you do not know when the end of your life will come. You cannot afford to postpone your spiritual work for a more convenient moment. There will never be a "better" time. You must prepare yourself by developing your soul at every opportunity.

Faithful and Wicked Servant
Who then is the faithful and wise steward, whom his lord will set over his household, to give them their portion of food at the right times? Blessed is that servant whom his lord will find doing so when he comes. Truly I tell you, that he will set him over all that he has. But if that servant says in his heart, "My lord delays his coming," and begins to beat the menservants and the maidservants, and to eat and drink, and to be drunken, then the lord of that servant will come in a day when he isn't expecting him, and in an hour that he doesn't know, and will cut him into pieces, and give his portion to the unbelievers.

That servant, who knew his lord's will, and didn't prepare, nor do what he wanted, will be beaten with many stripes, but he who didn't know, and did things worthy of stripes, will be beaten with few stripes. To whomever much is given, of him will much be required; and to whom much was entrusted, of him more will be asked.

The parable of *The Faithful and Wicked Servant*, found in Luke 12:42-48, defines the behavior of the wise servant and explains why that servant is wise. The images in juxtaposition are (a) the faithful and true servants contrasted with (b) the wicked servants. The underlying "unity of opposites" is (a) knowledge with responsibility and (b) knowledge without responsibility. Spiritual development is consistent with spiritual responsibility, and the *process* is one of developing spiritually, including being spiritually responsible.

Jesus is teaching us that someone who is rich in spirituality is expected to do much good in the world. And one who is entrusted with much inner knowledge (spiritual wisdom) is expected to do much with it. President John F. Kennedy mirrored this teaching in his presidential inaugural address when he said, "Do not ask what your country can do for you but ask what you can do for your country." Jesus also said life will eventually severely punish both those who lack spirituality as well as those who know what is expected of them but still behave poorly. However, one who does not know what is expected will be less severely punished.

These five parables explain who is wise and who is foolish in several different circumstances. Together they teach us that to be wise, you need to be proactive, watchful and to anticipate what you should do in and with your life. You must grow in your spirituality to the fullest extent you can. Not growing is not an option. You must seize every opportunity to develop spirituality and not postpone your efforts because you never know when the end of life will come. Finally, if you are rich in spirituality, you are required to do much good in the world.

Message For Those Who Teach His Message

The final set of parables in this chapter concerns messages Jesus gave to guide His followers, meaning those who would communicate His teaching to others. The Gospel of Mark restates many of the parables we analyze earlier in this chapter, but in Mark, Jesus directs His teaching specifically to His disciples. He tells them what they must do and what to expect as teachers.

Notice how the meaning of the parables stays approximately the same, but with the change of audience, you hear the message differently. As in many situations, the person who hears the message tends to alter what's being heard. In other words, the hearer's role and level of consciousness filter the content. Knowledge is structured by a person's consciousness.

That the message is heard differently is in itself an important understanding worthy of consideration. Often parables have different levels of meaning; people with different levels of consciousness can peel back the layers of meaning like an onion. The listeners can hear different messages, which result in different interpretations of the parables. A higher level of consciousness permits a listener to understand the deeper, more sophisticated meanings. The better parables provide important lessons again and again because as we foster our spirituality, we are able to understand the lessons at a deeper level.

The first parable in this group is about the sower, just as it is in the Kindom of Heaven section of this chapter.

Sower, in Mark
Jesus said, "There went out a sower to sow: And it came to pass, as he sowed, some fell by the way side, and the fowls of the air came and devoured it up. And some fell on stony ground, where it had not much earth; and immediately it sprang up, because it had not depth of earth; but when the sun was up, it was scorched; and because it had no root, it withered away. And some fell among thorns, and the thorns grew up, and choked it, and it yielded no fruit. And other fell on good ground, and did yield fruit that sprang up and increased; and brought forth some thirty, and some sixty, and some an hundred."

This Sower parable, in Mark 4:3-8, is about the wisdom of preparing yourself for the *process* of spirituality so that you can maximize its usefulness to you. In contrast, the Sower parable in Matthew is about where the sower decides to spread the seed. Jesus used an obscure style of communication, much like Heraclitus, but people with a developed consciousness would more easily understand the full message in His parables. Those capable of understanding would act to incorporate the deeper lessons into their lives. However, as we point out in our discussion of Matthew's version of *The Sower*, in this particular parable Jesus did something unique. He dropped His obscure style of communication and explained His meaning in greater detail to the disciples to be sure they understood.

Mark's version of the parable presents a complex juxtaposition depicting a cause-and-effect relationship. The juxtaposition is seen in (a) seeds that fell in different places (that is, fell by the way side, fell on stony ground, fell among thorns, and fell on good ground) and (b) what ultimately happened to those seeds (that is, the fowls devoured them, plants from the seeds immediately sprang up but the sun scorched them, the thorns choked the plants, whereas the well-nurtured seeds produced an excellent yield). The "unity of opposites" resides in (a) those prepared to receive the message and (b) those who are not.

Thus the teaching of spiritual wisdom effectively involves more than the quality of the teacher. It is also about the spiritual consciousness of the audience because only "good ground" can grow a truly remarkable "crop" of spiritually developed persons. The teacher of spirituality should anticipate that not all lessons will be understood and produce the desired action in an audience, especially if those lessons fall on "poor soil."

In some situations the listeners or audience will have little depth of understanding of spiritual concepts. As a result, they will be immediately elated about what they are hearing, but have little lasting spiritual development from the lessons because they just cannot understand the lessons' depths. Those who are easily tempted by materialism will hear the spiritual teacher, but the students' material and human desires will overcome the teacher's words.

In contrast, those with a positive spiritual consciousness will not only hear but also digest the teacher's lessons. This internalizing of the lesson will produce great spiritual development within the students, and the result will be significant goodness for themselves and the world.

In sum, this parable explains the missionary strategy of Jesus for His disciples and His other teachers of spirituality. He wanted them to take His message to the world. However, He wanted them to be realistic about what they should expect.

Candle Under a Bushel
He said, "Is a candle brought to be put under a bushel, or under a bed? And not be set on a candlestick? For there is nothing hid, which shall not be manifested; neither was any thing kept secret, but that it should come abroad."

This parable, found in Luke 4:21-22, stresses the importance of living your acquired spiritual wisdom and not trying to hide it. The juxtaposition lies in (a) a candle under a bushel or bed and (b) a candle on a candlestick. This simple parable shows the "unity of opposites" in (a) knowledge that is kept hidden, not shared and (b) knowledge that is shared with others. The light stands for the message of Jesus.

The *process* of communicating the message requires the teacher not to hide the message but to teach it openly to the students. As with the light of a candle, one need not cover it up, but rather hold it high so that its brilliance radiates as much as possible for others to receive its benefit. This injunction also reinforces the teachings from other parables: namely, those who have inner knowledge and spiritual wisdom are expected to do more with it.

A third parable Jesus gave to those followers who would teach His spiritual lessons was that of *The Mustard Seed*. Notice how this parable, as explained by Luke, parallels a similar parable in the Gospel of Matthew, although the conclusions differ.

Mustard Seed, in Luke
He said, "The Kingdom of God is like the mustard seed, which, when it is sown in the earth, is less than all the seeds that be in the earth; but when it is sown, it grows up and becomes greater than all herbs, and shoots out great

branches; so that the fowls of the air may lodge under the shadow of it."

The Mustard Seed, from Luke 4:30-32, emphasizes that spiritual wisdom may seem small, but it grows into something important. The juxtaposition of images appears in (a) the tiny mustard seed and (b) the huge mature plant. Here the "unity of opposites" consists of (a) the potential of the spiritual lessons and (b) the fulfillment of the teachings.

The *process* is the maturation of spiritual development. This famous parable makes the point that the goal for teachers of spirituality is to spread the message and give refuge to those who seek it. Each lesson is relatively small, but as the student matures, the lesson will also mature within the student and become huge.

Summary Of Four Observations

Our first observation is that Jesus faced a great challenge in communicating His message to people, including His own disciples. Like those who tried to understand the Greek philosopher Heraclitus, the audiences for Jesus' message found His ideas obscure. Perhaps this difficulty was because His audiences held an undeveloped spiritual consciousness that kept them from understanding the depth of the lessons. Possibly this difficulty was also because they lacked an in-depth background in Jewish thought and Greek philosophy. Regardless of the reason, Jesus resorted to using parables to explain His ideas.

Like any good teacher who soon realizes when communication with students is not working, He moved away from the teaching method He used in the Sermon on the Mount. He discovered that parables greatly helped to get at least some of His major lessons across to His direct and indirect audiences. The eight parables He used to explain His concept of the Kindom of Heaven illustrate the revised method He came to prefer when presenting these complex teachings.

Our second observation is that His goal was to move, with the help of His spiritual teachers, as many people as possible from the Kingdom of Man to the Kindom of Heaven. The Kingdom of Man is simply a paradigm, a consciousness in which ego-and-materially-driven persons find that their impulses control their behavior as they go through the process called life.

Typically, people do not even realize they have adopted the Kingdom of Man consciousness, but occasionally some intentionally choose it. The Kindom of Heaven is a paradigm or consciousness, but it is also a *process* that one must choose to create and engage with using *freewill*. To Jesus, the Kindom of Heaven *process* means:

- Spiritual food (lessons) enables those who seek to grow and develop spiritually, especially when they engage their freewill to do so.
- People can become spiritually valuable to God, to themselves, and to others.
- Spiritual food (lessons) can raise people up and bring to them to spiritual maturity.
- People with spiritual maturity are required to be active agents in the world and use the Kindom of Heaven *process* to act with righteousness.
- The Kindom of Heaven is always there, but is hidden from some; although hidden, those that seek it can find it.
- The Kindom of Heaven is of the greatest value possible to people, but it requires them to give up that which has no value, meaning their egocentric ways and the material desires that control them.
- The Kindom of Heaven involves people gathering and then sorting out what is truly good and righteous in their life experiences.

- The Kindom of Heaven requires learning from the Torah and the new interpretations taught by Jesus in His Sermon on the Mount.

Our third observation is that Jesus was teaching us the difference between being wise and being foolish. In stressing the importance of being wise, Jesus was apparently influenced by Aristotle (384-322 BCE), who also stressed that wisdom was essential to being ethical.

To be spiritually wise, you need to be proactive and anticipate what you can and should do with your life. Wise persons grow their spirituality to the greatest extent they can. Not trying to grow spiritually is not an option for the wise because a wise person realizes that spirituality can only be developed while one is alive and that not doing so is an irredeemable waste of an opportunity. Those rich in spirituality must do as much good in the world as they can with their spirituality.

Our fourth and last observation relates specifically to those who wish to carry forth the spiritual lessons of Jesus to others. He wanted them to have realistic expectations about spreading His message. His followers should anticipate that His message would not be understood or accepted by all. However, those who did understand it would find His message significant to their lives and the lives of those around them.

Jesus also wanted His followers not to hide their spirituality, but rather to manifest it as much as possible so that others could receive its influence. Finally, He wanted to assure His followers that spreading His message might seem like a small undertaking, but that it would eventually result in many people living His message to the betterment of themselves and the whole of society.

Chapter 11

Getting Off Message

In this chapter, we argue that the message of Jesus was distorted because of His experience on the cross. Remarkably, He somehow escaped alive from His ordeal on the cross, and, to keep from being captured and placed on the cross again, He and His friends created a cover story. That story, and the imaginations of the Apostle Paul and the Roman theologians, overwhelmed Jesus' message. That original message was not understood well in His time and was certainly not understood well by what became known as Christianity.

A Speculation on the Story of the Crucifixion

We speculate that Jesus, who was also known for His miracles, pulled off a grand illusion in which He apparently died on the cross while actually surviving the ordeal. Given the danger of the illusion, we doubt if it was planned as it occurred, but that possibility exists.

A more likely possibility is that Jesus planned for the crowd at His trial to vote to release Him, but Barabbas, the criminal, was released instead. That part of the plan did not work. As a result, an alternative plan was quickly hatched to save His life. It worked, but it required Jesus to endure significant pain and suffering even though He had drugs to help Him while on the cross.

Why Jesus developed the risky plan to go to trial is not clear, but we have hints. Certainly, the opposition from the chief priests to His reform Jewish ministry was making it hard for Him to be effective among the people. Apparently, He decided to do something dramatic that would capture the imagination of the people and His disciples.

His goal was to significantly elevate His ministry to a new level of acceptance. It worked in that it did capture the attention of people and awed His disciples—the Jesus Movement rapidly grew after His time on the cross. Ironically, the plan ultimately failed during the subsequent centuries because His message was mostly ignored and replaced by something largely foreign to His intent.

If His dying on the cross was an illusion, a trick, who needed to be involved? Clearly, the disciples were not involved, or at least most of the disciples were not, given that they did not play a role in the illusion and were clearly surprised by the developments. However, the head of the crucifixion detail of Roman soldiers, Joseph of Arimathaea, Nicodemus, the "angel" in white, and possibly Simon of Cyrene probably were co-conspirators in the trick.

Judas was involved in the early stages of the scheme, but he was not aware of the final illusion, the crucifixion. This could explain his suicide after Jesus was taken down from the cross. Pontius Pilate could have been involved to some degree, given that he made some strange decisions, such as allowing the body of Jesus to be taken to a private burial site soon after being removed from the cross.

Notice what the Roman soldier, who was head of the detail, did. In earlier gospel stories, Jesus had healed the slave of a Roman centurion (Luke 7:1-10). Could the ultimate actions of the Roman head of the detail have been a payback favor? Yes, the head of the detail allowed Jesus to be mocked, stripped, scourged and beaten. But this was obviously done primarily for the benefit of the chief priests, who considered Jesus their enemy. It was not done for the Romans, who had no strong reason to consider Jesus a political criminal. While the torture and mocking were nasty and most certainly painful, they were also necessary if anyone was to believe the crucifixion was real.

To conserve Jesus' strength for the cross, the Roman head of the detail compelled Simon of Cyrene to literally do the heavy lifting and carry the cross (Matthew 27:32). The head of the detail also allowed Jesus to have some drug potion that would have helped Him deal with the pain of being on the cross. Whether He was nailed or tied to the cross is unknown, but the Romans normally lashed the wrists and feet of their victims during crucifixions.

We do know there was a verbal signal from Jesus, but the gospels conflict on the actual wording. In Matthew and Mark, He said, "My God, my God, why have you forsaken me?" (Matthew 27:46; Mark 15:34). In Luke, He said, "Father, forgive them: for they know not what they do" (23:34). In John, He said, "It is finished" (19:30). The Matthew and Mark version was probably a poor translation from the Aramaic to the Greek. We do know that the head of the detail allowed Jesus to receive a drink from a sponge and that apparently Jesus "died" immediately thereafter.

The traditional breaking of the legs did not happen, but a spear thrust into the body of Jesus did happen, possibly because one of the soldiers in the detail was not in on the "trick" or was remarkably skilled in knowing where to place the spear to avoid any vital organs.

The Roman head of the detail allowed the "expired" body of Jesus to be taken down immediately from the cross after only a few hours. Such relatively quick action was unusual as normally a body was left to rot on the cross for many days and sometimes for weeks in order to send a message to the people that Rome did not tolerate actions such as were done by the crucified. Finally, Jesus was treated with loving care instead of disrespect, as was the normal practice, and He was transported to a place where His wounds were treated immediately.

Our speculation is that this arranged illusion went well, except for possibly the spear thrust to the side of Jesus. However, even that contributed to the argument that He died on the cross. Jesus was at once treated after being taken from the cross, and later He awoke from the drugs He took while apparently being crucified. The drugs had made Him appear to be dead, and after He awoke, He found He was wrapped in linen and His wounds treated with herbs and aloe.

Within about 36 hours, Jesus' friends, of whom at least one wore white, removed the stone door. He talked with Mary Magdalene briefly, and He was taken separately to the Galilee, where He eventually met His disciples.

Could such a crucifixion illusion be staged? The fact that many live staged "crucifixions" occur every Easter without killing the actor playing Jesus implies that staging a fake death is really quite possible.

A Speculation on What Happened After the Cross

The New Testament tells us that Jesus continued to teach the disciples after His experience on the cross, and they did preach Jesus' lessons following His instructions. We do not know how long Jesus stayed in Israel, but it must have been some months because it took time for Him to heal and be ready to travel long distances. We also know that His instruction and the preaching of His followers were hugely successful in expanding the Jesus Movement.

Mark Mason in his *In Search of the Living God* speculates that Jesus left the region and the Roman Empire. Mason notes that Bishop Irenaeus (114-202 CE) of Lyons, in the western part of the Roman Empire, wrote the landmark orthodox book *Against Heresies*. The bishop stated that Jesus lived to be an old man, until at least 98 CE.

Bishop Irenaeus was an important Christian theologian with impressive ties to early Christian leaders. He was a student of Bishop Polycarp of Ephesos (also spelled Ephesus), who in turn was a student of John the Evangelist of Ephesos, who is credited with writing the Gospel of John. *Against Heresies* was a refutation of Gnosticism. Bishop Irenaeus of Lyons, along with others, created the Alpha Interpretation, building on the works of the Apostle Paul and basing it upon Paul's interpretation as to what happened to Jesus and the cover story that Paul and later Christians took as the truth.

Possibly Jesus went to Damascus as soon as He was able and lived at an Essene center nearby. (The Essenes were members of an ascetic Jewish sect in Palestine.) From there, Mason argues, Jesus developed the plan that turned Saul into Paul, as we discuss later in this chapter.

Jesus may have assumed the name of Thaddeus and gone to the Kingdom of Osrhoenians in the Parthian Empire, which was East and North of Jerusalem and included parts of what is now Northern India. If so, He stayed with King Abgarus, whom He cured from what was called an "incurable disease" by Eusebius, the fourth-century church historian. "Thaddeus" converted the kingdom to what became known as Christianity. This accomplishment marked the first conversion of an entire kingdom.

Jesus might have left that kingdom about 50 CE, upon the death of the king. The new king, the old king's son, was not as favorable toward Christianity, and there was the continuing threat by the Romans that they might invade his kingdom, a threat they eventually made good on.

Another possibility, according to Mason, is that He went to Nisibis, which is near Edessa and is now called Nusabin. After Nisibis, He went to what is now North Turkey and Kurdish territory. Still another possibility is that eventually He and His mother followed the old Silk Road west and stayed near Ephesos on the West coast of Turkey in a dwelling now named the "House of Mary," which is very close to where John, the likely author of the Gospel of John and Acts, lived. The Roman Catholic Church recognizes the house as a former residence of Mary, the mother of Jesus.

We believe, as He then moved east on the Silk Road, Jesus Christ became known as Yus Asaf, meaning "leader of the healed"; and He was also called Isa or Issa, a mispronunciation of the Syrian version of Yeshu, meaning Jesus. Mason reports that Agha Mustafai spoke of Him, as did the court poet of Emperor Akbar of India. The Emperor used two different names for Jesus, Ai Ki Nam-I and Yuso Kristo, meaning "thou whose name is Yuz or Christ." The Acts of Thomas say that in 47 CE, Jesus and Thomas were together in Taxila, which is now in Pakistan, at the Court of King Gunda. East of Taxila is now the small town of Mari.

Mark Mason says that Mary, the mother of Jesus, died on the way to India when she was around 65. Jesus was then about 49. Mason also points out that in the town of Mari, there is a grave called "Mai Mari de Asthan," meaning "the final resting place of Mother Mary." Today it is still honored by Muslims. From Mari, Mason says that Jesus traveled to Kashmir and then to other places in India.

In North India He served as a spiritual advisor to King Shalivahan and King Gopanada. The Indian name of Jesus was Youza Asaf. He was particularly revered as one of the ancient Nath Yogis of the Nath sect. One king put Him in charge of repairing the Shiva Temple atop Gopadri Hill. King Kanishka issued a coin honoring Jesus on which He is referred to as Yuzo. While still in India, Yuzo (Jesus) also spent time in Baba-Zain-un Din Walin shrine in the ancient cave of Rishis. Apparently, He was a well-respected religious leader and was associated with the Buddhist faith.

At the end of Jesus' life, which more than one source says was around age 100, He became the major force behind the fourth Buddhist council in Harwan, located in the Srinagar

District of Kashmir. This council is associated with establishing Mahayana Buddhism, which holds that everyone, not just monks and nuns, could attain Buddhahood. There is a strong parallel between attaining Buddhahood and living in the Kindom of Heaven. In the middle of Srinagar, in a building called Rozabal, meaning "the tomb of a prophet," exists the grave of Yuz Asaf with an inscription that discusses Him.

The key to the survival of Jesus was the cover story that said He died on the cross and through a miracle, God then raised Him from the dead. One New Testament passage that is quoted to assert the cover story is Matthew 12:40. It says, "For as Jonas was three days and nights in the whale's belly, so shall the son of man be three days and three nights in the heart of the earth."

Those citing this passage fail to recall that Jonas did not die but survived his ordeal, and, we maintain, so did Jesus. Nevertheless, the cover story had to be created in order to prevent Jesus from being sought by Roman authorities on behalf of the Jewish high priests and put again on the cross. Of interest is that the cover story is similar to the story of the righteous one in the Wisdom of Solomon (Scott 216).

Given the Jewish story of Elijah being taken into heaven by God (2 Kings 2:8), the cover story for Jesus not surprisingly had Him also taken into heaven. In addition, given that His mother talked about the virgin birth, the cover story about His death seemed appropriate in that one story addressed His birth and the other His death. What is important to note is that the virgin birth and crucifixion stories became an integral part of the entire story and those myths overwhelmed His message.

The Problem of Saul (Later Called Paul)

For the early Jesus Movement, there was the problem of Saul. After Jesus was on the cross, Saul became the harshest and most successful critic of Jesus and the Jesus Movement.

Our speculation is that Jesus executed a plan that turned Saul into Paul, converting His most successful critic into His most successful advocate. Jesus somehow knew from His contacts that Saul was going to Damascus on a road through territory that was very familiar to Jesus.

We speculate that Jesus set up an ambush with a flash of light probably from a mirror or an explosion. Saul was overcome with shock and fell to the ground. He heard, "Saul, Saul why do you persecute me?" Saul said, "Who are you, Lord?" Jesus said, "I am Jesus whom you have persecuted . . . ." Saul trembled with astonishment and said, "What will you have me do?" Jesus replied, "Arise, and go into the city, and it shall be told you what you must do" (The Acts 9:4-6).

A simpler explanation of Saul's conversion is that he had a psychotropic experience on the road to Damascus. Given that Saul was a zealot against the Jesus Movement, once he converted he then became zealous for the Jesus Movement. His nature was to be a zealot, whatever the cause.

Regardless of how Saul was converted, the result of his conversion was amazing. After the conversion, even his name was changed from Saul to Paul. Paul went to Damascus and other places to train in the Jesus Movement. He soon became the most successful apostle in converting others.

However, Paul was assigned to convert the Gentiles in Asia Minor and was kept away from the Jesus Movement in Israel. In fact, his letters tell us he felt he was second rate compared to the other leaders of the Jesus Movement, in spite of his remarkable success in bringing converts to what soon became Christianity.

Once, when some of the closest followers of Jesus went to Corinth to preach, a place where Paul was also preaching, Paul felt they were preaching a different message than his (Scott 102). Maybe Paul was preaching a different message that included the resurrection, and the closest followers of Jesus were not.

Jesus asked Paul to focus His ministry on the Gentiles, possibly to keep him away from the Jews and the heart of the Jewish Movement. Regardless, Paul was extremely successful. He was responsible for a very large number of Gentiles converting to Christianity, especially in Asia Minor but also in Greece and later in Rome itself.

Paul preached a message similar to the one Jesus taught, with the difference that Paul embraced the cover story as not only truth but also integral to the importance of Jesus. The cover story significantly influenced Paul and shaped his understanding of Jesus. For Paul, the resurrection was everything. Christ died for man's sins, and God brought Him back to life.

In a short time the new Gentile form of Christianity that Paul created moved away from the theology of the Jesus Movement and its original Jewish roots. The new Christianity led to the beginnings of the Alpha Interpretation by building on Paul's quotations, and it later evolved into what is today recognized as Christianity. Ironically, given that Jesus and Paul were both Jews, the Christianity that they created within a few centuries became known for its anti-Jewish discrimination.

The conversion of Saul to Paul also meant that Jesus had another important reason to leave the Galilee and the Roman Empire. Clearly, Jesus did not want Paul to realize that he was tricked or had been maneuvered or that there was an untrue cover story at the heart of the Jesus story. Saul already had proved he could be a formidable enemy, and therefore, Jesus and the Jesus Movement did not want to see a return of the old Saul. In addition, the newborn movement did not want to lose Paul because he was their best and most successful advocate, even if he did create a new teaching different from that of Jesus.

The unintended consequence of the conversion of Saul to Paul was that Christianity eventually moved even faster away from the actual message of Jesus—the Omega Interpretation. The new Christianity of the Gentiles took the cover story and interpreted it to mean that the sacrifice of Jesus on the cross had to take place to overcome man's original sin—the Alpha Interpretation. That interpretation continues to define and dominate Christianity today.

So Where Did the Alpha Interpretation Come From?

In the first, second and third centuries, Christian theologians in the Roman Empire re-interpreted the message of Jesus and the events around His life to give us what today is called Christian theology. For three hundred years there had existed at least four competing interpretations (Ebionites, Marcionites, Gnostic, and Orthodox) of Jesus' message.

Then, in the fourth century, Roman Emperor Constantine recognized and even supported the previously outlawed Christian faith, with the understanding that only one interpretation of what was the Christian faith would be acceptable. Constantine had just successfully fought a civil war, and he was not interested in any more disharmonies that might result in conflict in this newly unified empire. He convened the Council at Nicaea in 325 CE, to demand from the Christian bishops a single interpretation for Christianity.

To achieve the "consensus," Constantine attended that Council with a supporting group of Roman soldiers. The attending Christian bishops voted, and the majority of votes agreed to the Orthodox interpretation that we call here the Alpha Interpretation and that the contemporary scholar Bart D. Ehrman calls the "proto-orthodox."

The two most significant Christian groups in the first 300 years were the Gnostics and the Orthodox. The Gnostic Christians built upon theology of the Gnostic Jews from Alexandria, the city that was the intellectual capital of the Roman Empire. Building on the Genesis story, the Gnostics created a complex myth that explained why the world was essentially evil in spite of there being a loving God.

The Orthodox group, which strongly opposed the Gnostics and developed the Alpha Interpretation, was based primarily in Rome. That proved to be a great advantage in eventually defining what was to become the belief structure for Christians.

Although the cover story of the resurrection and the ascension was a lie, in the Jewish mind, then and now, telling a lie in order to save a life is not improper but merely sensible. Probably Jesus and His key followers developed the story as part of a stratagem to discourage Romans and Jewish leaders from seeking Jesus to put Him back on the cross. Starting with Paul, the lie was accepted as truth and eventually integrated into the core of the Alpha Interpretation (Orthodox). Three hundred years after Christ, it triumphed over the other interpretations ("St. Irenaeus of Lyons").

Toward the end of the second century, Bishop Irenaeus, in his role as one of the leading theologians for the Orthodox group, had fixated on the idea that he needed to create a narrative integrity between the Old and New Testament. He believed the New Testament had to complement and fulfill the prophecies of the Old Testament. With the Omega Interpretation, which we discuss in Chapter 4, such an alignment between the Old and New Testament would be impossible because it would distort Jesus' message.

In Bishop Irenaeus' version, Christ's death by crucifixion atoned for Adam and Eve's disobedience in Genesis, a defiant act that was the source of what Orthodox theologians call "original sin." The concept that atonement for past sins was possible through human sacrifice is suggested by the story of Abraham and his son. The bishop knew the story in which God asked Abraham to sacrifice his son Isaac. But God did not allow Isaac to be sacrificed, and later Abraham sacrificed a ram instead. Yet, according to Irenaeus, God sacrificed His only son Jesus for the redemption of the human race.

The reasoning of Bishop Irenaeus ignores the fact that God

did not actually allow Abraham to kill his own son. We wonder why an all-powerful God would find such a sacrifice necessary; God could merely declare the original sin was forgiven. Why should the only Son of God make a totally unnecessary sacrifice? The logic of the bishop escapes us, but this nevertheless became the accepted interpretation that defines Christianity today.

Irenaeus had at his disposal most of the gospels and other texts considered sacred. Perhaps because the Gospel of Mary, the Gospel of Thomas, and the Gnostic gospels were associated with a competing Christian group, he took strong exception to those gospels. Irenaeus and others instead built on the writings of the Apostle Paul. Paul, a devout Jew who had not known Jesus directly, said "Christ died for our sins . . ." (First Corinthians 15:3).

From Paul's words, Bishop Irenaeus concluded that Jesus died for the original sin of Adam and Eve, a sin that supposedly applied to every human because human beings had committed the first sin. Note that Irenaeus used the Greek meaning of "sin" as a "wrong" rather than Aramaic, the first language of Jesus, which used the meanings "missing the mark" and "unripe." Chapter 7 of this book, which examines the Gospel of Mary, directly addresses why this Aramaic meaning defeats any argument for original sin.

The Gospel of Mark also impressed Bishop Irenaeus with its use of the word "ransom," and the bishop concluded that Jesus was truly the only Son of God. The bishop understood that the ransom (the death of the only Son of God on the cross) was the price paid for the original sin of Adam and Eve. Bishop Irenaeus and other Orthodox leaders argued that because of Jesus' sacrifice on the cross, anyone could be saved from eternal hell and damnation if they but accepted Jesus as their savior.

Episcopal Bishop John Shelby Spong refers to this redemption as the "rescuer mentality" and notes it relates to the Jewish holy day Yom Kippur, designed to be an occasion to pray for atonement or restoration. (The concept of the scapegoat has its roots in this holy day.)

Essentially, to be Jewish meant that although you had sought forgiveness from God and those you had harmed directly during the year, there might be things you did that hurt people and of which you were unaware, had forgotten or overlooked. Therefore, you needed to atone for all your past bad acts or sins on the last day of the Jewish year in order to renew and rebuild your relationship with God for the coming year (Spong, *New Christianity* 10).

In sum, the article of faith that said Jesus' death had atoned for humankind's original sin is the consequence of Bishop Irenaeus and other Christian theologians in the Roman Empire. They taught that we no longer needed to atone or accept responsibility for our personal deeds and actions through the Jewish ceremony of Yom Kippur. Instead, they taught that we must confess our wrongs in the confessional, offer penance, and accept Jesus as our savior. Although we think Bishop Irenaeus was wrong, we easily see how he reached his conclusion. It was based on selected passages in the New Testament, his faulty understanding of the Torah, and his misunderstanding of what happened on and after the cross.

In arguing against the rescue mentality, Bishop Spong questions the underlying assumption of Bishop Irenaeus, who believed that the Garden of Eden at one time was a perfect place rather than a work in progress. But if there was no fall from perfection, then the sacrifice of Jesus could not restore something that was never lost. If we are to accept the current scientific theory of evolution, at best, the Adam and Eve story is a legend, and there never was such a perfect place.

Using the Adam and Eve story, even symbolically, to conclude there was original sin for all humankind fails logically because we must accept that a perfect place once existed. It is not reasonable to make such an assumption. If we, like Bishop Spong, challenge and do not accept the assumption that there was a perfect place called the Garden of Eden, then there logically could not be a fall from perfection into an imperfection called original sin. Thus Bishop Spong argues that the logic of Bishop Irenaeus fails, and we argue so does the Alpha Interpretation fail.

In short, early Christian theologians—Roman not Jewish—connected the story of Abraham and Isaac from the Torah to somehow conclude that Jesus was God's sacrifice for the original sin of humankind committed by Adam and Eve. Interestingly, the Jewish community disagrees and even points out that God clearly outlawed human sacrifice. Therefore, the sacrifice of God's Son on the cross makes no sense to the Jewish mind, even if it did make sense to the Roman mind of Bishop Irenaeus and others. The Romans had sacrificed humans for entertainment in the arena for centuries, so sacrifice made sense to them.

In addition, in Jewish thinking, calling Jesus "God" or "the Son of God" was another amazing theological leap of logic, but again, it was not much of a leap for the Roman mind that already called the emperor "God" and "Son of God." To Jews, there is only one God, and the Roman theologians' concept of a three-in-one God is pure invention and possibly idolatry. To the Roman mind that was used to worshipping many gods, the notion of a three-in-one-God was reasonable, and it became acceptable even into our era when the Roman Empire has long since ceased to exist.

From the New Testament, we know that Jesus did use the terms "Son of Man" and "Son of God." But a literal use of language can lead someone, especially in the Roman context that commonly used the concept for its emperors, to conclude that Jesus was saying He was the Son of God. In addition, Jesus continually spoke about the Kingdom of Man and the Kingdom (Kindom) of God. So the Alpha Interpretation was easy for the Roman mind to accept, but is increasingly difficult for the twenty-first-century mind to accept.

We believe that Jesus was well schooled in Greek and quite familiar with the Platonic concept of the ideal. To Plato, the reality of a chair was not any given physical chair but rather the ideal concept, or "form," as he termed it, of a chair. This manner of thought is difficult for today's college students taking their first philosophy course to understand and would have been nearly impossible for the average uneducated Aramaic speaker to understand. Nevertheless, Jesus was working with ideal concepts when He spoke about the Kingdom (Kindom) of God, the Kingdom of Man, Son of Man, and the Son of God.

As we explain earlier, we think His notion of Kingdom of Man and Kindom of God corresponds today to what we would call a mind-set, paradigm, or state of consciousness. For Jesus in His time, there was no parallel word in the very simple Aramaic language He used in everyday conversation and discourse.

Jesus would have been challenged to present His message to His people because His concepts were sophisticated and probably beyond the experience of almost all of His listeners. They had virtually no formal education except basic training in the Torah and the rest of what Jews today call the Jewish Bible and Christians call the Old Testament. There is the high probability that His listeners misunderstood at least some small, or even large, portions of His message.

According to Eusebius of Caesarea, who recorded early Christian history around 300 CE, the story of Jesus and His message was not set down in writing immediately but took place over several decades after His experience on the cross. In addition, the first written version of His story and message was in Greek, which is a significantly more complex and sophisticated language than the Aramaic that Jesus spoke. Hence, memory and translation errors are very probable, as are errors and intentional additions by copyists over the centuries before moveable type was invented.

To Jesus, when a person was acting with a mindset that was ego-desire centered, he was in the consciousness of the Kingdom of Man and was the Son of Man. When a person was acting with the consciousness of a loving concern for the Oneness of All, he was in the Kindom of God and was the Son or Daughter of God.

Because of His own advanced spiritual development, Jesus was almost always, and maybe always, in that Kindom of God consciousness, so, in that sense, He was the Son of God. However, so was anyone else with such a consciousness. His choice of words was merely a description of how one's mindset is expressed in thought, speech, and behavior.

Although this literal interpretation of the term "Son of God" is reasonable for the twenty-first-century mind, we reiterate that one must understand the use of the term "Son of God" in the Roman context. As we point out earlier, Roman emperors used such language to declare themselves God and above any law. Chapter 6 discusses this point in terms of Philo and his meeting with the Roman Emperor.

Christian Roman Bishops maintained that Jesus was God, and this assertion strengthened their argument in the Roman context that Jesus was of greater stature than Roman emperors. Why? They stipulated that emperors could not be God and even got Roman Emperor Constantine to agree at the Council of Nicaea. They argued that Jesus was, therefore, worthy of being worshipped, as He was more significant than an emperor.

This language was so important that it became the centerpiece of the 325 CE Council of Nicaea. The new Emperor Constantine so much wanted a consistent empire-wide religion that he surrendered all his claims regarding the honorific epithets, such as "Very God of God," "King of Kings," "Son of God," in exchange for a single uniform "Roman" Catholic dogma and a pledge of allegiance that would help keep his empire unified and at peace. Well after the fall of the Roman Empire, the Nicene Creed or something very similar is still recited in thousands of churches very Sunday.

In the Jewish context, the phrase "Son of God" was provocative. Only God was God. To imply that any human was God was fundamentally not Jewish. So when Jesus used such language speaking to His Jewish audience, He was almost asking for His enemies to misinterpret His words. A reasonable guess is Jesus used those titles to provoke His audience to think and carefully consider what the Kindom of God or Heaven really meant. Unfortunately, His use of such language was the primary charge His enemies used against Him at His trial.

The idea of the death of Jesus on the cross was central to the Alpha Interpretation of the Bible. Yet almost every detail of the resurrection of Jesus differs from one gospel to another. However, the notion that He died and rose again is a necessary component of the Alpha Interpretation with its assertion that Jesus was the willing sacrifice of God for the redemption of humankind.

Let us assume here that Jesus did not die but somehow survived the experience on the cross. If that is true, the logic of the Alpha Interpretation fails completely. Furthermore, if Jesus had survived, some of what is said in the New Testament gospels was merely a ruse to discourage the Jewish and Roman authorities from seeking Him and trying to crucify Him again.

Interestingly, after the cross experience, the closest followers of Jesus did not soon use the Alpha Interpretation. Paul was the person who preached about the death of Jesus, which was a "fact" he did not witness. That so-called fact, which was really a cover story, evolved into the critical element of the Alpha Interpretation.

As we point out in Chapter 4, clear evidence exists that Jesus did not die on the cross if you are willing to disregard the discussion of miracles and adopt a more objective perspective. First, Josephus, who wrote a history of that period, said that Jesus was alive after being on the cross, and he also discussed a situation in which several men had also survived a similar experience. Second, we know from the New Testament that Jesus Himself said He was alive after being on the cross (Luke 24:39-43).

Third, Jesus spent significantly less time on the cross than was normal for a Roman crucifixion; and fourth, the Roman guards did not break His legs, as was the normal practice. Fifth, the sponge given Him could have contained a drug that rendered him unconscious. Sixth, one or more Roman guards could have been a part of the conspiracy to save His life, as Jesus had saved the life of a Roman centurion's slave a few years earlier. Of note from the Gospel of Mark, a Roman soldier standing at the cross did say, "Truly this man was the Son of God" (Mark 15:39). This comment suggests that a Roman soldier considered Jesus to be an extraordinary person like the Emperor of Rome who held that title.

Seventh, events after the so-called crucifixion also indicate Jesus survived the cross. As we explain in Chapter 4, according to the New Testament, He appeared alive to His friends several times over the months of His recovery, and His disciple Thomas even placed his hand into the wound of Jesus (John 20:27). Eighth, the very fact that a story was created to say Jesus ascended into *heaven* cleverly refutes the story itself. How could He ascend to a place that He Himself asserted did not exist as a place? The illogic supports that He was not only alive after supposedly dying on the cross and there was no *resurrection*. Ninth, as Mark Mason suggests, Jesus recovered and eventually fled Israel to a place such as Edessa (now Urfa), just outside of the Roman Empire's eastern border. The king of that city-state had invited Jesus to come, and Jesus would have been comfortable there because the people spoke His language. There is also the possibility that He returned to India, which He perhaps had visited as a young man.

In summary, there are reasonable grounds on which to doubt the Alpha Interpretation, in spite of its extreme popularity. The Alpha Interpretation was clearly the invention of those who lived after Jesus. It was based on a highly questionable set of assumptions that some Roman theologians, centuries after the death of Jesus, used to connect the statements of the Old Testament with those of the New Testament and thereby create a unified, but erroneous, dogma. Clearly, the Alpha Interpretation is not consistent with Jewish thought, and the fact that Jesus was Jewish raises more questions about the validity of the interpretation made by the Roman Christian theologians.

The Case For the Omega Interpretation

Can we prove beyond doubt that our speculation, what we call the Omega Interpretation, is what happened to Jesus? No, but neither can the advocates of the Alpha Interpretation prove that their version of the life, death, resurrection, and ascension of Jesus is correct, especially if they use accepted scientific means or rigorous reasoning. We all have to come to our beliefs based on leaps of faith. The question is how big those leaps will be. The advantage of our version of the story is that you do not have to believe in fantastic miracles to say that it occurred.

Another advantage is that our version makes the original message of Jesus the heart and center for why Jesus should be important to us today. With the Omega Interpretation, the believers in Jesus have good reason to seek out spiritual wisdom and to use that wisdom in their lives. We think that the Omega Interpretation could influence the world to evolve spiritually, to attain a state more fulfilling for the individual and more loving and peaceful for society. We also think the Omega Interpretation is more in keeping with the original end purpose of

Jesus, which was to provide "soul food" for those who would listen and learn.

Summary

Jesus wanted to reform the Jewish faith, but unintended consequences moved humanity away from His message. He had trouble explaining His message of brotherly love in the context of Heraclitus' process philosophy. He met significant and successful opposition from the Jewish religious establishment, which considered Him its enemy.

As a result, Jesus developed a bold trick—an illusion—to awe people and motivate His disciples. The planned trick at first might have been to have the crowd excuse Him from the charges of the priests, but that failed. Possibly, at the last minute, an illusion was put together, in which He apparently died on the cross.

What is amazing and might be considered a "miracle" is that it worked, except for a nasty gash on His side. Jesus recovered, the disciples spread the word, including the cover story, with great success, and He was able to convert His fiercest critic, Saul, into His most successful critic, Paul.

However, the success of Jesus also changed His whole message in an unintended direction. As we have pointed out, He probably left the Roman Empire, moved into the Parthian Empire, and eventually settled in India. He continued His ministry, possibly using another name, focused on reforming another religion, and finally was successful in achieving religious reform. We argue that He might have eventually moved to the extreme eastern portion of the Parthian Empire, into what is now Kashmir, and participated in the fourth Buddhist reform council in North India (Ross 83).

Christianity spread quickly in both the Roman and the Parthian Empires. However, the stories of the virgin birth and Jesus' death on the cross and later ascension became the most remembered and influential aspects of His evolved story, perhaps because they were the most dramatic and defied logic.

Jesus' message of brotherly love continued, but His sacrificial death for the forgiveness of humankind's original sin became central to what was understood as Christianity. Christians came to believe that Jesus was God. They also came to believe that if a person merely said he or she believed Jesus was God, after death that person would go to a place called heaven. Jesus' message about seeking spirituality was essentially lost and buried for centuries.

The irony of this loss is enormous. Jesus was focused on His Jewish faith and was trying to improve it. What happened was that instead He inadvertently created a new religion whose followers spent hundreds of years killing and otherwise persecuting His own people. His message of brotherly love became significantly less important than the alternative Alpha Interpretation in which you needed only ask for a favor, such as passage to heaven, say Jesus was your savior, and then you would receive eternal life in a place called heaven.

Jesus' teachings became political tools for the elite who cared little about the meek whom He championed. Jesus' love for God was turned into a distortion of what God meant to Him. His preaching of self-help through extensive spiritual development became almost entirely an ATM-like religion. The revised theology of the Roman Christian theologians required little personal effort, and the result was an expanded Kingdom of Man consciousness that Jesus thought was wrong. His message was not completely lost, but the elaborate consequences of His own cover story buried that message to the point it was almost forgotten.

Part 2

The Spirituality Enigma

Chapter 12

Introduction To Spirituality

The second part of this book addresses spirituality and the compelling enigma of spirituality found in the Gospel of Thomas. As we note earlier, this Coptic (Egyptian) document was discovered in a jar along with the Gospel of Mary and many other early Christian gospels and documents in December 1945. The Gospel of Thomas is said to be a collection of 114 mostly brief sayings of Jesus Christ recorded by Didymos Judas Thomas, who is also called the Apostle Thomas.

We believe these 114 sayings constitute a complex and certainly difficult enigma that can help the reader understand spirituality from the point of view of Jesus. Clearly, someone, or several people over time, who used the name Jesus had an understanding of spirituality and were willing to share that knowledge with their contemporaries and subsequent generations.

There is no way we can firmly assert that Jesus did or did not pronounce all of the sayings, but we can note a close similarity between many of the sayings and what is written in the New Testament. We suggest the reader examine Chapters 9 and 10 of this book, including the cited quotations, to notice how parallel the New Testament is to the Gospel of Thomas discussed here in Part 2.

An enigma is a puzzle or a mystery. Most people reading the Gospel of Thomas for the first time will agree that it is a puzzling mystery. Some might disagree with our solution to the enigma; however, we do believe our interpretation should help those interested in understanding the topic of spirituality.

Chapter 12

The version of spirituality set out in Part 2 of this book flows from the Omega Interpretation discussed in Chapters 4, 9 and 10. As the reader will observe, these subsequent chapters logically complement Part 1 by explaining what Jesus meant by the term "soul food."

As we point out in Chapter 2 and other chapters, a growing trend throughout the world is for people to identify themselves as being spiritual rather than religious. We have found that many who do so share a firm conviction that they disapprove of organized religious institutions but have a wide range of ideas about what spirituality means. The next several chapters should give everyone a reasonable idea as to what a profound thinker over two thousand years ago meant by spirituality.

The purpose of the chapters in Part 2 is not necessarily to encourage anyone to be spiritual. Instead, our purpose is to help readers understand the spiritual perspective developed by Jesus, its approach to living, its core beliefs and values, and its strong relationship to early Christianity and the Omega Interpretation.

In addressing the solution to the enigma in the Gospel of Thomas, we come from an interfaith perspective. Almost every religion has a mystical or so-called spiritual wing that is disharmonious with its fundamentalist, orthodox, conservative, and traditional wings. The literatures of the mystical wings in the various religions help us to solve the Gospel of Thomas spiritual enigma.

We draw upon the spiritual knowledge of the Hindu, Jewish, Buddhist, Christian, and Islamic faith traditions. We take this approach because we find the spiritual knowledge of these five traditions to be similar, and when synthesized, they provide a richer understanding of spirituality and permit a more meaningful solution to the enigma.

We agree with Robert Wright's observation in *The Evolution of God* that most human beings are genetically "hardwired," or at least have a tendency, to believe in something some call "God." From our ancestors, who worshipped the inexplicable elements such as sun, moon, and wind, to the classical Greeks who worshipped the indifferent gods of Mount Olympus, to the Jewish people who worship Yahweh, peoples have created a theology involving one or more gods.

Nevertheless, thinking people in modern and scientific western culture find traditional religious explanations of God logically difficult and wanting. Thus the rapidly growing spiritual-but-not-religious (SBNR) movement in the early 21st century is understandable. Spirituality has become increasingly popular. Such groups as ex-Catholics, searching Protestants who are not pleased with their churches' dogma and creed, and Jews, who are dissatisfied with their orthodox and conservative beliefs, look to spirituality.

Those who use the term "spirituality" are often vague as to its meaning, and the meanings vary widely. We believe in His time, Jesus would have considered Himself to be spiritual, but He would have defined spirituality as a process that involves acquiring spiritual wisdom and living that wisdom. We think His understanding of spirituality is not only powerful but also extremely useful to those who wish to live in a better world.

The growing SBNR group often feels places of worship are more like museums than places for spirituality. These individuals are increasingly dissatisfied with religions that tell them to practice a certain way and read a particular passage on a defined day. They find their religious leaders asking them to believe impossible assertions without allowing opportunity for questioning or doubting. They increasingly feel their organized religions are no longer relevant to the lives they wish to lead.

These people want self-discovery and spiritual growth. Some have decided there is no God, while others want an individual union with the Divine. For these groups, the "I have the answer" approach, with its lack of searching and its lack of opportunity to ask tough but important questions, compounds the void with its dearth of acceptable answers about spiritual matters.

Religio, the root of the English word "religion," means to bind to the absolute and to each other in a shared vision of who we are and why we are here. Disillusioned and disaffected people from the major religions feel such bonds no longer exist and nothing is absolute.

To fulfill their yearnings, these people have turned away from their traditional religions and reached out to the mystical wing of their respective religions or explored spirituality within other religions. They intuit that they are on the edge of something significant, but spirituality is unclear to them at the rational level. They read such contemporary spiritual philosophers and popular theologians as Matthew Fox, Deepak Chopra, Eckhart Tolle, and Barbara Marx Hubbard. They feel these thinkers are part of a global transformation of universal consciousness, but still the subject remains unclear.

These disaffected persons are often in tune with the contemporary postmodern context, and the very idea of religion evokes for them a sense of empty ritual and blind adherence to precepts that are dissonant with the times. Religion, to them, is increasingly a negative activity divorced from spirituality. They are spiritual—whatever that means to them—but *certainly* not religious. It's relevant that Jesus, in the Gospel of Thomas, clearly believed in God, but He mirrored the same anti-religious views so common in the twenty-first century,

What is spirituality? Part 2 of this book attempts to answer that question using the Gospel of Thomas, but, as we point out earlier in this chapter, not only in terms of one faith tradition but with the influence of five major faith traditions together speaking to us. We approach this challenge with an awareness that the mystical wings of all traditions have created a remarkable literature that is often difficult to understand.

The reader who is a person of faith will note that we refrain from using what some call "God talk" in these chapters. Mystical language from almost all traditions is filled with such "God talk," and it often renders the spiritual wisdom particularly difficult for the less religious person to comprehend. In addition, we have discovered that "God talk" so offends non-religious persons that they often cannot digest the spiritual wisdom.

Therefore, in the spirit of Oneness with both people-of-faith and non-religious people, our presentation here minimizes such language. In that way, both sets of people can more easily approach and then understand the mystery and puzzle of spirituality with its wisdom.

The major research source for these chapters is *The Word of the Light*, which we wrote and Hara Press published (1998). The book is organized using the 114 sayings of the Gospel of Thomas that the established Christian churches consider as apocryphal. *The Word of the Light* also presents over 900 quotations, not provided in this book, from the Holy Scriptures of the Hindu, Jewish, Buddhist, Christian, and Islamic traditions.

The *Word of the Light* demonstrates the remarkably parallel, and sometimes exact, message of spiritual wisdom that exists within the cited traditions. Therefore, when reading these chapters in Part 2, knowledgeable readers from the various traditions may recognize the inspirations from their own Holy Scriptures.

Although we present our interpretation of the sayings from the Gospel of Thomas, we do encourage readers to consider their own interpretations that could be quite different from ours. While some of the sayings, and therefore the questions we pose and their answers, may seem redundant, the reader will find that, on reflection, the repetition allows a closer examination of the nuances of spirituality.

Part 2 revisits themes a second and third time to allow not only an accumulated understanding from our previous discussions and chapters but also a different focus relevant to the chapter at hand. Thus the learning process builds sequentially on earlier material while addressing the theme of the chapter.

One last observation: we found in our reading of the Gospel of Thomas that Jesus was, for His time, very spiritual but not very religious in the contemporary literal meaning of that word. Nevertheless, He does speak to issues in our century, and His sayings are worthy of our careful study.

Chapter 13

Practical Spiritual Knowledge

The purpose of this chapter is to present the practical knowledge of spirituality we believe Jesus advocated in His ministry. In so doing, we address the word puzzle called the Gospel of Thomas. The chapter focuses on the search for spirituality, ways to learn it, elements of the spiritual process, spirituality at work in the world, and the qualities of a spiritual person.

Seeking Spirituality
In terms of practical knowledge about spirituality, what is critical?

> And He said, "Whoever discovers the interpretations of these sayings will not taste death." (Gospel of Thomas, 1)*

The interpretations of these sayings are eternal and do not experience death as do living entities. However, individuals must discover the interpretations and perhaps rediscover over time the same interpretations. Spirituality is the most precious process one can experience, and it is the way of happiness, pleasure, and peace.

What should I seek? How long must I be a seeker? What will I find?

---

* The sayings from the Gospel of Thomas are drawn from our book *The Word of the Light*, which used translations from James M. Robinson, Marvin Meyer, and Bentley Layton. We recommend Meyer's book, *The Gospel of Thomas*, as the best short treatment of the Gospel of Thomas.

> **Jesus said, "Let one who seeks not stop seeking until one finds; and upon finding, the person will be disturbed; and being disturbed, will be astounded, will reign and will reign over the entirety."** (Gospel of Thomas, 2)

The first and essential characteristic of spirituality is to be a seeker of it. Spirituality holds relevance for both people of faith and non-believers. Simply trying to gain inner knowledge is the most important key to finding spirituality. It is often, and should be, associated with the Tree of Life, which is a mystical concept alluding to the interconnection of all life. Spiritual wisdom tells you that by being a seeker, you will always gain, but by not seeking, you will always lose, and thus forfeit everything.

You should seek enlightenment, the inner Self, and spiritual wisdom to discover how to live a life worth living. Enlightenment is the uncontainable and the inexpressible that neither is nor is not. The inner Self resides in your heart. You should seek to grow the inner Self, using the eternal spiritual wisdom. And finally, you should seek the most practical of all knowledge—how to live a life worth living.

If you seek spirituality, you will eventually find it; but you must continually seek as long as you have life itself. Finding it is not a matter of memorization and recitation. Spirituality is the revelation that comes from insight, which, in turn, you gain through seeking. It embraces doubt as a friend, and it allows you to understand the most ancient and newest wisdom. Once you start finding through your seeking, you have a bond with the Oneness of life that is everlasting.

When you begin finding this wisdom, it will disturb and astound you. What you will find is how limited and illusory our material world is, but you will also find the greatness of your inner being, your Self. Once you find spirituality and its spiritual wisdom, you have found the greatest wealth possible, and with it you become aware of your Self and all that life can offer you.

Where is spirituality?

> Jesus said, "If those who attack you, say to you, 'See, the kingdom is in the heaven,' then the birds of heaven will precede you. If they say to you, 'It is in the sea,' the fish will precede you. But, the Kingdom of God is inside you. And it is outside you. When you become acquainted with yourselves, then you will be recognized. And you will understand that it is you who are children of the living father. But if you do not become acquainted with yourselves, then you are in poverty, and it is you who are the poverty." (Gospel of Thomas, 3)

Spirituality, which flows from spiritual wisdom, is not a particular place or thing, but is a process that arises out of interaction between the individual and his or her environment. It arises from an individual state of self-awareness, but it is a process of consciousness and being that emanates from the wholeness we call life. Each person has his or her own life-path, and each of us is free to choose to move along that path with or without spirituality. To find the ever-growing wisdom and practical knowledge that is spirituality, we must search within ourselves. We come to comprehend it as we move along our path and interact with life.

Is spirituality linked to being self-aware?

> Jesus said, "The person advanced in days will not hesitate to ask a little child seven days old about the place of life. And that person will live. For many of the first will be last, and they will become one." (Gospel of Thomas, 4)

Spirituality is a process of self-awareness that must originate within each person but also must be manifested outside a person. If we are not self-aware, we remain in the illusionary materialistic and ego-centered world with its poverty. Common manifestations of spirituality are (1) being peaceful, restrained, and disciplined, (2) being free from the desires that rule lives, (3) being self-existent with nothing lacking, (4) having no fear of death, and (5) being aware of the totality that is Oneness.

Where do you find spiritual wisdom?

> **Jesus said, "Recognize what is before your face and what is hidden to you will become disclosed unto you. For there is nothing hidden unto you. For there is nothing obscure that will not become shown forth and nothing buried that will not be raised." (Gospel of Thomas, 5)**

The lessons or elements of spirituality, called spiritual wisdom, are always before you and only *seem* hidden from you. They are available to all of us, and the lessons come to us in many forms, including through our everyday experiences, nature, and the Holy Scriptures from all traditions. Our spiritual lessons lie in the little occurrences and lessons of daily life, but also in the more dramatic events of life.

You may not recognize those life experiences as lessons right away, but eventually you will if you remain a seeker. The lessons come to you in the form of people, faces, personalities, and other phenomenal or human characteristics in our daily experiences, but our minds have difficulty looking past the physical manifestations to their absolute permanent truth.

Our minds act to screen, filter, and prevent us from fully seeing and understanding our experiences as life's spiritual lessons. Indeed, we create our own illusions, limitations, and diversions, even as we try to understand life's lessons, including those that come from various Holy Scriptures.

What is spirituality about?

> His followers asked him and said to him, "Do you want us to fast? How should we pray? Should we give to charity? What diet should we observe?" Jesus said, "Do not lie, and do not do what you hate, because all things are disclosed before heaven." (Gospel of Thomas, 6)

Spirituality is not about what you eat or do not eat, how you pray, or what you give to charity. It is about not being controlled by lust, hatred, and folly. It is not about being perfect or not making mistakes. It is about learning lessons from our experiences through having accurate insight, liberating our minds, and being unattached to this material world or some vision of the afterlife.

Spirituality is about being truthful, being honest with yourself, and not being hypocritical. Without truth you cannot find your higher inner Self, and without full knowledge of yourself you cannot be spiritual. It is about avoiding the ultimate ignorance, which is self-deception. It is about sincerely trying to be a good and righteous person. It is about seeking to grow spiritually as an individual but within the context of interacting with others.

In spirituality, why is being human of critical importance?

> Jesus said, "Fortunate is the lion that the human will eat, so that the lion becomes human. And foul is the human that the lion will eat, and the human will become lion." (Gospel of Thomas, 7)

Only through the human rather than the animal experience can spirituality be discovered. Our minds, with their ability to comprehend, permit us to transcend, but only if they are grounded in spiritual wisdom. Both humans and animals have souls and can love, but humans differ from animals in that we have the potential to think wisely and discern. This potential for wisdom and discernment allows us to grow spiritually and reach the highest state of consciousness. To be spiritual, you must choose to use that potential by transcending your "animal body" and growing your "spiritual body."

How do I focus on the spiritually significant in my life?

> **And He said, "Humankind is like a wise fisherman who cast his net into the sea and drew it up from the sea full of little fish. Among them the wise fisherman discovered a fine large fish. He threw all the little fish back into the sea and with no difficulty chose the large fish. Whoever has ears to hear should hear!" (Gospel of Thomas, 8)**

This question requires a three-part answer. First, you must realize that life continuously teaches each of us many lessons. Second, your many lessons are happening simultaneously. Therefore, you must release the lesser lessons and focus on the lesson that is most significant to you in terms of your greatest potential growth in spirituality. Third, you must treasure the significance of the lessons you receive with deep and abiding inner joy for what they bring.

How should I prepare myself to best make use of life's lessons?

> **Jesus said, "Look, the sower went out, took a handful of seeds, and scattered them. Some fell on the road, and the birds came and pecked them up. Others fell on rock, and they did not take root in the soil and did not produce heads of grain. Others fell on thorns, and they choked the seeds and worms devoured them. And others fell on good soil, and it brought forth a good crop:**

Practical Spiritual Knowledge

It yielded sixty per measure and one hundred twenty per measure." (Gospel of Thomas, 9)

Beyond recognizing life's lessons, you should see them as opportunities and be grateful for them. If you are to grow from those lessons to the maximum extent, you need to receive those lessons without emotion, free of anger, without silliness, and free of desire. This receiving of lessons should occur regardless of whether the experiences that bring the lessons are happy, sad, inconvenient, or even painful. People's abilities and dispositions naturally limit their growth, but the wiser among us try to maximize our capacity and center our dispositions to take full advantage of spiritual opportunities. Do *not* (1) squander, dissipate, or diffuse those lessons; (2) close your senses or your heart to those lessons; and most importantly, (3) stop or retard your spiritual growth.

How should I approach those opportunities and challenges?

Jesus said, "I have thrown fire upon the world, and look, I am watching it until it blazes." (Gospel of Thomas, 10)

As you grow spiritually, you need to know that life's opportunities and challenges change you and what you see in the world around you in very significant ways. Growing spiritually can separate you from some members of your family, friends and associates because it redefines you as a spiritual person in ways that can differ from the values and desires of non-spiritual persons.

Life's opportunities and challenges will include periodic tests that refine and clarify your understanding of earlier lessons. You need to see your life as a set of continuous learning experiences that are not easy to comprehend, may seem strange, require all your senses to be alert, and continually change you. You should not fear these changes but recognize and embrace them.

What will you do with your spirituality?

> Jesus said, "The heaven will pass away; and the one above it will pass away. The dead are not alive, and the living will not die. During the days when you are what is dead, you made it alive. When you are in the light, what will you do? On the day when you were one, you became two. But when you become two, what will you do?" (Gospel of Thomas, 11)

Because of your acquired spirituality, your former religious understandings will pass away, as will your prior understanding of God. You will see past your temporal illusions and comprehend permanent truths. As you become spiritual, you will discover you are living in two worlds at once: the finite material and the infinite spiritual. The important question is: What will you do with this new spirituality you have acquired?

Learning Spirituality
What are the characteristics of someone who can teach me spirituality?

> The followers said to Jesus, "We know that you are going to leave us. Who will be our leader?" Jesus said to them, "No matter where you are, you are to go to James the Just, for whose sake heaven and earth came into being." (Gospel of Thomas, 12)

One characteristic of spiritual teachers is that they are extraordinarily righteous in character (also see question and answer 45 in the next chapter, and see Chapter 10). Such teachers serve others, understand the temptations of life, willingly teach the young, avoid power struggles, and appreciate the wise ones who came before them. Such teachers are capable of praising others, are impeccable in their actions, controlled, intelligent, insightful, ethical, and are always composed. Such persons guide, restore the students' souls, lead them toward righteousness, give comfort in times of trouble, prepare them for troubled times, and applaud them when they are successful.

How should I deal with all that I can and should learn?

> Jesus said to his followers, "Compare me to something and tell me what I am like."
>
> Simon Peter said to him, "You are like a just messenger." Matthew said to him, "You are like a wise philosopher." Thomas said to him, "Teacher, my mouth is utterly unable to say what you are like."
>
> Jesus said, "I am not your teacher. Because you have drunk, you have become intoxicated from the bubbling spring that I have tended." And he took him, and withdrew, and spoke three sayings to him.
>
> When Thomas came back to his friends, they asked him, "What did Jesus say to you?"
>
> Thomas said to them, "If I tell you one of the sayings he spoke to me, you will pick up rocks and stone me, and fire will come from the rocks and consume you." (Gospel of Thomas, 13)

Spirituality is about acquiring inner knowledge, called wisdom, when you are ready to receive it. The source of inner knowledge is your life, and although this wisdom can grow within you only incrementally, ultimately it is potentially infinite. For each of us, life with its lessons is everywhere and is in everything: it is infinite and, therefore, impossible to explain fully with words. However, just because words cannot explain life and its spiritual wisdom completely and we cannot fully understand life, that does not mean we cannot benefit from even a little of its spiritual wisdom.

Will others know that I am spiritual?

> **Jesus said to them, "If you fast, you will bring sin upon yourselves, and if you pray, you will be condemned, and if you give to charity, you will harm your spirits.**
>
> **"When you go into any region and walk through the countryside, when people receive you, eat what they serve you and heal the sick among them. For what goes into your mouth will not defile you; rather, it is what comes out of your mouth that will defile you." (Gospel of Thomas, 14)**

Physical appearances, gestures of devotion, and rituals such as fasting, prayer, or even giving to charity do not define a spiritual person. Your words and actions toward others show your commitment to spirituality. A person lives spirituality because it is a mindset, a consciousness, an attitude one can adopt only with discipline and self-control.

Having pureness of heart and loving unconditionally are how we manifest spirituality. It can be seen when one does good deeds without seeking reward or recognition. Spirituality is not proselytizing or trying to convince others, but rather demonstrating your belief by living it. Spirituality is also accepting generosity without question from the heart of others.

Not letting outside events disturb your inner peace is also an expression of spirituality. Spiritual persons are thoughtful about what they say and do. They confidently live their spirituality by their own standards. They do not wait for others to define it by their standards.

Spiritual persons do not scorn others or act proudly. They know that their inner being correctly motivates their actions. Spiritual persons also know that their positive relationships with life are critical if they are to have personal fulfillment. They behave in life-supporting ways, and in every manner possible, they demonstrate a universal and unconditional love for all creation and all things.

As a spiritual person, how do I deal with others about the subject of God?

Jesus said, "When you see one who was not born of woman, fall on your faces and worship. That is your father." (Gospel of Thomas, 15)

A spiritual person realizes that trying to fully understand and explain a concept as infinite as God is impossible, but being human, we commonly wish to do so. A spiritual person accepts that various peoples have projected themselves and their culture into their understanding of God and the dogma related to that understanding.

Thus discussing God objectively becomes remarkably difficult, if not impossible. As a result, spiritual people learn to experience their life lessons internally. Furthermore, they comprehend the futility of trying to express any explanations of God.

As a spiritual person, how should I view life's conflicts and challenges?

> Jesus said, "Perhaps people think that I have come to impose peace upon the world. They do not know that I have come to impose conflicts upon the earth: fire, sword, war. For there will be five in a house: There will be three against two and two against three, father against son and son against father, and they will stand alone." (Gospel of Thomas, 16)

While on your spiritual path, realize that your closest loved ones may become your strongest enemies in your quest for spirituality. Each soul's path, regardless of status or position, has its own hardships and conflict from unexpected directions, but every person can prevail if he or she has patience and diligence. One should view conflicts and challenges as opportunities in which significant spiritual learning can take place.

What is life's perfect gift?

> Jesus said, "I shall give you what no eye has seen, what no ear has heard, what no hand has touched, what has not arisen in the human heart." (Gospel of Thomas, 17)

Life helps us grow spiritually, and with that growth, we become our own gift, which is as perfect as we can become, to others and to ourselves. This gift of life is far more valuable and precious than all the treasures of the universe. With our developed inner awareness, life allows us to see more deeply and live more completely with greater and more profound understanding.

The Spiritual Process
What are the beginning, middle, and end of spirituality?

> The followers said to Jesus, "Tell us how our end will be." Jesus said, "Have you discovered the beginning, so that

you are seeking the end? For where the beginning is, the end will be. Fortunate is one who stands at the beginning: That one will know the end and will not taste death." (Gospel of Thomas, 18)

The beginning of the spiritual process is our seeking to understand the mysteries of life, a seeking which often begins when we sense and care about the existence of suffering. The middle of the spiritual process is when life gives us lessons, which many of us will ignore or not even notice. The end of our path and final end of our quest for spirituality is our full and complete self-realization that everything is One, and the One is life itself.

What are the sources of spiritual nourishment?

Jesus said, "Blessed is the person who existed before coming into being. If you exist as my disciples and listen to my sayings, these stones will minister unto you.

"Indeed you have five trees in paradise which do not move in summer or winter, and whose leaves do not fall. Whoever is acquainted with them will not taste death." (Gospel of Thomas, 19)

There are five sources of spiritual nourishment. First is the seeking, which we discuss earlier in the chapter. In addition, understanding the importance of doubt and the limitations of faith are of corollary importance. Second is increasing self-awareness and the realizations it gives us. Third is the mind, which must be stilled so that we can see, hear, and understand the lessons. Fourth is life with all its lessons, which together are the Tree of Life. Fifth is our struggle to understand and discern what is good and evil, while using our hearts to love everything.

How does spirituality grow within me?

> The followers said to Jesus, "Tell us what heaven's kingdom is like."
>
> He said to them, "It is like a mustard seed. It is the smallest of all seeds, but when it falls on prepared soil, it produces a large plant and becomes a shelter for birds of heaven." (Gospel of Thomas, 20)

Spirituality starts through the smallest bit of self-awareness and grows rapidly if a person has a strong desire to seek. It can eventually produce a great person who, in turn, can become a source of peace and enlightenment for many. Your inner Self, which is the product of your spirituality, begins in your heart. The inner Self grows not only a healthy love of self but also extends that love to the Oneness some call the universe. The inner Self, through the process of spirituality, grows and develops within you. It works in harmony with your pure and clear mind, filtering out ego and materialism, which cloud your perceptions of the world.

What are students of spirituality like?

> Mary said to Jesus, "What do your disciples resemble?"
>
> He said, "What they resemble is children living in a plot of land that is not theirs.
>
> "When the owners of the land come they will say, 'Surrender our land to us.'
>
> "They, for their part, strip naked in their presence in order to give it back to them, and they give them their land.

> "Thus I say that the owner of an estate, knowing that a bandit is coming, will keep watch before the bandit comes and not let the bandit break into the house of his kingdom and steal the possessions. You, then, be on your guard against the world. Arm yourself with great power lest the brigands find a way to get to you; for the trouble that you expect will come. Let an experienced person dwell in your midst!
>
> "When the crop had matured, that person came in haste, sickle in hand, and harvested it. Whoever has ears to hear should listen." (Gospel of Thomas, 21)

Serious students of spirituality have a childlike innocence that shows an unawareness of their challenging circumstances or the potential possibilities of their opportunities. But they are willing to learn when confronted by their mistakes. They need to acquire a quality of watchfulness so that they can maintain and grow their spirituality. Without it, excessiveness, laziness, and weakness can easily overwhelm them to the point that they lose their self-awareness and are overcome by worldly desires.

A true student of spirituality must recognize the traps of life and remain on guard at all times because some misdeeds cannot be reversed. Students must also realize that their opportunities to grow stop with death. Only life provides opportunities for spiritual growth. Thus serious students do not procrastinate but maximize such opportunities to achieve the greatest spiritual growth possible during their lifetimes.

If I am to become completely spiritual, what must I be like?

> Jesus saw some babies nursing. He said to His followers, "These nursing babies are like those who enter the kingdom."

> They said to Him, "Then shall we enter the kingdom as babies."
>
> Jesus said to them, "When you make the two into one, and when you make the inner like the outer and the outer like the inner, and the upper like the lower, and when you make male and female into a single one, so that the male will not be male or the female be female, when you make eyes in place of an eye, a hand in place of a hand, a foot in place of a foot, and image in place of an image, then you will enter the kingdom." (Gospel of Thomas, 22)

You must make two into One without diminishing either by thinking in terms of the "unity of opposites" (see Chapter 5). Without this view you are left with dualism, but with this view you see two as One. When you do so, you become One, and this "unity of opposites" means the inner is no longer the inner and the outer is no longer the outer. Instead, the two are part and parcel of a unity; and in achieving unity, you have reached and entered the Kindom of Heaven.

Your actions and words must be like your inner Self: free of human divisions and reflecting a consciousness totally changed to that of Oneness. You must follow the middle path. Namely, you must have the right view, right thoughts, right speech, right action, right livelihood, right effort, right mindfulness, and right consciousness. This middle path gives you vision, which gives you knowledge, which leads to calmness, insight, and eventually to your enlightenment.

Can spirituality be universal in humankind?

> Jesus said, "I shall choose you, one from a thousand and two from ten thousand, and they will stand as a single one." (Gospel of Thomas, 23)

Everyone can be spiritual, but to be spiritual a person must choose to be so freely, and few will do that. Few will be spiritual because, although life sends its spiritual lessons, most will never see or hear them. Many who do see or hear will not understand the lessons. Many who do understand will not want to exert the discipline required or will simply prefer to let the world of physical desire control them. So, ultimately, only a few will ever fully participate and live the process called spirituality. Those who do will stand as a single One.

Where do I place my acquired spirituality?

> His disciples said, "Show us the place where you are, for we must seek it."
>
> He said to them, "Whoever has ears should listen! There is a light existing within a person of light. And it enlightens the whole world: And it does not enlighten, if it is darkness." (Gospel of Thomas, 24)

Individuals must always center the spiritual process within themselves, and that spirituality enlightens the whole world. Individuals must also cultivate and grow their hearts so that the process of spirituality becomes part of their entirety. That expanding spirituality must replace all non-spiritual attributes, such as malice, jealousy, greed, and so on. Spirituality does not grow in individuals simply because they declare they are spiritual; it comes into existence through their sincere daily actions that bear witness to it and create it.

How do I manifest my spirituality?

> Jesus said, "Love your brother like your soul, protect that person like the pupil of your eye." (Gospel of Thomas, 25)

You start to manifest your spirituality by loving and protecting your spiritual brothers and sisters. Spirituality becomes real with the process of co-creation. Life's lessons give you insights, and you use them to shift your mindset to one of loving. That is the beginning, but you also need to move your feelings of love to others by not hating anyone and by renouncing any selfish attitude within yourself. When you adopt a more detached but loving approach to life, everything looks different because your appreciation of all things and all people changes dramatically.

Is spirituality a matter of focusing on human limitations?

> **Jesus said, "You see the speck that is in your brother's eye, but you do not see the beam that is in your own eye. When you take the beam out of your own eye, then you see clearly to take the speck out of your brother's eye." (Gospel of Thomas, 26)**

Spirituality grows by first noticing and dealing with your own faults and then noticing the human limitations of others. Most of us are quick to see even the smallest faults in someone else's behavior while never detecting our own. Spirituality requires shifting your focus to your faults and making the necessary reforms within yourself. Once you are free of at least your major faults, if not most of them, then you are in a position to see the limitations of others and possibly help them. If you are spiritually wealthy, meaning you are advanced in your spiritual process, you have a responsibility to pardon and forgive the problems and shortcomings of others, especially if they are subordinates or those entrusted to your care.

Must I take seeking spirituality quite seriously?

> Jesus said, "If you do not fast unto the world you will not find the Kingdom of God. If you do not make the Sabbath a Sabbath, you will not behold the father." (Gospel of Thomas, 27)

Seeking spirituality is about not letting worldly desires control you. It is also about making a conscious commitment to grow spiritually and live a spiritual life. This is a serious undertaking, but also a source of great joy. Religious rituals and other religious acts have the purpose of inspiring us and keeping us focused. They can help in not letting worldly desires control or overwhelm us. However, they are not enough, and if not done seriously, may even be dysfunctional.

Such activities focus our energy on the daily flux of the world and may even distract us from learning and living the spiritual lessons given by life. Ideally, when we are spiritually committed, every moment of our lives is a Sabbath and every breath we take is a meditation. Our daily actions and our gratitude are our true gifts to life.

Getting Spiritual
When will humanity become spiritual?

> Jesus said, "I stood at rest in the midst of the world. And unto them I shown forth incarnate; I found them all intoxicated. And I found none of them thirsty. And my soul was pained for the children of humankind, for they are blind in their hearts and cannot see. For, empty did they enter the world, and again empty they seek to leave the world. But now they are intoxicated. When they shake off their wine, then they will repent." (Gospel of Thomas, 28)

People will turn to spirituality when they realize that their egos and desires for the material things of life control them and others around them. As long as humanity is focused on the material world, it has no thirst for, nor sees any value in, spirituality. People will discover spirituality when they realize that the systemic deficiencies, such as those found in human relationships, politics, and business, and the problems they experience in their lives, arise from unhealthy egos, desires, and materialism.

When this realization occurs, they will develop beyond seeing life as a set of problems or challenges created by unmet desires and ego gratification. People will begin to realize that (a) the world their minds create is impermanent; (b) this impermanent world contains the seeds of suffering; (c) their own minds are the source of most of their confusion; (d) and their own bodies and their worship of materialism are where their problems reside. When humanity makes these realizations, humanity will become spiritual.

Given that assessment, is it not amazing to see any spirituality in the world?

> **Jesus said, "It is amazing if it was for the spirit that flesh came into existence. And it is amazing indeed if spirit (came into existence) for the sake of the body. But as for me, I am amazed at how this great wealth has come to dwell in this poverty." (Gospel of Thomas, 29)**

Yes, to find spirituality in a world dominated by materialism, egoism, and desire is surprising, but it exists. Remarkably, life uses humanity's materialism, ego, and desire to provide spiritual lessons that, with love, transform some individuals into spiritual beings. Thereby life assures there will be at least some meritorious self-controlled people receptive to spirituality.

What should I identify with when I am spiritual?

Jesus said, "Where there are three, they are godless. And where there is one alone, I say that I myself am with that one. Lift a stone and you will find me there. Split a piece of wood, and I am there." (Gospel of Thomas, 30)

When you are spiritual, life becomes part of you, and you identify with everything. There is no separation between you and *any*thing and *every*thing else. Given that there are always a few who are spiritual among us, a debate on unity and duality will always continue. Rather than engage in this debate, you are wiser merely to point out that life's lessons are always present in the events of the day, and the words of the spiritually wise are always available. However, you must realize that when someone assumes life is anything less than everything, that person merely lacks the spiritual understanding that separations and divisions in life are only illusions.

Why do people have difficulty in seeing the wise among them and profiting from their wisdom?

Jesus said, "A prophet is not acceptable in the prophet's own town; a doctor does not heal those who know the doctor." (Gospel of Thomas, 31)

Wisdom comes with many different forms and faces. Yet, we often cannot believe or honor spiritual wisdom if it comes from a familiar face. Why? Most people are ego-and-desire-driven, so they cannot believe anyone can be unlike them, such as the wise. Unless people are spiritual, in some small measure, they cannot fully appreciate the accomplishment of someone who is spiritually wise and cannot gain from the teaching of a wise one.

Will spirituality help me meet the challenges of life that will come to me just because I am trying to be spiritual?

> **Jesus said, "A city built upon a high hill and fortified cannot fail, nor can it be hidden." (Gospel of Thomas, 32)**

With spirituality, you will have a firm basis to deal with life's challenges. For example, people who are not spiritual might confront, challenge and even assault you. Their minds are focused on desire and ego, and they see and hear differently from you. They may feel challenged and threatened by you and be unable to accept the views of someone spiritual. But you cannot hide the fact that you are spiritual because they will sense it. They cannot escape from their behavioral realities of being ego and materially driven that determine who they are, just as you cannot deny your spiritual wisdom. Thus you will always be subject to challenges from them, but you will always be able to meet their challenges with your spirituality.

Can I hide my spirituality from others?

> **Jesus said, "What you hear in your ear, proclaim upon your rooftop into some else's ear. Indeed, no one lights a lamp and puts it under a vessel, nor puts it in a hidden place. Rather, it is put on a lamp stand so that each who enters and leaves might see its light." (Gospel of Thomas, 33)**

As a spiritual person, you can never hide who and what you are. It is obvious to others that you are a different type of person. For example, because of spirituality, you become even more aware of the suffering and hardship of others, and you must act out of love for them because that is who you have become. If you are spiritual, you cannot hide or deny it because spirituality does not exist unless it is lived, and living requires thoughts, words and deeds that demonstrate its meaning to those around you. You do not need to brag about it, for if you do, you will have lost it.

Should I have a spiritual teacher?

> **Jesus said, "If a blind person leads a blind person, both of them will fall into a hole." (Gospel of Thomas, 34)**

We need teachers, mentors and guides, but we must choose our teachers wisely. If your teacher is not well-developed spiritually, he or she will not only fail to teach spirituality but will also cause your spiritual growth to regress. If you wish to learn spirituality, you must select your teacher not by his or her agreeable personality but by his or her egoless wisdom. The true teacher provides a path of learning but requires you to walk down that path yourself because learning is not an event but a process requiring your active participation. An acceptable teacher will let you know when you have learned everything that teacher can teach you and when it is time to move on to your next teacher.

Spiritual Qualities
Are resolve and forethought essential qualities for learning spirituality?

> **Jesus said, "No one can enter the house of the strong and wreck it without first tying that person's hands. Thereafter, one can overturn the person's house." (Gospel of Thomas, 35)**

Indeed, *resolve and forethought* are essential qualities needed to learn spirituality. Other essential qualities include being able to reject ignorance and desires for the material world. Even the strongest of people can find resolve and forethought difficult to achieve and even more difficult to maintain. Often they find they are divided within themselves. Resolve and forethought come from self-awareness and self-realization, which start with the very act of breathing. You overcome the vital physical world with discipline, concentration, and extensive preparation, but you also do it with the assistance of those around you.

Is vanity one of the qualities I should try to overcome?

Jesus said, "Do not worry, from dawn to dusk and from dusk to dawn, about what food you will eat, for what clothing you will wear." (Gospel of Thomas, 36)

Vanity, involving food, clothing, position, and status symbols, seriously hinders achieving spirituality. You cannot gain spirituality from outer manifestations of custom, desire, or security. Spirituality is about the infinite and is not gained from the finite. However, your consciousness in dealing with the finite determines how you grow in the infinite of spirituality.

Should I be ashamed of my position in life?

His followers said, "When will you appear to us and when shall we see you?"

Jesus said, "When you strip without being ashamed and you take your clothes and put them under your feet like little children and trample them, then you will see the child of the living one and you will not be afraid." (Gospel of Thomas, 37)

When you fully comprehend life, you cannot be ashamed or embarrassed about being spiritual. In liberating yourself from desires that drive you, you liberate your mind from the bondage of your emotions. You become as free and happy as the little children whose joys are rooted in the depth of their souls and radiate outwardly. Spirituality needs to be approached with innocence that transcends the world of ego and desire, the world of anger and revenge. If you liberate yourself in this way, then you start understanding the meaning of life, and you exude an inner confidence of who and what you are.

Will there be times that I do not understand life's lessons?

Jesus said, "Often you have desired to hear these sayings that I am speaking to you, and you have no one else from whom to hear them. There will be days when you will seek me and you will not find me." (Gospel of Thomas, 38)

Life will not always provide you the lessons when you want or expect them, primarily because you will have difficulty hearing them above the chatter of your mind. Every human mind is limited to some extent, but with patience you will find the lessons come. You may have trouble hearing the lessons at first because you are too involved with your daily concerns. Realize that life, which is providing your lessons for growth, is something that moves at its own pace. Patience, diligence and perseverance will be necessary on this journey.

Are religious leaders and scholars teachers of spirituality?

Jesus said, "The Pharisees and the scribes have taken the keys of knowledge and have hidden them. They have not entered, nor have they allowed those who want to

enter to do so. As for you, be as shrewd as snakes and as innocent as doves." (Gospel of Thomas, 39)

Seldom will religious leaders and scholars prove to be good spiritual teachers; too often they are ego-driven and unable to control their desires. Also some religious leaders deliberately withhold spiritual teachings because of their personal agendas for professional advancement, material status, dogma, and protection of their jobs, pensions or sectarian positions. Scholars also often spin and misrepresent spiritual lessons to suit their own academic agendas.

Therefore, for purposes of spirituality, approach religious leaders carefully. Analyze their actions and not just their words. And approach scholars by looking at the quality of their research and the dogma that they may be serving. Ultimately, life itself is your guide to spirituality, and only you can grow your own spirituality. Do so by being mindful of the lessons, and be guided by your own loving heart.

A Summary of the Spiritual Process

Jesus saw spirituality as something highly practical for anyone who wished to live the good life. His message taught us how to discover spiritual wisdom by using the spirituality process and then applying that wisdom to better live our lives. To Jesus, spiritual wisdom is the nourishment of the soul. It feeds your inner being so that you can nurture and increase your accumulated spirituality and rise above your mere animal instincts. Spirituality is not a set of rules or even a list of virtues; it is a process of inquiry and a higher consciousness resulting from that process of inquiry.

The spiritual process is something each person can find and apply but only with the use of *freewill*. The process is an activity over time that permits a person to transcend the illusionary and finite material world. The person then sees and understands that infinite wisdom can govern and influence actions and behavior. Spirituality is *both* a process found and created within, *and* a lived mindset or consciousness. It is not about traditional activities associated with organized institutional religions. It is something only humans can accomplish because humans have the ability to discover and discern at abstract levels of thinking. Spirituality is the most valuable gift life gives each of us, but we must actively and freely choose to accept and apply it in our lives.

You can learn spiritual wisdom and thus grow your spirituality. However, as you learn, you will be changed. One is wise to have a spiritual teacher, but good ones are rare. If you are successful at seeking spirituality, a change will occur in your heart, and you will find that you start loving others unconditionally but not naively. You will discover deep and abiding inner peace.

However, you will also discover some topics, such as God, cannot be explained very well, if at all, to those who are ego, desire-, or materialistically-centered. Normally you should avoid such topics, except in your communications with more advanced spiritual persons. As you become more spiritual, you will discover that your former friends and often your relatives will not accept you and may try to change you back to your old ways.

With spirituality you will have a better understanding of the mysteries of life, particularly the self-realization that everything, including yourself, is part of the One. Your ego-driven self will disappear. Your life will become a journey of continuing discovery because of your new self-awareness and realizations. You will appreciate that the "unity of opposites" applies to everyone and everything.

You will accept that far more people in the world are not spiritual. Nevertheless, you will know that there are people who are spiritual, and their numbers can increase if still others wish to learn and avail themselves of proper training. Such training teaches spiritual wisdom through the process of spirituality.

Part of spirituality is using your developed heart and learned spiritual wisdom in relations with others. This part of spirituality starts with noticing your own faults and developing and implementing a strategy to eliminate them. This removal of your faults is especially pertinent when it comes to not letting worldly desires control you.

An important note to those who are spiritual: you cannot and should not hide your spirituality because it will help you deal with life's challenges. In addition, your actions and behavior will serve as role models to those who also might wish to become spiritual. Nevertheless, because you do not hide it, you can count on the fact that some people without spirituality will make it their business to confront and challenge you.

If you are spiritual, you will have certain needs and qualities. You will need strong resolve and forethought to reject ignorance and desires for the material world. You will escape vanity because fancy clothes, position, and status will mean little to you. You will be liberated from the bondage of your emotions. You will appreciate that you will not always understand life's lessons. And you will know that religious leaders and scholars are typically not the best teachers of spirituality.

Chapter 14

Discerning Between Good and Evil

This chapter explains the role of spirituality in discerning between good and evil. Most of us are aware of good and evil even if we disagree on what is good and what is evil. However, discerning the difference is a challenge. This chapter helps us determine one from the other, including knowing what to avoid and what to acquire. It also examines ways to recognize the attributes of discernment and how to make ethical decisions.

How to Discern
Where does our understanding of how to discern good from evil come from?

> Jesus said, "A grapevine has been planted outside the father. And because it is not sound, it will be plucked out by the root and will perish." (Gospel of Thomas, 40)

Our ability to discern good from evil emanates from life, and life emanates from Oneness. All life is interconnected, and all life is contained in everything. It is simultaneously infinite and granular. Yet most of us discern between good and evil by applying a much lower standard that separates us from the Oneness. For example, we commonly distinguish good from evil based on (a) using our senses, such as wanting pleasure; (b) using our minds, such as following rules; or (c) using our ego, such as furthering our power or wealth.

Thus we separate ourselves from the interconnectedness of life by limiting ourselves to our senses, our minds, or our egos. In doing so, we limit our search for a standard in judging what is good and evil. We fail to look to virtuous people and the lessons they can teach us. However, as we grow in spirituality, we shift to the standard of Oneness, meaning the interconnectedness of life, and we reach out to what life teaches us and use that to discern good from evil.

What is the source of the knowledge of good and evil?

Jesus said, "Whoever has something in hand will be given more, and whoever has nothing will be deprived of even the little that person has." (Gospel of Thomas, 41)

The source of the knowledge of good and evil is the spirituality that life and our self-awareness reveal within us. The ability to determine good from evil increases within the person who grows and acts with spirituality. That ability diminishes within the person who has little or no spirituality. Those who vigilantly and enthusiastically gain in spirituality also gain in discernment, and those who neglect their spiritual growth are essentially unable to make such discernment.

How should I avoid evil?

Jesus said, "Be a passerby." (Gospel of Thomas, 42)

Because of life, you are in the world, but you do not have to be caught in its ego and material attachments. You should approach worldly matters by appreciating that life presents to you an illusion; however, you must look past it and not be taken in. Although you live in the illusion, you must allow life's lessons to nourish your spiritual growth. Be a passerby to its desires and material focus. This does not mean you are indifferent to others. On the contrary, you must still engage in life with compassion. Allow its lessons to guide and inspire you, but also allow yourself to feel its love.

How do I recognize who is telling me useful information about good and evil?

> **His followers said to him, "Who are you to say these things to us. You do not know who I am from what I say to you. Rather, you have become like the Jewish people, for they love the tree but hate its fruit, or they love the fruit and hate the tree." (Gospel of Thomas, 43)**

You cannot know someone is giving you useful information about good and evil solely by what he or she says. A person's judgment about good and evil is a function of the maturity of the inner Self that flows from spiritual wisdom. By living the consequences of their actions in life, the spiritually-wise learn that being good begets more good, and conversely, being evil begets even more evil. Good and evil actions are self-reinforcing.

As Karmic law and Newtonian physics explain, every action produces a reaction. Learning discernment between good and evil comes from studying with spiritually-developed people. Such people have defined virtues and developed codes of conduct for living spiritual lives.

What is a common critical mistake in discerning between good and evil?

> **Jesus said, "Whoever blasphemes against the father will be forgiven, and whoever blasphemes against the son will be forgiven, but whoever blasphemes against the**

> **Holy Spirit will not be forgiven, either on earth or in heaven." (Gospel of Thomas, 44)**

A common mistake seekers make is cutting themselves off from life and the spiritually-wise. But a worse mistake is cutting themselves off from their essence as a spiritual being. Cutting yourself off from life with its lessons of spiritual wisdom and from the spiritually-wise is a mistake because it radically reduces progress in your spiritual process, even though you can nevertheless still make discernments. However, renouncing your inner Self is a critical mistake. If you do not accept that you have an inner Self or you refuse to listen to its small voice of reason within, it cannot guide you in deciding what is good and what is evil. Without acknowledging your inner essence, you will not be able to discern between good and evil.

From where within me does the discernment between good and evil come?

> **Jesus said, "Grapes are not harvested from thorn trees, nor are figs gathered from thistles, for they yield not fruit. A good person brings forth good from the storehouse; a bad person brings forth evil things from the corrupt storehouse in the heart and says evil things. For from the abundance of the heart this person brings forth evil things." (Gospel of Thomas, 45)**

The discernment between good and evil comes from the spiritually-developed heart. Such a heart loves everything, is righteousness (see Sayings 12 and 46, as well as Chapter 10), and is the storehouse of knowledge from which one can tell good from evil. People who are especially good are filled with awe from life and have stored in their hearts the spirituality gained from their life's lessons so they may draw on it later.

What must I do to be an exceptional spiritual person?

> Jesus said, "From Adam to John the Baptist, there has been none among the off-spring of women who has been more exalted than John the Baptist, so that such a person's eyes might be broken. But I have said that whoever among you becomes a little one will become acquainted with the kingdom and will become more exalted than John." (Gospel of Thomas, 46)

To be an exceptional spiritual person (see Saying 12), you need to lead a childlike life with the virtues of purity (see Saying 5), innocence, and humility. You acquire knowledge of such virtues from life and from the words of the spiritually-wise. The most important way to become righteous and be exceptional is to gain greater spirituality.

To Avoid and Acquire
What should I avoid in order to make proper decisions about good and evil?

> Jesus said, "A person cannot mount two horses or bend two bows. And a servant cannot serve two masters, or that servant will honor the one and offend the other. No person drinks aged wine and immediately desires to drink new wine. New wine is not poured into aged wineskins, or they might break, and aged wine is not poured into a new wineskin, or it might spoil. An old patch is not sewn onto a new garment, for there would be a tear." (Gospel of Thomas, 47)

To be able to distinguish correctly between good and evil, you must reject all forms of dualism and remain emotionally neutral. Your loyalty and love must go only to the Oneness.

"Emotional neutrality" means (1) you have self-control of passions, and you will not let them control you; (2) you are free from pride; and (3) you have no compulsions towards materialism or your desires.

Again, emotional neutrality is not *indifference* to the plight of others. You must care about others as a way of manifesting your own spirituality. Emotional neutrality is an essential protection of your inner Self as you make decisions about good and evil. Without emotional neutrality, life's circumstances negatively influence your decisions.

Is peace important in my, and our collective, ability to discern between good and evil?

> **Jesus said, "If two make peace with one another within a single house, they will say to a mountain, 'Go elsewhere,' and it will go elsewhere." (Gospel of Thomas, 48)**

If you are to discern good from evil, you must make peace within yourself and find and experience peace with the outer world. Collectively, we need to make peace with each other if together we are to tell good from evil. With peace comes the ability to have emotional neutrality within us and among others. Finding peace does not necessarily mean doing nothing. Peace is a mindset and consciousness that permits us to be fearless, dispassionate, and unattached. Emotional neutrality transforms our feelings so that our compassion is directed to the whole of creation, and we become united in a common goodwill for one another.

How can I expand my understanding of good from evil?

> **Jesus said, "Blessed are the solitaires and the select person for you will find the kingdom; for since you**

have come from it you shall return to it." (Gospel of Thomas, 49)

The ability to understand good and evil builds from successfully engaging in the spiritual process. Because it is a process, with practice the ability grows in each of us over time. The understanding also builds within us as we read the works of sages from the past. These writings are yet another gift of spiritual knowledge to subsequent generations. Such wisdom does not die. It is eternal. It lives beyond its author but must be discovered and rediscovered in every generation.

Where, outside me, does my discernment of good and evil come from?

Jesus said, "If they say to you, 'Where are you from?' say to them, 'It is from the light that we have come—from the place where light, on its own accord alone, came into existence and stood at rest. And it has been shown forth in their images. If they say to you, 'Is it you?' say, 'We are its offspring, and we are the chosen of the living father.' If they ask you, 'What is the sign of your father within you?' say to them, 'It is movement and repose.'" (Gospel of Thomas, 50)

Your ability to discern flows from life's spiritual wisdom. Life gives us the "unity of opposites" of good and evil so that we can learn to distinguish between the two. Learning to determine good from evil is partially an evolutionary and experiential process that flows from life's lessons. We develop discernment by alternately taking time to reflect on an upcoming action, taking the action, then again reflecting upon what we have done. Through the process of reflection and action, we come to internalize and thus embody the lessons we learn.

When will I be able to judge good from evil?

> **His disciples said to him, "When will the repose for the dead come to pass, and when will the new world come?" He said to them, "That repose which you are waiting for has come, but for your part you do not recognize it." (Gospel of Thomas, 51)**

You can distinguish good from evil now, but you do not realize you can. The "unity of opposites" called life consists of the finite, meaning the mortal being that lives and dies, and the infinite, meaning the immortal that exists as lessons that can be lost but never die. Lessons are learned through experiencing and observing life.

Sometimes we are able to learn from the lessons and sometimes not. Sometimes we are not ready or do not see them, but the lessons themselves never die. Sometimes they may revisit us many times before we "get" a lesson. Sometimes we may need to learn the lessons on various subtle levels before we are able to truly understand it in its totality.

If you are on a spiritual path, you have absorbed at least some of the lessons, and you reflect those lessons in your actions toward others. You will continually reflect and learn even more as you embody the larger meaning of those lessons. Life is an opportunity to be a receptacle for those infinite lessons. You become increasingly better at discerning good from evil as you grow in the process of spirituality.

Learning lessons that hone your discernment of good and evil identifies you more with the Oneness of life. As you move closer to that Oneness, you better understand the meaning of life in both its mortal and immortal aspects. And as you move closer to that Oneness, you begin to see you are on a spiritual journey that is transforming you from the finite world into the eternal world. Those not on this journey can see only the finite and cannot comprehend the infinite or its significance.

Discerning Between Good and Evil

How should I regard past and present spiritual teachers?

> His followers said to him, "Twenty-four prophets have spoken in Israel, and they all spoke of you."
> He said to them, "You have disregarded the living one who is in your presence and have spoken of the dead." (Gospel of Thomas, 52)

As you proceed on your spiritual journey, you should appreciate wise spiritual teachers from the past, but do not disregard the living teachers who have built upon those past teachings. Life has given you the great teachers of the past to help you discover for yourself the eternal lessons that will help you on your spiritual journey. Life is now also giving you a person near you who can help you discover even more lessons important for your journey. You should be alert for potentially important people in your life. You should honor both the great teachers of the past and the one near you who may also be offering you spiritual lessons.

Attributes of Discernment

In discerning good and evil, is there an important physical attribute I need to have?

> His followers said to him, "Is circumcision useful or not?" He said to them, "If it were useful, children's fathers would produce them already circumcised from their mothers. Rather, the true circumcision in spirit has become valuable in every respect." (Gospel of Thomas, 53)

In every respect, there is no more important attribute that you bring to discerning good from evil than the spirit of life. You must understand that your soul, which you develop through life's lessons, guides your body, while your mind acts as executive director. However, life owns your body, and the spirit of life is within you. What is most important is to improve your soul through life's lessons by using your spirit and self-awareness to cut through the illusions.

Does being poor make the discerning of good and evil easier for me?

> **Jesus said, "Fortunate are the poor; for yours is heaven's kingdom." (Gospel of Thomas, 54)**

In some circumstances, poverty and hardship may make it easier to understand what is good or evil, but there is no special virtue to those conditions. In fact, extreme hardship, such as poverty, does create in some people hatred and anger, which can result in a vicious cycle of negative thoughts and activities.

However, the spirit of life is often strong in the poor. They can better understand what is good and evil because of their perspective, especially if they endure with fortitude and forgiveness. Those in hardship often more easily understand that work alone is the true reward and not any fruit it might produce. Rich or poor, you need to perceive success and failure as being the same.

How is single-minded focus important in discerning good from evil?

> **Jesus said, "Those who do not hate their fathers and mothers cannot be disciples of mine, and those who do not hate their brothers and their sisters and take up their cross like me will not become equal to me." (Gospel of Thomas, 55)**

Our single-minded focus must be unconditional love. You cannot understand good and evil if there is hatred in your soul, nor can you handle the condemnation towards you that will often come. Correct discernment requires one to love life unconditionally, meaning all things and all people. Such a love is possible only with detachment from the values of the material world. Single-minded focus on loving the Oneness of life sets the proper context, and from this all other relationships will flow.

In discerning good and evil, how should I value the material world?

> **Jesus said, "Whoever has become acquainted with the world has found a corpse, and the world is not worthy of the one who has found the corpse." (Gospel of Thomas, 56)**

You must understand in your heart that the values of the material world are worthless to the spiritual person except as a tool or means of learning and growing spiritually. Understand the proper role for the material world's values, and focus on controlling your ego's desires.

To discern good from evil, find the middle path between self-indulgence and self-denial. Even if it is difficult, you must purge both extremes from your being. You will come to realize that life "owns" everything, and it merely permits you to dwell here so you can make spiritual progress. Center yourself in knowledge gained from your spiritual lessons.

Is evil a necessary aspect of life?

> **Jesus said, "The father's kingdom is like a person who had good seed. His enemy came at night and sowed**

weeds among the good seed. The person did not let them pull up the weeds, and said to them, 'No, or you might go to pull up the weeds and pull up the wheat along with them.' For on the day of the harvest the weeds will be conspicuous and will be pulled up and burned." (Gospel of Thomas, 57)

The existence of evil is absolutely necessary. The "unity of opposites" called good and evil makes it possible to discern one from the other. But we cannot fully comprehend one without the other. When the difference between good and evil is conspicuous, then you need to confront evil and transform it by appropriate means.

The challenge of discerning good and evil sometimes appears as a slowly unraveling series of mysteries. Their appearance is coupled with continuing advice from most of humankind that deflects you from solving those mysteries. As a spiritual person, you grow by using your *freewill* to avoid evil, and you benefit from the challenge of learning how to discern and properly deal with it.

Work of Discernment
Is discerning good from evil hard work?

> Jesus said, "Fortunate is the person who has worked hard and has found life." (Gospel of Thomas, 58)

Of course, discerning good from evil requires *willpower*, meaning self-control and mental focus. The greatest enemy in life is almost always ourselves. Discernment is hard work, partly because we can easily make the mistake of trying to gain some advantage in the material world or an imagined afterlife. Instead, wishing only to do "the right thing" for the benefit of the Oneness of all should be our motivation. It takes hard work to reach that understanding and continue the journey. Nevertheless, that work is central to the meaning and purpose of life, and it is essential in discerning good from evil.

What is the role of a spiritual teacher in my efforts to learn how to better discern good from evil?

Jesus said, "Look to the living one as long as you live, or you might die and then try to see the living one, and will be unable to see." (Gospel of Thomas, 59)

Guidance from a spiritual teacher is important because we acquire not only the ability to discern good from evil but also the meaning of selfless and unconditional love. The teacher can help us appreciate that the enemy of love is fear, which comes from doubting that everything is One.

A spiritual teacher can help you learn that Oneness includes good and even evil. Both are necessary if you are to understand the lessons of spirituality. A teacher helps you not only look to the positive lessons of life and achieve better discernment, but also helps you benefit positively from wrong choices and negative lessons.

How important is quiet reflection?

They saw a Samaritan carrying a lamb as he went to Judea.
He said to his disciples, "This <...> the lamb."

They said to him, "So that he might slaughter it and have it to eat."

He said to them, "He will not eat it while it is alive, but rather when he has slaughtered so it becomes a carcass."

They said, "Otherwise he cannot do it."
He said to them, "You, too, seek for yourself a place of repose, lest you might become a carcass and be devoured." (Gospel of Thomas, 60)
Note: The symbol <...> means part of the original manuscript is missing.

Both a time and a place for quiet reflection are very important. Finding the inner Self, where your answers exist, can be difficult; but practices such as silence and meditation help you reach your inner place. When you know the techniques to access it, you can go there anywhere and anytime. You will not find the answers in the material world. Only you can choose to look in the correct place and realize that many so-called wise people and world leaders have made the mistake of looking in the wrong place.

Should I be single-mindedly guided by my spirituality?

Jesus said, "Two will rest on a couch; one will die, one will live."

Salome said, "Who are you, mister? You have climbed onto my couch and eaten from my table as if you are from someone."

Jesus said to her, "I am the one who comes from what is whole. I was given from the things of my father."

"I am your follower."

"For this reason I say, if one is whole, one will be filled with light, but if one is divided, one will be filled with darkness." (Gospel of Thomas, 61)

Being detached from desire is important, but more importantly, you need focus and determined concentration to allow spirituality, including its virtues, to guide you. In other words, you should be of one mind and not be distracted or easily swayed from your chosen path. You should master yourself. Be as perfect as you can be.

Should I announce widely my thoughts and decisions on good and evil?

> **Jesus said, "I disclose my mysteries to those who are worthy of my mysteries. Do not let your left hand know what your right hand is doing." (Gospel of Thomas, 62)**

Announce your thoughts and decisions about good and evil only to those who are ready, eager, and can properly understand. Guard your words and your decisions, selectively announcing them only to those closest to you who share your spirituality and who will respect and value your sharing. You should not share with those who might mock or ridicule you. Writing down your thoughts and decisions about good and evil is a useful exercise, but share them carefully with others.

Am I wiser to delay making decisions about good and evil?

> **Jesus said, "There was a rich person who had a great deal of money. He said, 'I shall invest my money so that I may sow, reap, plant, and fill my storehouses with produce, that I may lack nothing.' These were the things he was thinking to his heart, but that very night he died. Whoever has ears should hear." (Gospel of Thomas, 63)**

When it comes to making decisions about good and evil, realize that matters involving material aspects of your life are not important. But spiritual concerns, such as your self-worth and honesty, are extremely important. Typically, spiritual concerns are time sensitive, and a delay in making decisions fosters doubt and inappropriate second thoughts. Thus time is always important in such circumstances, and delay can be a serious mistake. Always appreciate that a non-decision *is* a decision, often with important consequences.

Ethical Decisions
Do all people react to ethical decisions in the same way?

> Jesus said, "A person was receiving guests. When he had prepared the dinner, he sent his servant to invite the guests.
>
> "The servant went to the first and said to that one, 'My master invites you.'
>
> "That person said, 'Some merchants owe me money; they are coming to me tonight. I must go and give them instructions. Please excuse me from dinner.'
>
> "The servant went to another and said to that one, 'My master has invited you.'
>
> "That person said to the servant, 'I have bought a house and I have been called away for a day. I shall have no time.'
>
> "The servant went to another and said to that one, 'My master invites you.'
>
> "That person said to the servant, 'My friend is to be married and I am to arrange the banquet. I shall not be

able to come. Please excuse me from dinner.'

"The servant went to another and said to that one, 'My master invites you.'

"That person said to the servant, "I have bought an estate and I am going to collect the rent. I shall not be able to come. Please excuse me.'

"The servant returned and said to his master, 'The people whom you invited to dinner have asked to be excused.'

"The master said to his servant, 'Go out on the streets and bring back whomever you find to have dinner.'

"Buyers and merchants will not enter the place of my father." (Gospel of Thomas, 64)

Not all people react to ethical decisions in the same manner. When inviting people to hear about ethical matters, realize that those who are materialistic and ego-centered are not really interested unless those matters impact their material situation or make a difference in terms of their power or prestige. If those conditions are not met, you are wasting your time. In contrast, those who are spiritual would like to hear about ethical matters; they appreciate how such ethical insights can help them grow spiritually. Materialistic and ego-centered people are oblivious to such insight.

Do all people react to matters of fairness in the same way?

He said, "A kind man owned a vineyard, and put it in the hands of cultivators for them to cultivate, so that he might get its produce from them. He sent his slave so that the cultivators might give the produce of the vineyard to the slave. They seized, beat, and all but killed his slave, and the slave went and spoke to its owner. Its owner said, 'Perhaps they did not recognize it (the slave), and he sent another slave. The cultivators beat the other slave. Next the owner sent his son and said, 'Perhaps they will show respect for my son.' Those cultivators, since they recognized that it was he was heir to the vineyard, seized him and killed him. Whoever has ears should listen!"(Gospel of Thomas, 65)

Some materialistic and ego-centered people cannot grasp the meaning of fairness in a relationship, and they will act only in their perceived self-interest. Regardless of your best efforts to understand and reach out to them, their true character will govern how they tend to react to you. Wiser spiritual persons recognize such people exist and will take the necessary precautions.

When it comes to ethical decisions, are non-spiritual and spiritual people fundamentally different?

Jesus said, "Show me the stone that the builders rejected: That is the corner stone." (Gospel of Thomas, 66)

Non-spiritual and spiritual persons have fundamentally different values and, consequently, see ethical questions differently. What is foolishness to a non-spiritual person can be fundamental to the value system of a spiritual person. For example, materialistic persons may lie to make a profit in a business relationship while spiritual persons would think lying to be fundamentally wrong. When a wrong is done to a non-spiritual person, punishment of the wrongdoer is essential. When a wrong is done to a spiritual person, the primary concern is that the wrong doer not be permitted to do that wrong to others.

Spiritual people grow their inner Selves by learning lessons from life, and they value Oneness. They manifest those lessons by applying their learned values in ethical decision-making. Spiritual people might easily find the rejected ethical point of non-spiritual persons to be critical to their ethical argument and embrace it as their key point in their argument and decision. For example, a non-spiritual person might have no problem holding back information in order to make a sale, but spiritual persons would reject that out of hand. Their ethical view is to be honest and provide all information critical to a proper sale.

Why are the values of materialistic people so opposite to spiritual ones?

Jesus said, "If anyone should become acquainted with the entirety and should fall short at all, that person falls short of the whole place." (Gospel of Thomas, 67)

Spiritual and materialistic people literally perceive the world differently, and therefore their values are radically different. For example, as noted in Saying 66, what is worthless and unimportant to the materialistic person, such as the rejected stone, can be of central importance to the spiritual person. Materialistic people believe that everyone acts for the purpose of receiving rewards or avoiding punishments. Spiritual people believe they must do "the right thing" because it makes sense in terms of Oneness. They assume that doing good works is ethically valuable, and conversely, doing evil deeds is ethically wrong.

However, spiritual people know that spirituality does not increase because they do good works or diminish by their "missing the mark" on any occasion. They know instead that causality runs not from good works to spirituality but from spirituality to good works. Spiritual people know spirituality shapes their values and attitudes, and those values and attitudes define ethics for them. Their ethics are more important than the good works their actions may accomplish.

Can I gain anything from the hate and persecution perpetrated by non-spiritual people?

> Jesus said, "Blessed are you whenever they hated you and persecuted you. And wherever they have persecuted you, they will find no place." (Gospel of Thomas, 68)

As a spiritual person, you can gain from negative experiences, especially when they stem from ethical matters. You should view hate and persecution coming from non-spiritual people as a life-test. Such treatment can help you understand the value of enduring with fortitude. You also eventually discover how to transcend your suffering through detachment. Do not condemn those who hurt you in anger, do not keep grudges, and do not feel sorry for your unfortunate circumstances.

Can I gain anything if I am heartsick from some person or some institution assaulting me because of my ethics?

> Jesus said, "Blessed are those who have been persecuted in their hearts. It is they who have truly come to be acquainted with the father. Blessed are they who hunger for the belly of the needy to be satisfied." (Gospel of Thomas, 69)*

The fact that you feel the assaults in your heart helps you understand the lesson in spiritual wisdom that should result

*Bentley Layton, *The Gnostic Scriptures*

from those attacks because it is easier to grasp the positive inner lesson when it emerges from emotional experiences. The heart is the essential place to transcend from the egocentric and materialistic to the spiritual. Sadness and sorrow can bring spiritual growth because they cause you to enter your inmost being to find strength and answers to your burning questions. Being heartsick from persecution of others or yourself can help you learn that a mental attitude and outlook, such as returning hate with hate, is not spiritual. Transcending hate with good actions and thoughts is spiritual.

What is the difference between the ethical decisions of a spiritual person versus a non-spiritual person?

Jesus said, "If you bring forth what is within you, what you have will save you. If you do not have that within you, what you do not have within you will kill you." (Gospel of Thomas, 70)

Spiritual persons manifest their spirituality by making good, lasting ethical decisions for everyone, whereas non-spiritual persons make decisions only in terms of how those decisions affect themselves.

Although some people might say that non-spiritual persons can act ethically, those people do not understand that intention and awareness are essential to being spiritual and ethical. A non-spiritual person can appear to act ethically but such an act is not motivated from being spiritual. Non-spiritual persons can never manifest an ethical action from a spiritual lesson that they did not learn in the first place. Non-spiritual persons are clueless as to the spiritual basis for their decisions, and such persons do not realize that their decisions must proceed from a heart that cares for everyone.

Once I have become spiritual, can non-spiritual arguments influence my ethical decision-making?

> **Jesus said, "I shall destroy this house and no one will be able to build it <. . . .>"** (Gospel of Thomas, 71)
> Note: The symbol <. . . .> means part of the original manuscript is missing.

Non-spiritual arguments no longer have power to influence a spiritual person. Spiritual persons must manifest their inner Self and turn their understanding of what is ethical into actions. Their previous materialistic or egocentric nature no longer exists, and it cannot be re-established as it was before. Spiritual persons feel that they cannot waste their life's lessons. They see life and its lessons as a special gift. They do not wish to squander their gift senselessly but instead wish to maximize the lessons in their lifetime. Even procrastination is a separation from life's spiritual lessons because it results in the person missing opportunities.

What should I do if the decision (or question) concerns choosing one thing or person over another?

> **A person said to Him, "Tell my brothers to divide my father's possessions with me."**
>
> **He said to the person, "Mister, who made me a divider?"**
>
> **He turned to his disciples and said to them, "I am not a divider, am I?"** (Gospel of Thomas, 72)

If the ethical decision concerns taking a whole and subdividing it or not, the answer must favor Oneness. For spiritual persons, life is Oneness because they believe everything is connected and that our minds must see through and past the illusion of division. Therefore, when spiritual persons make ethical decisions, one party is not the victor over another, but the decisions serve the Oneness of us all. Everything lives in Oneness, which includes love, sharing, forgiveness, mercy, compassion, and all else that brings about the "unity of opposites."

After I have made my ethical decisions, should I seek help in implementing those decisions?

> **Jesus said, "The harvest is plentiful but the workers are few. So plead with the lord to dispatch workers for the harvest." (Gospel of Thomas, 73)**

Making spiritually-guided decisions may involve you alone or perhaps only a few; but often implementing them requires many helpers if all the appropriate people are to receive full and proper benefits. Therefore, you should ask for assistance, especially if the implementation will be a significant challenge. Similarly, if you see other people need help in implementing such decisions, and you are in a position to do so, you should provide assistance, even if you are not in a position of leadership.

If many seek a decision from me and the answer is not apparent, what should I do?

> **He said, "Master, there are many around the drinking trough, but there is nothing in the well." (Gospel of Thomas, 74)**

You are wise to take time to meditate on the situation, including the decision to be made. Your inner voice is a reservoir of learned lessons. Still your mind long enough to hear it. As a source of guidance, look to your inner Self and the lessons you have discovered from life. As a spiritual person, you will have much to draw upon, whereas the non-spiritual person has little or nothing.

Is making ethical decisions a group or an individual matter?

Jesus said, "There are many standing at the door, but those who are alone will enter the wedding chamber." (Gospel of Thomas, 75)

One of the paradoxes related to spirituality is the relationship between the individual and Oneness because it also is a "unity of opposites." Like a drop of water entering the vast ocean from a mountain stream, we are simultaneously both the drop and the ocean, as the drop is the individual and the ocean is the Oneness.

However, for spiritual persons making an ethical decision, each should always act as an individual even if his or her decision is made in a group context. Or to put the point another way, if the person makes an ethical decision within a group, the spiritual person must act independently of the group context because ethical decisions should arise out of the person's individual consciousness shaped by spirituality.

Spiritual persons are rare. They have at least the emergence of enlightenment and are teachers of truth. Thus their independent voice will produce a valued harmony, plus the necessary discipline and dedication within the group. Spiritual persons must bear their own burden in making decisions because they are accountable to themselves in the context of "Oneness."

A Summary of Spiritual Discernment

A person has many opportunities in life to decide between good and evil. How does a person make such discernments? Jesus makes the point that a spiritual person and a non-spiritual person will approach such decisions differently. Spiritual persons make decisions from a mature and spiritually-developed heart. For example, spiritual people see interconnections rather than separations, and they embrace emotional neutrality. They do this with a peace of mind and a discernment that flows from their life's accumulated spiritual wisdom, a wisdom coming from not only their experiences but also wise spiritual teachers.

A vital attribute that allows spiritual persons to discern accurately is their spirit of life. It helps them overcome hardships, such as poverty, with a single-minded focus on unconditional love. To them, the material world is worthless, except as a means to acquire life's lessons of spiritual wisdom. They understand that evil will always exist, and that distinguishing good from evil requires of them *willpower*, self-control, and mental focus.

What demonstrates spirituality to the larger world is the ability of spiritual persons to discern good from evil throughout their lives. For spiritual persons, Oneness is the yardstick that determines how they perceive a situation and how they measure what they perceive.

Chapter 15

Spiritual Love

Why is love a much-misunderstood phenomenon, and spiritual love is even more misunderstood? Spiritual love is not lust or passion. It exists in a heart that is deeply caring and with no thought of gain or benefit. It wants the individual Self to grow in spirituality and, in that process, give of itself. Spiritual love helps you appreciate that the body is merely the container of the Self, but within that container, you manifest the inner progress of your soul while giving to others.

What Is It?
What is most valuable about spirituality?

> Jesus said, "The father's kingdom is like a merchant who had a supply of merchandise and then found a pearl. That merchant was prudent; he sold the merchandise and bought the single pearl for himself. So also with you, seek his treasure that is unfailing, that is enduring, where no moth comes to devour and no worm destroys." (Gospel of Thomas, 76)

Unconditional love is the most valuable aspect of spirituality because it is unfailing, enduring, cannot be destroyed, and cannot be stolen. Spiritual love resides in the heart, and it brings treasure to the world. From such love comes the understanding of your spiritual lessons, which help you develop your inner Self. It can never spoil, rot, or fade away.

Where does spiritual love come from?

> **Jesus said, "It is I who am the light that presides over all. It is I who am the entirety: it is from me that the entirety has come, and to me that the entirety goes. Split a piece of wood: I am there. Lift a stone, and you will find me there." (Gospel of Thomas, 77)**

Spiritual love emanates from life found in the whole of creation. Life is the Oneness of *everything*, of which we are a part. Thus love emanates from the Oneness, meaning all life, and it guides and nurtures us. You can reciprocate that love by understanding that you are part of the *all* and *spiritual love* is in you.

Why does spiritual love have to be unconditional?

> **Jesus said, "Why have you come out to the countryside? To see a reed shaken by the wind? And to see a person dressed in soft clothes, like your rulers and your powerful one? They are dressed in soft clothes, and they cannot understand truth." (Gospel of Thomas, 78)**

People should embrace unconditional love only because it is simply the right thing to do. They should not look for any benefits or try to avoid any punishments. Life lets individuals accept or reject spiritual love. That is their free choice.

If people do not accept spiritual love, life will proceed; but they will not be able to see or understand the lessons life offers them. Eventually, their own unattended character flaws will control them. Their own actions and beliefs will seal their fate, which by default will be based on the material world's values of vanity and avarice. Such people will live with a worldly consciousness full of ego and desire and therefore will not know the deep joy and peace of unconditional love.

Anyone who embraces unconditional love must be detached not only from actions flowing out of that love but also from the value of those actions. The moment we have an expectation of the fruits of our actions, even when those expectations are lofty in nature, we are doomed to frustration, disappointment and perhaps resentment.

We should not approach an act of kindness with the desire to feel good about ourselves but only with the desire to do what is right. If we make the mistake of being kind or doing good in order to feel satisfied with ourselves, then we will feel frustrated if the recipients of our action (1) are not grateful enough for our efforts, (2) are not respectful enough, or (3) in response to our obvious good deed, do not change their behavior in some fashion agreeable to us. Life lets non-seekers and false seekers place conditions on their love (for example, "What is in it for me?"). The irony of spiritual love is that the moment you perform an action for its fruit, you are no longer in spiritual love.

What is the context in which spiritual love should be understood?

> **A woman in the crowd said to him, "Fortunate are the womb that bore you and the breasts that fed you."**
>
> **He said to her, "Fortunate are those who have heard the word of the father and have truly kept it. For there will be days when you will say, 'Fortunate are the womb that has not conceived and the breasts that have not given milk.'" (Gospel of Thomas, 79)**

You must understand spiritual love only in the context of spirituality. Do not allow the desire for children, wealth, or high social standing misdirect your thinking, as none of it will produce long-lasting satisfaction. Love can exist only with knowledge and truth. Love comes from life itself. You should consider spiritual lessons with their acquired wisdom a gift of love from life itself.

What is and is not spiritual love?

> **Jesus said, "Whoever has come to know the world has discovered the body; and whoever has discovered the body, of that person the world is not worthy." (Gospel of Thomas, 80)**

What we normally call love is built on a false perception that grows out of false values. For example, a life of self-control that avoids worldly desires appears to be a form of sacrifice, but it really is just an expression of love. Spiritual love means having the breath of life and a fully conscious soul. Spiritual love is not passion, greed, thirst for sense pleasures, or the wanting of wealth and children.

How should I return the spiritual love given to me by life?

> **Jesus said, "Let one who has become wealthy rule, and let one who has power renounce it." (Gospel of Thomas, 81)**

You should return life's love by freeing your mind to see past the false perceptions and values of the material world. Knowledge from those false perceptions and values will distort your ability to comprehend and to make sound decisions. You need to take the love given by life and grow it within you as much as you possibly can. As you mature in spirituality, focus life's love in your heart, and naturally give of yourself without seeking anything in return.

Relationships
What is the relationship between love and spirituality?

> Jesus said, "Whoever is near me is near the fire, and whoever is far from me is far from the kingdom." (Gospel of Thomas, 82)

Whoever is near spirituality is near love, and whoever is far from spirituality is far from life. Spirituality with its love can be found in the spiritual wisdom of all religions and their teachings. If love is in your heart, you will hear life's spiritual lessons. Life is often consuming and difficult, but with unconditional and compassionate love for life in your heart, you will gain inner knowledge that will strengthen you and help you reject fear, doubt, false perceptions, and false values.

Why do many misunderstand what spiritual love is?

> Jesus said, "Images are visible to human beings. And the light within these images is hidden by the image of the father's light: it will be disclosed. And his image is hidden by his light." (Gospel of Thomas, 83)

The human mind understands love in terms of physical emotions and desires that are binding in a relationship; thus the illusions of the world cloud and confuse our understanding of what life's unconditional love is. However, as a seeker, you learn and grow your spirituality; you begin to understand the loving kindness that flows from life's spiritual lessons. You discover that because of this kindness, righteousness flows naturally from your heart, and with that understanding, you grasp the meaning of unconditional love that focuses on Oneness.

Does spiritual love include loving myself?

Jesus said, "When you see your resemblance you are happy: But when you see your images that came into existence before you and are neither moral nor visible, how much you have to bear!" (Gospel of Thomas, 84)

Each of us has a body, and we identify our individual self as being contained within the body. We do not necessarily understand that there is also a higher inner self, or Self, with a capital "S." It is the Self that grows with life's spiritual lessons. The individual self often sees itself as a separate entity subject to the currents of nature. The result is that the individual self is often unstable, fickle, full of desire, and restless. The self also identifies with the terms "me, my, mine." Growing spirituality, through awareness of the Self and through learning life's lessons, guides you to walk your path to spirituality. Without doing so, we cannot fully understand spiritual love and, more importantly, live it.

Why do the wealthy and powerful have a more difficult time understanding spiritual love?

Jesus said, "Adam came from power and great wealth, but he was not worthy of you. For had he been worthy, he would not have tasted death." (Gospel of Thomas, 85)

Individuals with material wealth and power typically see life in terms of physical bodies, buildings, possessions, proper names, heritage, positions and titles rather than in terms of spiritual love. They believe they have rightly earned or are otherwise entitled to their wealth and power. This belief blinds them from seeing that true goodness flows naturally from the heart and from spiritual love that focuses on Oneness. They cannot see life as a gift of love providing unlimited opportunities and giving Self its meaning.

What does spiritual love require of me?

Jesus said, "Foxes have their dens and birds have their nests. But a child of humankind has no place to lay his head and gain repose." (Gospel of Thomas, 86)

The gift of spiritual love requires your continuous focus and attention, with the result that there is no end to your potential for learning and living those lessons. Your love should be spiritual work that becomes part of the very purpose of your life. Your spiritual journey begins with love; therefore, you should celebrate life by embracing its lessons with gusto, and, in turn, not be overwhelmed by its challenges, which undoubtedly will occur. Even though life's experiences make you spiritually rich by challenging, sustaining, and assisting you in your inner growth, you cannot take those lessons for granted.

How does spiritual love result in my happiness?

Jesus said, "How miserable is the body that depends on a body, and how miserable is the soul that depends on these two." (Gospel of Thomas, 87)

Spiritual love prevents you from going down two false paths: (1) allowing physical appetites and material desires to drive you, and (2) becoming dependent on those appetites and desires experienced through the body. Spiritual love helps you appreciate that the body is merely the house of the Self, and hence it is a place of dynamic action and inner progress for the soul. Spiritual love teaches you that the means to happiness is being wise enough to use the right view, right thought, right speech, right action, right livelihood, right effort, right mindfulness, and right concentration. This way you can avoid sorrow and frustration and achieve inner peace, which is bliss.

Perceiving Love
How can I perceive spiritual love?

> Jesus said, "The messengers and the prophets are coming to you, and they will give you the things that you possess. And you, too—give them the things that you have, and say among yourselves, 'When are they coming to take their own?'" (Gospel of Thomas, 88)

Messengers of spiritual love communicate directly from their hearts to the hearts of seekers. We cannot speak or hear past life's illusions except through the love that is in the heart. You perceive this new reality of love in your heart when you give up ignorance and life's illusions and seek spiritual wisdom, first through your heart and then your mind. You perceive this love when you unconditionally give spiritual love back to everyone and everything without any expectations. Such love is without fragmentation or divisiveness.

Should I direct my spiritual love to both life and those who live in life?

> Jesus said, "Why do you wash the outside of the cup? Do you not understand that the one who made the inside is also the one who made the outside?" (Gospel of Thomas, 89)

To return spiritual love, you must love the internal, life itself, but also the external—all people and all other living things. The true nature of life is Oneness, but Oneness is also within our hearts, which are the means through which our spirituality grows. Spiritual love means loving others as you do yourself, but it also means loving yourself by fostering the spirituality within you so that you give more to others daily.

Is living spiritual love a hardship?

> **Jesus said, "Come to me, for my yoke is easy to use and my lordship is mild, and you will find repose for yourselves." (Gospel of Thomas, 90)**

Spiritual love is not a hardship. It comes from restful and satisfying "work." You will not feel lost. You will feel satisfied and successful. Spiritual love is not a hardship but a joy. Spiritual work, given with love, is like a virtuoso playing music. The musician is filled with joy simply from playing the instrument and does not feel it is work. He or she feels only the joy of the music.

What can help me believe spiritual love exists?

> **They said to him, "Tell us who you are, so that we may believe in you."**
>
> **He said to them, "You are testing the face of heaven and earth, and you have not recognized the one who is in your presence! And you do not recognize how to test this time of crisis." (Gospel of Thomas, 91)**

We know that spiritual love exists because many wise people throughout the world and ages have talked about it. Realistically, you cannot grasp it with the material characteristics our minds create; but you can perceive signs that such a love exists. You also know it exists because you see the evidence that you are developing your inner Self.

Spiritual Love

With spiritual love, must you be a constant seeker?

Jesus said, "Seek and you will find. In the past, however, I did not tell you the things about which you asked me them. Now I am willing to tell them, but you are not seeking them." (Gospel of Thomas, 92)

Spiritual love requires that you must not only be a constant seeker of spirituality but you must seek to discover an increasingly complex and critical understanding of it. You do not *acquire* spiritual love; but you uncover, complete, and perfect it while realizing there is always more to find and perfect. Learning spiritual love is done incrementally. Time is an important aspect of the learning process because it takes time to digest the lessons and practice applying them to life. Thus, being a life-long seeker is essential.

Once I understand spiritual love, should I try to explain it to others?

"Do not give what is holy to dogs, or they might throw them upon a manure pile. Do not throw pearls to swine, or they might < > it < > " (Gospel of Thomas, 93)

Note: The symbol <...> means part of the original manuscript is missing.

Not everyone is capable of understanding the full measure of spiritual love. Therefore, you must first know how much individuals can understand. Giving them too much at once would be a waste of their and your time and effort. If someone is indulgent, devoid of love and loyalty, envious of others, or lacks self-discipline, then perhaps that person is not ready to understand spiritual love. If so, you should not try to explain it. When you do explain spiritual love to others, you must always be courteous, wise, and kind, and also realize that spiritual love can be explained in many ways. However, it might be easier and more effective to just demonstrate it through your actions.

Necessary for Love
Besides seeking, what else is necessary for spiritual love?

> **Jesus said, "One who seeks will find; for one who knocks it will be opened." (Gospel of Thomas, 94)**

Four conditions are necessary for spiritual love. First, as implied before (see Saying 2), if you seek, you will find; and if you also seek with love in your heart, spiritual love will open to you. Second, you can use your *willpower* to diminish your desires to the point they no longer control you. Third, focus on the righteousness you have learned from life. Fourth, when others ask you about spiritual love, be willing to teach them to the extent they are able and ready to learn.

When helping others with my spiritual love, what should I do?

> **Jesus said, "If you have money; do not lend it at interest. Rather, give it to someone from whom you will not get it back." (Gospel of Thomas, 95)**

Help others with grace, modesty, awe, conscientiousness and sincerity. You should help others with your love, but also with wisdom and discernment. As the psychologists explain, enabling is not helping because your generosity can be dysfunctional for the recipient. For example, giving money to a drug addict is not an act of love but merely enables him or her to buy more drugs and continue the problem. Give help freely to all sincere seekers. Give it without expecting any merit for what you are doing. Do not turn anyone away or hide anything the person can understand. Even to non-spiritual people, give love, do good, and lend your help with no expectations of reward.

What happens when I give spiritual love?

> **Jesus said, "The father's kingdom is like a woman. She took a little yeast, hid it in dough, and made it into large loaves of bread. Whoever has ears should hear!" (Gospel of Thomas, 96)**

For most people who have little spiritual development, the love you give will seem small in terms of what they can grasp, but they will grow to appreciate it. If they are spiritual people, this righteous love (see Saying 50 and Chapter 10) will grow infinitely. Do not talk about what you are giving. Instead put your spiritual love into practice with your actions. The result of your gift to seekers is that many will improve the quality of their lives and, in turn, give more to others; in contrast, non-seekers may not even notice or appreciate your gift, and the illusions in their lives will continue to control them.

After discovering spiritual love, can I lose it?

> **Jesus said, "What the kingdom of the father resembles is a woman who was conveying a jar full of meal. When she had traveled far along the road, the handle of the jar broke and the meal spilled out after her along the road. She was not aware of the fact; she had not understood how to toil. When she reached home she put down the jar and found it empty." (Gospel of Thomas, 97)**

Even if you have been a spiritual seeker and have practiced spiritual love for some time, you can lose it as you travel life's path. You must always be aware of how you can lose it, whether such threats are present, and what you should do to counter those threats. For example, guard your spiritual wealth by associating with spiritually-wise people.

Should I prepare to defend myself against my spiritual enemies?

Jesus said, "What the kingdom of the father resembles is a man who wanted to assassinate a member of court. At home, he drew the dagger and stabbed it into the wall in order to know whether his hand would be firm. Next, he murdered the member of court." (Gospel of Thomas, 98)

You must prepare to defend yourself against your spiritual enemies by practicing your defenses and being resolved in using those defenses. Defenses include speaking the truth, continuing to study spiritual wisdom, and doing what is right. In other words, do not become complacent, do not let your guard down, do not be afraid of confrontation, and when the time comes, exercise your defenses with emotional neutrality. If conflict is necessary, your spiritual wisdom and love will easily equip you to deal with it.

How should I deal with my spiritual enemies?

The followers said to him, "Your brothers and your mother are standing outside."

He said to them, "Those here who do the will of my father are my brothers and my mother. They are the ones who will enter my father's kingdom." (Gospel of Thomas, 99)

Those who are spiritual in their habits and actions are your real family, but they might not be your biological family. People of other faith traditions, if they are spiritual, are not among your spiritual enemies. They are your spiritual family. The people who claim to love you the most might, in fact, may be your worst spiritual enemies. You must treat them as persons who can take away your spiritual love and may try to do so. Minimize their contact with you, and reject those who would stand against your progress. Maximize your contact with your spiritual family while appreciating and even loving anyone who assists you on your spiritual path.

Loving Whom
How should I deal with the government and other institutions in my life?

> They showed Jesus a gold coin and said to him, "Caesar's people demand taxes from us."
>
> He said to them, "Give Caesar the things that are Caesar's, give God the things that are God's, and give me what is mine." (Gospel of Thomas, 100)

Although you live in the temporal world, your challenge is to transcend it—not to reject it—meaning you should participate in the material world, including paying your taxes, because it is part of life and how you learn and grow spiritually. In important situations, you must go deep within your heart to know the right action to take, which must always be based on your righteousness and spiritual love. There are three simple rules: (1) Always speak the truth unless harm can result, but maybe even then; (2) Be detached and objective; (3) Be generous. Having spiritual love means you show kindness and compassion to all creatures and all people.

How and why should I love my family?

> "Whoever does not hate father and mother as I do cannot be a follower of me, and whoever does not love father and mother as I do cannot be a follower of me. For my mother <. . .>, but my true mother gave me life." (Gospel of Thomas, 101)

Note: The symbol <…> means part of the original manuscript is missing.

Your relationship toward family members should stem from whether they help you grow spiritually or whether they try to deter you. Love life itself and try to have no hatred for any being. Honor your father and mother with your heart-felt love because they provided you the life that permits you to do spiritual work. Spiritual love of Self means you assume responsibility for the care of your own spiritual progress while appreciating the loving care given you by your mother, father and other relatives.

Should I love all religious leaders?

> **Jesus said, "Damn the Pharisees, for they are like a dog sleeping in the cattle manger, for it does not eat or let the cattle eat." (Gospel of Thomas, 102)**

Do not be swept away by religious leaders who try to charm you with flowery words or who cling to pleasure and power. Worthy religious leaders must be free from impurity and have strong self-control. If a religious leader claims—or worse, boasts—that he or she is holy, then that person is possibly a fraud. Such religious leaders prevent people from learning spirituality because their actions and words lead people away from spirituality and into division.

How do I protect myself against such religious leaders and others?

> **Jesus said, "Fortunate is the person who knows where the robbers are going to enter, so that he may arise, bring together his estate, and arm himself before they enter." (Gospel of Thomas, 103)**

You must arm yourself and use your resources to defend yourself. Through inner peace, you can hear the warnings. Protect yourself by using such actions as asking questions, meditating, saying mantras, using chants, and deliberately avoiding fraudulent religious leaders. Being forearmed takes great practice and discipline because it requires being ego-free, understanding Oneness, and not letting passion invade your consciousness.

What is the gift of spiritual love?

> **They said to Jesus, "Come, let us pray today and let us fast." Jesus said, "What sin have I committed, or how have I been undone? Rather, when the bridegroom leaves the wedding chamber, then let people fast and pray." (Gospel of Thomas, 104)**

The gift is life with Oneness. Every action and thought performed with spiritual love is a continuous prayer of gratitude. You may learn spiritual lessons in theory, but such theory is useless unless it is manifested with your being and actions. Expressing your spiritual love for everyone and everything is critically important. Fasting and praying for material success is foolish. Our most important prayers use our free choice to liberate us from selfhood, the ego and a separate individuality by asking for the strength to do so.

Is strength of purpose and courage important in having spiritual love?

> Jesus said, "Whoever knows the father and mother will be called the child of a whore." (Gospel of Thomas, 105)

You must show strength of purpose and courage while remaining righteous (see Saying 50 and Chapter 10). Although righteousness is a vital aspect of spiritual love, it often elicits condemnation from peers. A spiritual person should consider such condemnation from friends and foes alike as a positive rather than negative sign because railing against what they cannot fathom is a normal human trait. Rather than feeling discouraged at such condemnation, feel compassion, and *love them all the more.*

Is there strength in spiritual love?

> Jesus said, "When you make the two into one and you will become children of humanity, and when you say, 'Mountain, move from here,' it will move." (Gospel of Thomas, 106)

Spiritual love is the source of great strength for accomplishing anything. When you free yourself from hate and passion and achieve serenity, sorrows flee. Your thoughts become calm. Your spiritual love grows into the Oneness of spirituality. With Oneness, you are one with life and everything in the universe. That is why you have such great strength and can accomplish anything.

Even when I go astray, does life love me if I have spirituality?

> Jesus said, "The kingdom is like a shepherd who had a hundred sheep. One of them, the largest, went astray.

> He left the ninety-nine and sought the one until he found it. After he had gone to this trouble, he said to the sheep, 'I love you more than the ninety-nine.'" (Gospel of Thomas, 107)

You will find that if you stray from spirituality and you wish to come back, life will seek you out and with great love return you to spirituality. Life happens to all of us and is continually giving spiritual lessons, even if we ignore them. But life particularly gives lessons to those who have gained spirituality, even if they go astray for a time. You need to realize that few seek spirituality, and fewer yet grow it within themselves. Thus those who have achieved some spirituality, even if they wander from their spiritual path, are remarkable persons worthy of an extra effort to bring them back.

A Summary of Spiritual Love

Spiritual love is a "unity of opposites:" your love for life, and love that life has for you. Together, they represent an ideal unity. Fortunately, the love that life has for you always exists, and it is absolutely unconditional. Too often a person's love for life does not exist, and if it does exist, it is often conditioned on wanting something in return. True spiritual love is a two-way unconditional relationship.

You perceive spiritual love from the hearts of others and from the realization of the valuable gifts you are always receiving from life. Because of that love, you need to be a constant seeker who looks beyond the illusions and sees the spiritual wisdom given to you. Because of that love, you are aware of the positive impacts those gifts can have on your being, and you can determine how to live those gifts through your thoughts and actions.

Spiritual love is a necessity because without it you cannot understand and act in Oneness. Spiritual love helps you always be a seeker, but it also allows you to see past illusions to the infinite truths that make life deeply meaningful. Spiritual love has the striking effect of multiplying itself from a small to a large gift that positively impacts you and others.

Your spiritual love should be given to everything and everyone, even those who are not spiritual. But it should not be given naively. For those recipients who are in the Kingdom of Man, the givers must realize that their gift of spiritual love will not be fully appreciated or even understood. This does not mean that the spiritual love should not be given, but it does mean that such love should be bestowed with much care.

In addition, because spiritual persons are always in a minority compared to those who live in the Kingdom of Man, a spiritual person can anticipate misunderstandings and attacks. Therefore, a spiritual person needs to develop spiritually-oriented defenses. For example, you may be in a place where a collection plate is passed around and you have only a large denomination bill. You need change, and that change exists in the collection plate. It would be naive to just reach in and make change. Spiritual persons should ask someone to make change, as they do not want anyone thinking they are robbing the collection plate.

Spiritual love always comes from life, but it does not always come in a form we immediately recognize or appreciate. Sometimes the lessons seem harsh and even mean-spirited. We need to look past those types of illusions and feel the deeper love of caring that is always there. Seek the wisdom behind the deep love, profit from that gift, and appreciate its value.

Chapter 16

Conclusions about Spirituality

There is a hunger in the world for what Jesus called soul food, as evidenced by the worldwide crisis in religion. Unfortunately, but understandably, first Paul and later the Roman theologians corrupted the message of Jesus over centuries. The almost forgotten message of Jesus concerned spirituality: what it is, why it is important, how to go about developing it, and, finally, how to live it. Jesus was brilliant, and we need not only appreciate that brilliance but also start living what He so generously gave us.

To Jesus, God is real and is life itself. God is the ultimate loving teacher of spiritual wisdom for those who "have ears to hear and eyes to see." To Jesus, those lessons, which are infinite and exist forever, are exceedingly more valuable than anything else that can be imagined. God's gifts to humankind include life, *freewill*, and spiritual wisdom. Our challenge is to appreciate those gifts and to use them to reach the Oneness that is the Divine.

Owning Spirituality
If I internalize the teachings of a spiritual leader like Jesus, what then?

> Jesus said, "Whoever drinks from my mouth will become like me; I myself shall become that person, and the hidden things will be revealed to that person." (Gospel of Thomas, 108)

You will notice that as you internalize a spiritual leader's teachings, you become more like your teacher. You can then understand life in a way you could not have before. In order to internalize those lessons, you must contemplate them in your spiritual and loving heart to understand their message of wisdom. Once you understand the wisdom, you can use it as a bridge for yourself into the Oneness.

Isn't spirituality always there to be discovered?

> **Jesus said, "The kingdom is like a person who had a treasure hidden in his field but did not know it. And when he died, he left it to his son. The son did no know about it. He took over the field and sold it. The buyer when plowing, discovered the treasure, and began to lend money at interest to whomever he wished." (Gospel of Thomas, 109)**

You have to uncover, reveal, and manifest spirituality's treasure through your actions, but it is always within you. With spirituality, we realize that the materialism of the world is worthless, but the treasure within us is worth everything. Life's gift to us is an opportunity beyond description, with the ultimate treasure being Oneness. Once we find the treasure, we manifest it with our actions, and thus we benefit those around us. Eventually those benefits come back to us in greater measure than we give out.

Once I have become spiritual, what should I do?

> **Jesus said, "The one who has found the world and has become wealthy should renounce the world." (Gospel of Thomas, 110)**

Once you discover the treasure of spirituality, you recognize that the material world, with its illusions, is useless to you.

Your interests and desires change. The material world provides you with life's valuable lessons although, paradoxically, you must look beyond them to learn spirituality. The material world will not disappear with this realization, but the illusion, with its power over you, will disappear, and you will grasp the true treasures. This realization will free you; with that freedom, you will grow into the infinite immortality of Oneness.

Once I understand spirituality, what will I understand?

Jesus said, "The heavens and the earth will roll-up in your presence. And the living from the living will not see death." (Gospel of Thomas, 111)

You will understand that there is no place called heaven, what you call earth is an illusion, and Oneness is life. With spirituality, you understand and know everything differently, as your inner Self becomes the bridge to the freedom of Oneness. For example, you will grasp the significance of human suffering, and it will no longer affect you, except as a means for learning and a way to manifest your spirituality. Once you understand spirituality, you are awed by life, its infinite potential, and its majesty.

Last Lessons
Then is there no relationship between flesh and our soul?

Jesus said, "Damn the flesh that depends on the soul. Damn the soul that depends on the flesh." (Gospel of Thomas, 112)

With spirituality, your soul and body are not contingent upon each other because with spirituality you transcend the many bodily desires and limitations that drive you. When more and more people awaken to spirituality, the collective consciousness of the world increases, and the world changes its view on permitting suffering, strife, disputes, and controversy to exist. Future progress of the world does not depend on desires but rather on the aspirations of the heart.

When will spirituality come to this world?

His followers said to him, "When will the kingdom come?"

"It will not come by watching for it. It will not be said, 'Look, here it is,' or 'Look, there it is.' Rather, the father's kingdom is spread out upon the earth and people do not see it." (Gospel of Thomas, 113)

Spirituality is already here but spread thinly throughout the world. It will not expand by watching for it, but by our actions. Step-by-step, life is establishing greater spirituality within the world as more seekers become aware of Oneness. To perceive this change, we must still our minds and listen with our hearts in calmness and quiet. We must not judge others as good or bad or as being spiritual or not; instead, we must live our own spirituality and trust in life.

Who should be included or excluded from spirituality?

Simon Peter said to them, "Mary should leave us, for females are not worthy of life."

Jesus said, "Look, I shall guide her to make her male, so that she too may become a living spirit resembling you males. For every female who makes herself male will enter heaven's kingdom." (Gospel of Thomas, 114)

None shall be excluded from the opportunity to learn spirituality, but ultimately each person must freely choose, without external pressure, whether and to what extent he or she wishes to become spiritual. Free conscious choice is critical to spirituality because such choice is essential at the beginning of the journey, during each decisive moment on the path, and at the end of the quest. *Freewill* does not exist without a person first being willing to seek and engage in the spiritual process. A seeker must have the correct attitude. Inner progress does not occur because one is wise, intelligent, or agreeable to others, but because of self-awareness and life's lessons learned. The wisest way to establish the correct attitude is to live a simple life with few desires and to be controlled by none.

Implications

If the Omega Interpretation of the teachings of Jesus is correct, and we believe it is, we need to affirm, first, that misunderstanding has hidden His message. Second, it is now visible again, as more people comprehend it and become like Him. Certainly, His message was always there to be found. Now with religious institutions in crisis, we can more easily uncover and bring to light His message so that many more in the world will grasp and then engage in the spirituality process—to the benefit of everyone.

For those who adopt this Omega Interpretation of His message, massive changes are in order. For example, the Alpha Interpretation with its understanding of heaven will disappear into history. And the soul's existence will no longer be associated with the flesh. Omega followers will realize that the Kindom of Heaven with its focus on spirituality already is here and has been here for a very long time. No one is excluded from the Kindom of Heaven, but all who eventually uncover it must choose it with their *freewill*.

A Case Study

Thomas, one of the authors of this book, served as a volunteer chaplain for a city's hospice organization. In that capacity, he visited a man who was within a month of dying from cancer. The man was a devoted Lutheran, and like many near death, he worried about whether he had lived his life correctly and about the mistakes of his past. We all make mistakes; and, despite the forgiveness factor built into their faith, many Christians wonder if they will be granted a positive afterlife. The dying man wondered and talked about big questions, such as why God would send His Son to die for him and whether he was worthy.

As chaplain, Thomas pointed out that, in the Aramaic language in which Jesus preached, the word "sin" meant "unripe" and not "bad, evil," or "a committed wrong." Therefore, when we sin, from the point of view of Jesus, such an act reflects a lack of spiritual development and maturity on our part rather than an evil that we committed or that we are. Thomas stressed to the patient that clearly he was spiritually mature because he recognized the lessons life had given him. The mistakes of his past were merely learning opportunities, which he had and used to be "re-born" into the mindset and consciousness that Jesus taught.

To many Christians, being "re-born" means acknowledging that Jesus is their personal savior who died for their sins. But being "re-born" is not just some big conversion of a moment. It is normally a slow learning process we call spiritual maturation. What Jesus taught was spiritual love, and that means we must love everyone. Of course, that does not mean we should be foolish, such as enabling someone's bad behavior. The spiritual love of God is why Jesus lived, and the lessons He taught are why God "sent" Him or possibly why God was happy to co-create with Him. In the Alpha Interpretation, God sent His only Son to die for the sins of humankind. In the Omega Interpretation, the work of Jesus manifested God's spiritual love, to the ultimate benefit of humankind.

Thomas, as chaplain, also pointed out that it is not doing good that is solely important in life for a Christian, but rather it is learning the lessons of Jesus and manifesting those lessons through good deeds. This is a significant difference that many misunderstand. Heaven is not a place, but a mind-set, a consciousness, a paradigm, **and** a living process.

Volunteering as a teacher's aide out of spiritual love or helping a person get past a crisis are examples of what heaven represents. It is the process around us all the time, and it is of our own making. Evil and hell are the unripe or immature non-spiritual behaviors that hurt others. Those behaviors result from actions that are ego-centered and often done for material gain, and can, with conscious effort, be out-grown.

From the patient's many conversations with Thomas about spirituality, he gradually stopped denigrating himself as a failure and accepted that he truly was a good man who had learned many of the lessons Jesus taught. He learned that he had indeed lived a life worth living, and that is the best any of us can do. There is a remarkable and satisfying feeling that comes with understanding spiritual love. With it, the patient realized he had made significant progress in his life, gaining the lessons that God wanted him to learn so that he came to embody the love that comes from spiritual maturity.

Regardless of what the patient perceived as existing after death, when he passed he was at peace with himself and his life's work. It was a beautiful process to witness. It was like watching a flower bloom and sing in silence, "Look at what I truly am." We hope that, after reading this book, many more people will see the wisdom of spirituality in the Omega Interpretation of Christianity. If they do, they will also bloom and sing in that same joyful silence, and we will all benefit from their amazing discovery.

Appendix A
References & Suggested Readings

The following references are organized in two sections, first by chapter and then for the book overall. References cited within the text are marked by an asterisk.

By Chapter

Preface

Holy Bible. King James Version. 1611. Cleveland, Ohio: The World Publishing Company, n.d. Print.

*Priests for Equity. *The Inclusive New Testament*. West Hyattsville, Maryland: AltaMira Press, 2004. Print.

Chapter 1

*Glines, C. V. "They Wait for the Ships and Aircraft to Return–This Time Carrying Goods for Them. The Cargo Cults." *Air Force Magazine*. Online Journal of the Air Force Association. Jan. 1991: n. pag. Web. 18 Oct. 2013.

*West, Cornel. *Democracy Matters*. New York: Penguin Books, 2004. Print.

Chapter 2

*Armstrong, Karen. *A History of God*. New York: Random House-Ballantine Books, 1993. Print.

Callaway, Ewen. "Ancient Warfare: Fighting for the Greater Good." *New Scientist,* Life section. 4 June 2009. Print and Web. 21 Jan. 2014. <newscientist.com/article/dn17255-ancient-warfare-fighting-for-the-greater-good.html>.

Crossan, John Dominic. *The Historical Jesus: The Life of a Mediterranean Jewish Peasant.* HarperSanFrancisco, 1991. Print.

---. *Jesus: A Revolutionary Biography.* HarperSanFrancisco, 1989. Print.

Dawkins, Richard. *The God Delusion.* Boston: Houghton Mifflin, 2006. Print.

Ehrman, Bart D. *Lost Christianities.* New York: Oxford University Press, 2003. Print.

---. *Lost Christianities: Christian Scriptures and the Battle over Authentication.* The Teaching Company Great Courses, 2002. DVD, Print.

---. *Misquoting Jesus.* HarperSanFrancisco, 2005. Print.

*Frankl, Viktor. *Man's Search for Meaning.* New York: Random House-Rider, 2004. Print.

Harris, Sam. *The End of Faith.* New York: W. W. Norton & Company, 2004. Print.

---. *Letter to a Christian Nation.* New York: Alfred A. Knopf, 2006. Print.

*Kushner, Harold S. *Why Bad Things Happen to Good People.* New York: HarperCollins Publishers, 1981. Print.

Kung, Hans. *On Being a Christian.* New York: Doubleday & Company, 1976. Print.

*Lynch, Thomas D., and Cynthia E. Lynch. *The Word of the Light.* Seattle: Hara Publishing, 1998. Print.

Putnam, Robert D., and David E. Campbell. *American Grace: How Religion Divides and Unites Us.* New York: Simon & Schuster Paperbacks, 2010. Print.

Spong, John Shelby. *A New Christianity for a New World.* HarperSanFrancisco, 2001. Print.

---. *The Sins of Scripture.* HarperSanFrancisco, 2005. Print.

---. *Why Christianity Must Change or Die.* HarperSanFrancisco, 1999. Print.

*Vivekananda, Swami. *Vedanta Society of New York.* 2013. Web. 26 Feb. 2013. <vedantany.org>.

Wells, H. G. 1922. *A Short History of the World.* Lawrence, Kansas: *Digiread.com*, Great Books Online, 2010. Web. 27 Apr. 2013. <bartleby.com/86/38.html>.

Whitehead, Alfred North. *Religion in the Making.* New York: Fordham University Press, 1996. Print.

Wilbur, Ken. *Integral Spirituality: A Startling New Role for Religion in the Modern and Postmodern World.* Boston: Integral Books, 2007. Print.

Wright, Robert. *The Evolution of God.* Boston: Little, Brown and Co., 2009. Print.

Chapter 3

Barnstone, Willis, and Marvin Meyer. *The Gnostic Bible*. Boston: Shambhala, 2003. Print.

*Callaway, Ewen. "Ancient Warfare: Fighting for the Greater Good." *New Scientist*, Life section. 4 June 2009. Print and Web. 21 Jan. 2014. <newscientist.com/article/dn17255-ancient-warfare-fighting-for-the-greater-good.html>.

*Cleary, Thomas. *Dhammapada: The Sayings of Buddha*. New York: Bantam Books, 1995. Print.

*Colby, Ann, Lawrence Kohlberg, et al. *The Measurement of Moral Judgment*. Vol. 1. New York: Oxford University Press, 2011. Print.

*Dawkins, Richard. *The Selfish Gene*. 30th Anniversary Edition. New York: Oxford University Press, 2006. Print.

*Epstein, Mark. *Psychotherapy Without the Self: A Buddhist Perspective*. New Haven: Yale University Press, 2007. Print.

*Fehr, Ernst, and Urs Fischbacher. "The Nature of Human Altruism." *Nature* 425 (23 Oct. 2003): 785-791. Print.

Fehr, Ernst, and Simon Gachter. "Altruistic Punishment in Humans." *Nature* 415 (10 Jan. 2002): 137-140. Print.

Fehr, Ernst, and Bettina Rochenbach. "Detrimental Effects of Sanctions on Human Altruism." *Nature* 422 (13 Mar. 2003): 137-140. Print.

*French, Howard W. "E. O. Wilson's Theory of Everything." *Atlantic Magazine* Nov. 2011: 70-82. Print.

Ions, Veronica. *Egyptian Mythology.* Trans. Paul L. Maier. Grand Rapids: Kregel Publications, 1988. Print.

Jasper, Karl. *Way to Wisdom.* New Haven: Yale University Press, 1951. Print.

*Judson, Olivia. "The Selfless Gene." *Atlantic Magazine* Oct. 2007: 90-98. Print.

*Kohlberg, Lawrence. "Moral Stages and Moralization: The Cognitive Development Approach." *Moral Development and Behavior Theory, Research, and Social Issues.* Ed. Thomas Lickona. New York: Holt, Rinehart and Winston, 1976. Print.

*Krubitzer, Leah, and Kelly J. Huffman. "A Realization of the Neocortex in Mammals: Genetic and Epigenetic Contribution to the Phenotype." *Brain Behavior Evolution* 55.6 (June 2000): 322-335. Print.

Rest, James R. *Development in Judging Moral Issues.* Minneapolis: University of Minnesota Press, 1979. Print.

*Rest, James R., Darcia Narvaez, Muriel J. Bebeau, and Stephen J. Thoma. *Postconventional Moral Thinking: A Neo-Kohlbergian Approach.* Mahwah, New Jersey: Lawrence Erlbaum Associates, 1999. Print.

*Satterly, David. "Piaget and Education." *The Oxford Companion to the Mind.* Ed. R. L. Gregory. New York: Oxford University Press, 1987. Print.

*Silberman, Neil Asher, and Israel Finkelstein. *The Bible Unearthed.* New York: Simon & Schuster-Touchstone, 2001. Print.

*Simpson, E. L. "Moral Development Research." *Human Development* 17.2 (1974): 81-106. Print.

*Trevino, Linda K. "Ethical Decision-Making in Organizations: A Person-Situation Interactionist Model." *Academy of Management Review* 11.3 (July 1986): 601-617. Print.

Tucker, Abigail. "Born to be Mild." *Atlantic Magazine* Jan. 2013. 43.9: 26-41. Print.

*"What is Williams Syndrome?" *Heart to Heart*. Web. 26 Feb 2013. <williams-syndrome.org>.

Chapter 4

"Calaphas." *High Priest's* [Sic] *of New Testament Times*. Web. 30 May 2012. <bible-history.com/HighPriests/index.html>.

Colby, Ann, Lawrence Kohlberg, et al. *The Measurement of Moral Judgment* Vol. 1. New York: Oxford University Press, 2011. Print.

Crossan, John Dominic. *The Historical Jesus: The Life of a Mediterranean Jewish Peasant*. HarperSanFrancisco, 1991. Print.

---. *Jesus: A Revolutionary Biography*. HarperSanFrancisco, 1989. Print.

Ehrman, Bart D. *Lost Christianities*. New York: Oxford University Press. 2003. Print.

---. *Lost Christianities: Christian Scriptures and the Battle over Authentication*. Chantilly, Virginia: The Teaching Company Great Courses, 2002. DVD, Print.

---. *Misquoting Jesus*. HarperSanFrancisco, 2005. Print.

---. *The Orthodox Corruption of Scripture: The Effect of Early Christological Controversies on the Text of the New Testament*. New York: Oxford University Press, 1993. Print.

*Errico, Rocco A., and George M. Lamsa. *Aramaic Light on the Gospel of Matthew*. Santa Fe, New Mexico: Noohra Foundation, 2000. Print.

*Eusebius of Caesarea. 300 CE. "Church History." *New Advent*. Web. 8 Aug. 2013. <newadvent.org/fathers/2501.htm>.

*Hiroshi, Sugihara, and Phil Gibbs. 1996, updated 1997. *What is Occam's Razor?* Web. 19 June 2013. <phys.ncku.edu.tw/mirrors/physicsfaq/General/occam.html>.

**Holy Bible*. King James version, 1611. Cleveland, Ohio: The World Publishing Company, n.d. Print.

**Josephus: The Essential Writings*. Trans. Paul L. Maier. Grand Rapids: Kregel Publications, 1988. Print.

Kohlberg, Lawrence. "Moral Stages and Moralization: The Cognitive Development Approach." *Moral Development and Behavior Theory Research and Social Issues*. Ed. Thomas Lickona. New York: Holt Rinehart and Winston, 1976. Print.

*Lamsa, George M. *Gospel Light*. Philadelphia: A. J. Holman Company. Reprint, HarperSan Francisco, 1969. Print.

"Leontopolis." *The Jewish Encyclopedia*. Web. 8 Aug. 2013.

*Notovitch, Nicholas. 1894. *The Unknown Life of Jesus Christ*. Chicago: Leaves of Healing Publications, 1990. Print.

*"Philo of Alexandria." *The Internet Encyclopedia of Philosophy*. Web. 30 May 2010. <iep.utm.edu/philo>.

Philo of Alexandria. *Selected Writings*. Ed. Hans Lewy Mineola. New York: Dover Publications, 2004. Print.

*Philo of Alexandria. *Works*. Trans. Charles Duke Yonge. 10 vols. 2 supplements. Massachusetts: Harvard University Press/London: William Heinemann Publishing, 1929-1953. Print.

Rest, James R., Darcia Narvaez, Muriel J. Bebeau and Stephen J. Thoma. *Postconventional Moral Thinking: A Neo-Kohlbergian Approach*. Mahwah, New Jersey: Lawrence Erlbaum Associates, 1999. Print.

*Scott, Bernard Brandon. *The Trouble with Resurrection*. Salem, Oregon: Polebridge Press, 2010. Print.

Spong, John Shelby. *A New Christianity for a New World*. HarperSanFrancisco, 2001. Print.

---. *The Sins of Scripture*. HarperSanFrancisco, 2005. Print.

"St. Irenaeus of Lyons." *Religion Facts*. Web. 30 May 2012. <religionfacts.com/christianity/people/irenaeus.htm>.

*"Therapeutae." *The Britannica Online Encyclopedia*. Web. 30 May 2012. <britannica.com/EBchecked/topic/591173/Therapeutae>.

*"Therapeutae." *New World Encyclopedia*. Web. 10 June 2012. <newworldencyclopedia.org/entry/Therapeutae>.

*Wells, H. G. 1922. *A Short History of the World*. Lawrence, Kansas: Digiread.com, Great Books Online, 2010. Web. 26 Feb. 2013. <bartleby.com/86/38.html>.

Wilson, Edward O. *The Social Conquest of Earth*. New York: Liveright Publishing, 2012. Print.

The Works of Philo Judaeus Vol. 1. Trans. Charles Duke Yonge. London: George Bell & Sons, 1894. Print.

Yonge, Charles Duke, trans. "The Works of Philo Judaeus." *Early Christian Writings*. 2001-2013 Peter Kirby. Transcribed from the 1993 reprint. Web. 19 June 2013. <earlychristianwritings.com/yonge>.

Chapter 5

"Alfred North Whitehead." *Stanford Encyclopedia of Philosophy*. Web. 30 May 2010. <plato.stanford.edu/entries/whitehead/>.

Cobb, Jr., John B., and David Ray Griffin. *Process Theory: An Introductory Exposition*. London: Westminster Press, 1976. Print.

*Ehrman, Bart D. *Lost Christianities*. New York: Oxford University Press, 2003. Print.

*Eusebius of Caesarea. 300 CE. "Church History." *New Advent*. Web. 26 Feb. 2013. <newadvent.org/fathers/2501.htm>.

*"Heraclitus." *Stanford Encyclopedia of Philosophy.* Web. 12 Apr. 2013. <plato.stanford.edu/entries/heraclitus>.

**Holy Bible.* King James version, 1611. Cleveland, Ohio: The World Publishing Company, n.d. Print.

*Lynch, Thomas D., and Cynthia E. Lynch. *The Word of the Light.* Seattle: Hara Publishing, 1998. Print.

*Mesle, C. Robert. *Process–Relational Philosophy: An Introduction to Alfred North Whitehead.* West Conshohocken, Pennsylvania: Templeton Press, 2008. Print.

---. *Process Theology: A Basic Introduction.* Atlanta: Chalice Press, 1993. Print.

"Philo of Alexandria." *The Internet Encyclopedia of Philosophy.* Web. 30 May 2010. <iep.utm.edu/philo>.

*"Process Philosophy." *Stanford Encyclopedia of Philosophy.* Web. 30 May 2010. <plato.stanford.edu/entries/process-philosophy>.

*Robinson, James M., ed. *The Nag Hammadi Library.* New York: Harper & Row, 1987. Print.

"Therapeutae." *The Britannica Online Encyclopedia.* Web. 30 May 2012. <britannica.com/EBchecked/topic/591173/Therapeutae>.

"Therapeutae." New World Encyclopedia. Web. 10 June 2012. <newworldencyclopedia.org/entry/Therapeutae>.

*Whitehead, Alfred North. *Religion in the Making*. New York: Fordham University Press, 1996. Print.

Chapter 6

*"About the Seminary." *New Seminary*. Web. June 2011. <newseminary.org/>.

*Goodenough, Edwin R. *An Introduction to Philo Judaeus*. 2nd ed. Lanham, Maryland: University Press of America, 1986. Print.

**Holy Bible*. King James version. 1611. Cleveland, Ohio: The World Publishing Company, n.d. Print.

*Lynch, Thomas D. and Cynthia E. Lynch. *The Word of the Light*. Seattle: Hara Publishing, 1988. Print.

*"Philo of Alexandria." *The Internet Encyclopedia of Philosophy*. Web. 30 May 2010. <iep.utm.edu/philo/>.

Philo of Alexandria. *Selected Writings*. Ed. Hans Lewy Mineola. New York: Dover Publications, 2004. Print.

*Philo of Alexandria. *Works*. Trans. Charles Duke Yonge. 10 vols, 2 supplements. Massachusetts: Harvard University Press/London: William Heinemann Publishing, 1929-1953. Print.

*Rad, Von Gerhard. *Wisdom in Israel*. London: Trinity Press International, 1972. Print.

Runia, David T. "Philo, Alexandrian and Jew." *Exegesis and Philosophy*. Surrey, United Kingdom: Variorum Collection Studies (Ashgate), 1990. Print.

*Wright, Robert. *The Evolution of God*. Boston: Little, Brown and Co., 2009. Print.

Yonge, Charles Duke, trans. *The Works of Philo Judaeus*. Vol. 1. London: George Bell & Sons, 1894. Print.

Chapter 7

Aristotle. *Nicomachean Ethics*. Trans. Martin Ostwald. Englewood Cliffs, New Jersey: Prentice Hall, 1962. Print.

*Ehrman, Bart D. *Lost Christianities*. New York: Oxford University Press, 2003. Print.

---. *Lost Christianities: Christian Scriptures and the Battle over Authentication*. Chantilly, Virginia: The Teaching Company Great Courses. DVD, Print, 2005.

---. *Misquoting Jesus*. HarperSanFrancisco, 2005. Print.

---. *The Orthodox Corruption of Scripture: The Effect of Early Christological Controversies on the Text of the New Testament*. New York: Oxford University Press, 1993. Print.

*King, Karen L. *The Gospel of Mary Magdala*. Santa Rosa, California: Polebridge Press, 2003. Print.

*Leloup, Jean-Yves. *The Gospel of Mary Magdalene*. Rochester, Vermont: Inner Traditions International, 2002. Print.

*Lynch, Thomas D., and Cynthia E. Lynch. *The Word of the Light*. Seattle: Hara Publishing, 1998. Print.

Chapter 8

Goodenough, Edwin R. *An Introduction to Philo Judaeus*. 2nd ed. Lanham, Maryland: University Press of America, 1986. Print.

Holy Bible. King James Version, 1611. Cleveland, Ohio: The World Publishing Co., n.d. Print.

Lynch, Thomas D., and Cynthia E. Lynch. *The Word of the Light*. Seattle: Hara Publishing, 1998. Print.

Philo of Alexandrea. *The Internet Encyclopedia of Philosophy*. 30 May 2010. <iep.utm.edu/philo>.

Philo of Alexandria. *Works*. Trans. Charles Duke Yonge. 10 vols. 2 supplements. Massachusetts: Harvard University/London: William Heinemann, 1929-53. Print.

Rad, Von Gerhard. *Wisdom in Israel*. London: Trinity Press International, 1972. Print.

Runia, David T. "Philo, Alexandrian and Jew." *Exegesis and Philosophy*. Surrey, United Kingdom: Variorum Collection Studies (Ashgate), 1990. Print.

Wright, Robert. *The Evolution of God*. Boston: Little, Brown and Co., 2009. Print.

Yonge, Charles Duke, author and translator, and Aristotle. *The Works of Philo Judaeus*. Vol. 1. London: George Bell & Sons, 1894. Print.

Chapter 9

*Errico, Rocco A., and George M. Lamsa. *Aramaic Light on the Gospel of Matthew*. Santa Fe, New Mexico: Noohra Foundation, 2000. Print.

*Fox, Emmet. *The Sermon on the Mount*. San Francisco: Harper & Row, 1996. Print.

Holy Bible. King James Version, 1611. Cleveland, Ohio: The World Publishing Co., n.d. Print.

Lamsa, George M. *Gospel Light*. Philadelphia: A. J. Holman Co., 1936. Reprint, HarperSan Francisco, 1969. Print.

Chapter 10

Aesop's Fables. University of Massachusetts Amherst. Web. 20 Oct. 2012. <umass.edu/aesop>.

Aristotle. *Nicomachean Ethics*. Trans. Martin Ostwald. Englewood Cliffs, New Jersey: Prentice Hall, 1962. Print.

*Freire, Paulo. *Pedagogy of the Oppressed*. New York: Herder & Herder (Crossroads Publishing Co.), 1970. Print.

Holy Bible. King James version. Cleveland, Ohio: The World Publishing Company, n.d. Print.

Chapter 11

"Calaphas." *High Priest's* [sic] *of New Testament Times*. Web. May 2011. <bible-history.com/HighPriests/index.html>.

*Ehrman, Bart D. *Lost Christianities*. New York: Oxford University Press, 2003. Print.

---. *Lost Christianities: Christian Scriptures and the Battle over Authentication.* Chantilly, Virginia: The Teaching Company Great Courses, 2002. DVD, Print.

---. *Misquoting Jesus.* HarperSanFrancisco, 2005. Print.

---. *The Orthodox Corruption of Scripture: The Effect of Early Christological Controversies on the Text of the New Testament.* New York: Oxford University Press, 1993. Print.

*Eusebius of Caesarea. 300 CE. "Church History." *New Advent*. Web. 8 Aug. 2013. <newadvent.org/f-thers/2501.htm>.

Evans, G. R., ed. *The First Christian Theologians: An Introduction to Theology in the Early Church.* Hoboken, New Jersey: Blackwell Publishing, 2004. Print.

**Holy Bible.* King James version. 1611. Cleveland, Ohio: The World Publishing Company, n.d. Print.

Josephus: The Essential Writings. Trans. Paul L. Maier. Grand Rapids: Krege Publications, 1988. Print.

Mason, Mark. *In Search of the Loving God.* Eugene, Oregon: Dwapara Press, 1997. Print.

Notovitch, Nicholas. 1894. *The Unknown Life of Jesus Christ.* Chicago: Leaves of Healing Publications, 1990. Print.

Philo of Alexandria. *Works.* Trans. Charles Duke Yonge. 10 vols., 2 supplements. Massachusetts: Harvard University Press/London: William Heinemann, 1929-1953. Print.

Ross, Nancy Wilson. *Three Ways of Asian Wisdom*. New York: Simon & Schuster, 1966. Print.

*Scott, Bernard Brandon. *The Trouble with Resurrection*. Salem, Oregon: Polebridge Press, 2010. Print.

*Spong, John Shelby. *A New Christianity for a New World*. HarperSanFrancisco, 2001. Print.

*---. *The Sins of Scripture*. HarperSanFrancisco, 2005. Print.

*"St. Irenaeus of Lyons." *Religion Facts*. Web. 30 May 2012. <religionfacts.com/christianity/people/irenaeus.htm>.

Yonge, Charles Duke. *The Works of Philo Judaeus*. Vol. 1. London: George Bell & Sons, 1894. Print.

Chapter 12

*Lynch, Thomas D., and Cynthia E. Lynch. *The Word of the Light*. Seattle: Hara Publishing, 1998. Print.

Meyer, Marvin. *The Gospel of Thomas*. HarperSanFrancisco, 1992. Print.

*Wright, Robert. *The Evolution of God*. Boston: Little, Brown and Co., 2009. Print.

Chapter 13

Janis, Sharon. *Spirituality for Dummies*. Boston: IDG Books Worldwide, 2000. Print.

*Lynch, Thomas D., and Cynthia E. Lynch. *The Word of the Light*. Seattle: Hara Publishing, 1998. Print.

Meyer, Marvin. *The Gospel of Thomas*. HarperSanFrancisco, 1992. Print.

Robinson, James M. *The Nag Hammadi Library*. New York: Harper & Row, 1987. Print.

Wright, Robert. *The Evolution of God*. Boston: Little, Brown and Co., 2009. Print.

Chapter 14

*Layton, Bentley, trans. "Saying 69," *The Gnostic Scriptures*. Garden City, New York: Doubleday & Company, 1987. Print.

*Lynch, Thomas D., and Cynthia E. Lynch. *The Word of the Light*. Seattle: Hara Publishing, 1998. Print.

Meyer, Marvin. *The Gospel of Thomas*. HarperSanFrancisco, 1992. Print.

Robinson, James M. *The Nag Hammadi Library*. New York: Harper & Row, 1987. Print.

Chapters 15 and 16

*Lynch, Thomas D., and Cynthia E. Lynch. *The Word of the Light*. Seattle: Hara Publishing, 1998. Print.

Meyer, Marvin. *The Gospel of Thomas*. HarperSanFrancisco, 1992. Print.

Robinson, James M. *The Nag Hammadi Library*. New York: Harper & Row, 1987. Print.

References and Suggested Readings

For Entire Book

"About the Seminary." *New Seminary*. Web. June 2011. <newseminary.org>.

Aesop's Fables. University of Massachusetts Amherst. Web. 20 Oct. 2012. <umass.edu/aesop>.

"Alfred North Whitehead." *Stanford Encyclopedia of Philosophy*. Web. 30 May 2010. <plato.stanford.edu/entries/whitehead>.

Aristotle. *Nicomachean Ethics*. Trans. Martin Ostwald. Englewood Cliffs, New Jersey: Prentice Hall, 1962. Print.

Armstrong, Karen. *A History of God*. New York: Random House-Ballantine Books, 1993. Print.

Barnstone, Willis, and Marvin Meyer. *The Gnostic Bible*. Boston: Shambhala, 2003. Print.

"Calaphas." *High Priest's* [sic] *of New Testament Times*. Web. May 2011. <bible-history.com/HighPriests/index.html>.

*Callaway, Ewen. "Ancient Warfare: Fighting for the Greater Good." *New Scientist*, Life section. 4 June 2009. Print and Web. 21 Jan. 2014. <newscientist.com/article/dn17255-ancient-warfare-fighting-for-the-greater-good.html>.

Casillas Rodríguez, General Luis Rey. Photograph taken as a colonel in Kashmir, India. Winter 1949. From a personal interview by Thomas D. Lynch with Casillas's son, Dr. Luis Rey Casillas Celis. 26 Apr. 2013.

Cleary, Thomas. *Dhammapada: The Sayings of Buddha*. New York: Bantam Books, 1995. Print.

Cobb, Jr., John B., and David Ray Griffin. *Process Theory: An Introductory Exposition*. London: Westminster Press, 1976. Print.

Colby, Ann, Lawrence Kohlberg, et al. *The Measurement of Moral Judgment*. Vol. 1. New York: Oxford University Press, 2011. Print.

Crossan, John Dominic. *The Historical Jesus: The Life of a Mediterranean Jewish Peasant*. HarperSanFrancisco, 1991. Print.

---. *Jesus: A Revolutionary Biography*. HarperSanFrancisco, 1989. Print.

Dawkins, Richard. *The God Delusion*. Boston: Houghton Mifflin, 2006. Print.

---. *The Selfish Gene*. 30th Anniversary Edition. New York: Oxford University Press, 2006. Print.

Ehrman, Bart D. *Lost Christianities*. New York: Oxford University Press, 2003. Print.

---. *Lost Christianities: Christian Scriptures and the Battle over Authentication*. Chantilly, Virginia: The Teaching Company Great Courses, 2002. DVD, Print.

---. *Misquoting Jesus*. HarperSanFrancisco, 2005. Print.

---. *The Orthodox Corruption of Scripture: The Effect of Early*

Christological Controversies on the Text of the New Testament. New York: Oxford University Press, 1993. Print.

Epstein, Mark. *Psychotherapy Without the Self: A Buddhist Perspective*. New Haven: Yale University Press, 2007. Print.

Errico, Rocco A., and George M. Lamsa. *Aramaic Light on the Gospel of Matthew*. Santa Fe, New Mexico: Noohra Foundation, 2000. Print.

Eusebius of Caesarea. 300 CE. "Church History." *New Advent*. Web. 8 Aug. 2013. <newadvent.org/fathers/2501.htm>.

Evans, G. R., ed. *The First Christian Theologians: An Introduction to Theology in the Early Church*. Hoboken, New Jersey: Blackwell Publishing, 2004. Print.

Fehr, Ernst, and Urs Fischbacher. "The Nature of Human Altruism." *Nature* 425 (23 Oct. 2003): 785-791. Print.

Fehr, Ernst, and Simon Gachter. "Altruistic Punishment in Humans." *Nature* 415 (10 Jan. 2002): 137-140. Print.

Fehr, Ernst, and Bettina Rochenbach. "Detrimental Effects of Sanctions on Human Altruism." *Nature* 422 (13 Mar. 2003): 137-140. Print.

Frankl, Viktor. *Man's Search for Meaning*. New York: Random House-Rider, 2004. Print.

Freire, Paulo. *Pedagogy of the Oppressed*. New York: Herder & Herder-Crossroads Publishing, 1970. Print.

French, Howard. W. "E. O. Wilson's Theory of Everything." *Atlantic Magazine* Nov. 2011: 70-82. Print.

Fox, Emmet. *The Sermon on the Mount.* San Francisco: Harper & Row, 1996. Print.

Glines, C. V. "They Wait for the Ships and Aircraft to Return– This Time Carrying Goods for Them. The Cargo Cults." *Air Force Magazine.* Online Journal of the Air Force Association Jan. 1991: n. pag. <airforcemag.com/Magazine/Archive/Pages/1991/January%201999/0191/cargo.aspx>.

Goodenough, Edwin R. *An Introduction to Philo Judaeus.* 2nd ed. Lanham, Maryland: University Press of America, 1986. Print.

Harris, Sam. *The End of Faith.* New York: W. W. Norton & Company, 2004. Print.

---. *Letter to a Christian Nation.* New York: Alfred A. Knopf, 2006. Print.

"Heraclitus." *Stanford Encyclopedia of Philosophy.* Web. 30 May 2010. <plato.stanford.edu/entries/Heraclitus>.

Hiroshi, Sugihara, and Phil Gibbs. 1996, updated 1997. *What is Occam's Razor?* Web. 19 June 2013. <phys.ncku.edu.tw/mirrors/physicsfaq/General/occam.html>.

Holy Bible. King James version. 1611. Cleveland, Ohio: The World Publishing Company, n.d. Print.

Ions, Veronica. *Egyptian Mythology.* London: Hamlyn Publishing Group, 1986. Print.

Janis, Sharon. *Spirituality for Dummies*. Boston: IDG Books Worldwide, 2000. Print.

Jasper, Karl. *Way to Wisdom*. New Haven: Yale University Press, 1951. Print.

Josephus: The Essential Writings. Trans. Paul L. Maier. Grand Rapids: Kregel Publications, 1988. Print.

Judson, Olivia. "The Selfless Gene." *Atlantic Magazine* Oct. 2007: 90-98. Print.

Kennedy, John F. Presidential Inaugural Address. 20 January 1961. Web. <jfklibrary.org>.

King, Karen L. *The Gospel of Mary Magdala*. Santa Rosa, California: Polebridge Press, 2003. Print.

Kohlberg, Lawrence. "Moral Stages and Moralization: The Cognitive Development Approach." *Moral Development and Behavior Theory Research and Social Issues*. Ed. Thomas Lickona. New York: Holt, Rinehart and Winston, 1976. Print.

Krubitzer, Leah, and Kelly J. Huffman. "A Realization of the Neocortex in Mammals: Genetic and Epigenetic Contribution to the Phenotype." *Brain Behavior Evolution* 55.6 (June 2000): 322-335. Print.

Kung, Hans. *On Being a Christian*. New York: Doubleday & Company, 1976. Print.

Kushner, Harold S. *Why Bad Things Happen to Good People*. New York: HarperCollins Publishers, 1981. Print.

Lamsa, George M. *Gospel Light.* Philadelphia: A. J. Holman Company, Reprint, HarperSan Francisco, 1969. Print.

Layton, Bentley, trans. "Saying 69," *The Gnostic Scriptures.* Garden City, New York: Doubleday & Company, 1987. Print.

Leloup, Jean-Yves. *The Gospel of Mary Magadalene.* Rochester, Vermont: Inner Traditions International, 2002. Print.

"Leontopolis." *The Jewish Encyclopedia.* Web. 8 Aug. 2013. <jewishencyclopedia.com/view.jsp?artid=206&letter=L>.

Lynch, Thomas D., and Cynthia E. Lynch. *The Word of the Light.* Seattle: Hara Publishing, 1998. Print.

Mason, Mark. *In Search of the Loving God.* Eugene, Oregon: Dwapara Press, 1997. Print.

Mesle, C. Robert. *Process–Relational Philosophy: An Introduction to Alfred North Whitehead.* West Conshohocken, Pennsylvania: Templeton Press, 2008. Print.

---. *Process Theology: A Basic Introduction.* Atlanta, Georgia: Chalice Press, 1993. Print.

Meyer, Marvin. *The Gospel of Thomas.* HarperSanFrancisco, 1992. Print.

Notovitch, Nicholas. 1894. *The Unknown Life of Jesus Christ.* Chicago: Leaves of Healing Publications, 1990. Print.

"Philo of Alexandria." *The Internet Encyclopedia of Philosophy.* Web. 30 May 2010. <iep.utm.edu/philo>.

Philo of Alexandria. *Selected Writings*. Ed. Hans Lewy Mineola. New York: Dover Publications, 2004. Print.

Philo of Alexandria. *Works*. Trans. Charles Duke Yonge. 10 vols., 2 supplements. Massachusetts: Harvard University Press/London: William Heinemann; Putnam, 1929-1953. Print.

Priests for Equity. *The Inclusive New Testament*. W. Hyattsville, Maryland: AltaMira Press, 2004. Print.

"Process Philosophy." *The Internet Encyclopedia of Philosophy*. Web. 30 May 2010. <iep.utm.edu/processp/>.

"Process Philosophy." *Stanford Encyclopedia of Philosophy*. Web. 30 May 2010. <plato.stanford.edu/entries/process-philosophy>.

Putnam, Robert D., and David E. Campbell. *American Grace: How Religion Divides and Unites Us*. New York: Simon & Schuster Paperbacks, 2010. Print.

Rad, Von Gerhard. *Wisdom in Israel*. London: Trinity Press International, 1972. Print.

Rest, James R. *Development in Judging Moral Issues*. Minneapolis: University of Minnesota Press, 1979. Print.

Rest, James R., Darcia Narvaez,, Muriel J. Bebeau, and Stephen J. Thoma. *Postconventional Moral Thinking: A Neo-Kohlbergian Approach*. Mahwah, New Jersey: Lawrence Erlbaum Associates, 1999. Print.

Robinson, James M., ed. *The Nag Hammadi Library*. New York: Harper & Row, 1987. Print.

Ross, Nancy Wilson. *Three Ways of Asian Wisdom*. New York: Simon & Schuster, 1966. Print.

Runia, David T. "Philo, Alexandrian and Jew." *Exegesis and Philosophy*. Surrey, United Kingdom: Variorum Collection Studies (Ashgate), 1990. Print.

Satterly, David. "Piaget and Education," *The Oxford Companion to the Mind*. Ed. R.L. Gregory, New York: Oxford University Press, 1987. Print.

Scott, Bernard Brandon. *The Trouble with Resurrection*. Salem, Oregon: Polebridge Press, 2010. Print.

Silberman, Neil Asher, and Israel Finkelstein. *The Bible Unearthed*. New York: Simon & Schuster-Touchstone, 2001. Print.

Simpson, E. L. "Moral Development Research." *Human Development* 17.2 (1974): 81-106. Print.

Spong, John Shelby. *A New Christianity for a New World*. HarperSanFrancisco, 2001. Print.

---. *The Sins of Scripture*. HarperSanFrancisco, 2005 Print.

"St. Irenaeus of Lyons." *Religion Facts*. Web. 30 May 2012. <religionfacts.com/christianity/people/irenaeus.htm>.

"Therapeutae." *The Britannica Online Encyclopedia*. Web. 30 May 2012.

"Therapeutae." *New World Encyclopedia*. Web. 10 June 2012.

The Tomb of Jesus Christ. The Online Centre for 'Jesus in India' Studies. 1999. Web. 30 Mar. 2012. <tombofJesus.com>.

Trevino, Linda K. "Ethical Decision-Making in Organizations: A Person-Situation Interactionist Model." *Academy of Management Review* 11.3. (July): 601-617. Print.

Tucker, Abigail. "Born to be Mild," *Atlantic Magazine* Jan 2013. 43.9: 26-41. Print.

Vivekananda, Swami. *Vedanta Society of New York*. 2013. Web. 26 Feb. 2013. <vedantany.org>.

Wells, H. G. 1922. *A Short History of the World*. Lawrence, Kansas: Digiread.com, Great Books Online, 2010. Web. 27 Apr. 2013. <bartleby.com/86/38/html>.

West, Cornel. *Democracy Matters*. New York: Penguin Books, 2004. Print.

"What is Williams Syndrome?" *Heart to Heart*. Williams Syndrome Association. 2011. Web. 26 Feb. 2013. <williams-syndrome.org>.

Whitehead, Alfred North. *Religion in the Making*. New York: Fordham University Press, 1996. Print.

Wilbur, Ken. *Integral Spirituality: A Startling New Role for Religion in the Modern and Postmodern World*. Boston: Integral Books, 2007. Print.

Wilson, Edward O. *The Social Conquest of Earth*. New York: Liveright Publishing, 2012. Print.

Wright, Robert. *The Evolution of God*. Boston: Little, Brown and Co., 2009. Print.

Yonge, Charles Duke, trans. "The Works of Philo Judaeus." *Early Christian Writings*. 2001-2013 Peter Kirby. Transcribed from the 1993 reprint. Web. 19 June 2013. <earlychristianwritings.com/yonge>.

Yonge, Charles Duke, author and translator, and Aristotle. *The Works of Philo Judaeus*. Vol. 1. London: George Bell & Sons, 1894. Print.

Appendix B

Spirituality Coordinate System

The Gospel of Thomas is one of the world's best summaries of spirituality, and social scientists can build upon this gospel to explain why spirituality is important and how humankind can best achieve it. By using the Spiritual Coordinate System presented in this appendix, scientists can apply the rigor of the scientific method to further our understanding of spirituality. With such research findings, political, educational and religious leaders can more intelligently advance the cause of peace on earth.

Researching Spirituality

As we discuss at length in previous chapters, spirituality, as understood by Jesus, is about moving an individual's consciousness from the Kingdom of Man to the Kindom of Heaven. In doing so, two variables are critical: Seeking and Oneness. A person must have self-awareness, want to learn spiritual wisdom, and have the *willpower* to change upon discovering spiritual wisdom. Those three qualities comprise the Seeking variable (see Saying 2 of the Gospel of Thomas). In addition, a person must have spiritual love, meaning deep caring in his or her heart that extends from the self to the Oneness that is everything. That extended love is the Oneness variable (see Saying 61 of the Gospel of Thomas.)

Seeking is about wanting to learn and grow spiritually. However, such spiritual seeking is impossible unless we have the ability to be self-aware and absolutely honest with ourselves as we use that self-awareness. We must be able to see our own faults and confront them. Once we attain self-awareness, we must *want* to learn spiritual wisdom and then have the added capacity to use *willpower* to let that wisdom change us. Social scientists can build a scale of the Seeking variable using a person or group's self-awareness, self-honesty, desire to learn spiritual wisdom, and use of willpower to let that wisdom change their behavior.

Oneness is about caring and love but also who is included in that caring and love. The negative of love is disdain and hate. Thus, for research purposes, scientists can say that love of everyone and everything is the most positive version of Oneness. In contrast, the emotions of disdain and hate directed at everything and everyone are the negative of Oneness, which we call Non-Oneness. From those two extremes, scientists can construct a continuum from the most positive version of Oneness to the most negative version of Non-Oneness.

Social scientists can place a person or a group on this scale of Oneness and Non-Oneness by starting with disdaining and hating everything and everyone and finishing by reaching the point of loving and caring about everyone and everything. A person or a group moves to "Maximum Oneness" by extending its circle of caring and love to the family, to associates and ultimately to everyone and everything.

In the seventeenth century, René Descartes invented what is called the Cartesian Coordinate System, which is shown by using a graph with an X and a Y axis. This tool is particularly powerful in scientific research because one can take two variables and plot them in terms of each other. For research into spirituality, our two variables are Seeking (the X axis) and Oneness (the Y axis). The following illustration presents the model for the Spirituality Coordinate System.

Spirituality Coordinate System Model

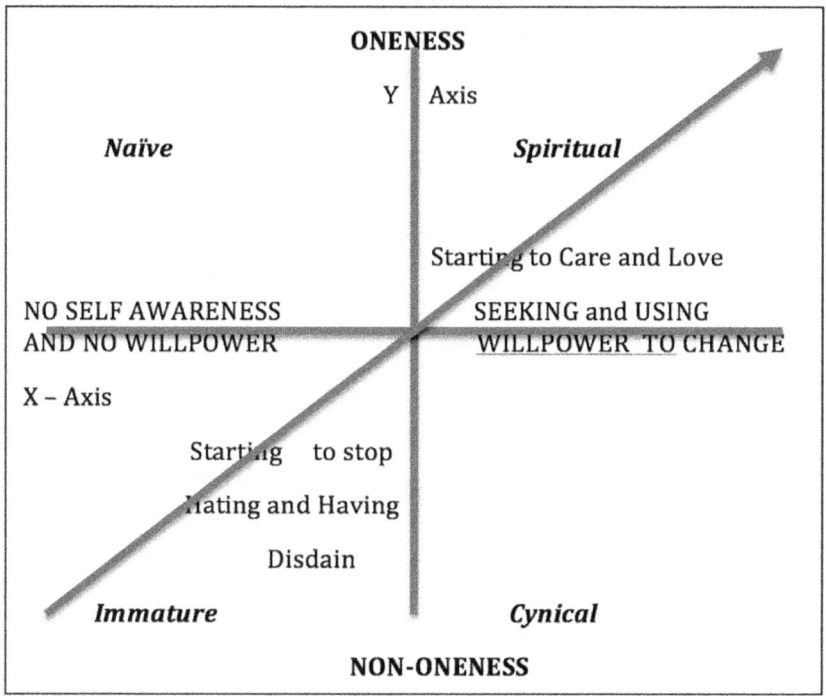

The model for the Spirituality Coordinate System consists of three lines. The horizontal line is the X-axis: it represents the *Seeking Continuum* that goes on the left from a person not being self-aware and having no *willpower*, to being a seeker at the point of origin (0, 0), to seeking wisdom and using *willpower* to change and improve his or her spiritual being. The vertical line is the Y-axis; it represents the *Oneness Continuum* that goes from disdaining and hating everyone and everything, to caring for and loving oneself at the origin (0, 0), to caring and loving everyone and everything.

The diagonal line represents the process of moving from the Kingdom of Man to the Kindom of Heaven advocated by Jesus. The diagonal progression starts with a person being immature, having little self-awareness, and feeling hate or disdain for everyone including the Self. This point represents living in the Kingdom of Man at its maximum. If spiritual progress is made in the process of moving to the Kindom of Heaven, the individual starts to care for and love his or her Self, begins to become self-aware, and starts to have the willpower to change spiritually. This means the person is starting to live in the Kindom of God. The process can continue until finally the individual reaches full Oneness and succeeds in seeking greater and greater spiritual wisdom and using it to become a greater spiritual being.

The model has four quadrants. The top left represents a *naïve* understanding of the meaning of life. The lower left represents an *immature* understanding of it. The lower right represents a *cynical* understanding. The upper right represents a full *spiritual* understanding of the meaning of life, which is a continuing seeking to be a complete spiritual being. Social scientists view each quadrant as a lens of understanding through which various individuals and groups interpret what is happening around them.

These lenses determine what and how individuals and groups understand information from their environment. As they move-up the diagonal line, they see and understand "reality" differently and therefore react to what happens in their lives differently. For example, they change from ego-centered materialists to a caring people who are motivated by wishing to grow spiritually and do something worthwhile for others.

Of course, these two factors are not sufficient for understanding the complete process of spirituality, as this book clearly demonstrate. However, these two variables working together as a unity capture the essence of spiritual growth. What is important to science is that this model opens the possibility that social scientists can do empirical research on the topic of spirituality. Researchers can create questionnaires and other kinds of research instruments to place individuals and groups on each continuum, thereby providing a means to measure spiritual development. Scientists can determine to what extent a person is spiritual, what factors help a person become more spiritual, as well as what factors strongly correlate with spirituality and its negative of materialism and egocentric thought and behavior.

Achieving Peace on Earth

Most observers of life today think people need to develop physically and intellectually if they are to be healthy and live up to their potential. Jesus, however, believed that a paramount need was for people to develop themselves spiritually. If they did that, they would gain spiritual wisdom from their life lessons given to them by God and become positive, contributing persons to themselves and society.

We believe Jesus was correct but that social scientists can use modern research tools to learn a great deal more about spirituality and how to foster it in the twenty-first century and beyond. Science can help us address important questions such as:

- What phenomena are associated with spirituality?
- What do we lose by not having spirituality in our lives?
- What diminishes the chances that spirituality can be learned?
- What increases the chances that we can learn and apply spiritual lessons to our lives?

Science, thus, can help us better understand this process of spiritual growth and in what ways it influences our well-being. We hope that, with such research, we can all move further toward achieving peace on earth.

Appendix C

Versions of the Golden Rule

There are many versions of the Golden Rule, as can be seen in the following quotations from selected faith traditions. We argue that the "true" Golden Rule is beyond words and one can best understand it by reading the various versions. Together they inform us of the meaning behind this fundamental lesson of spiritual wisdom.

Christianity
All things whatsoever ye would that men should do to you, do ye so to them; for this is the law and the prophets.
Matthew 7:1

Confucianism
Do not do to others what you would not like yourself. Then there will be no resentment against you, either in the family or in the state.
Analects 12:2

Buddhism
Hurt not others in ways that you yourself would find hurtful.
Udana-Varga 5,1

Hinduism
This is the sum of duty; do naught onto others what you would not have them do unto you.
Mahabharata 5,1517

Islam

No one of you is a believer until he desires for his brother that which he desires for himself.

Sunnah

Judaism

What is hateful to you, do not do to your fellowman. This is the entire Law; all the rest is commentary.

Talmud, Shabbat 3id

Taoism

Regard your neighbor's gain as your gain, and your neighbor's loss as your own loss.

Tai Shang Kan Yin P'ien

Zoroastrianism

That nature alone is good which refrains from doing another whatsoever is not good for itself.

Dadisten-I-dinik, 94,5

About the Authors

Rev. Dr. Thomas D. Lynch is founder and president of the International Academy for Interfaith Studies and is Professor Emeritus, Louisiana State University. The Academy trains individuals to be Interfaith Ministers. He is the author and editor of many publications, including *The Word of the Light*, which he co-authored with Rev. Dr. Cynthia E. Lynch. More can be learned about him at his website—***thomaslynch.me***—and the Academy website—*www.interfaithacademy.org*.

Rev. Dr. Cynthia E. Lynch is co-founder in the International Academy for Interfaith Studies and is Associate Professor, University of Texas Pan America (UTPA). She serves as editor of the *Global Virtue Ethics Review* and manages the Nonprofit Organization Training Program for University of Texas Pan America. More can be learned about her at the UTPA website—*www.utpa.edu*—and the Academy website.

www.ingramcontent.com/pod-product-compliance
Lightning Source LLC
Chambersburg PA
CBHW072003150426
43194CB00008B/975